The Expanding
European Union

The Expanding European Union

Past, Present, Future

edited by
John Redmond
Glenda G. Rosenthal

LYNNE
RIENNER
PUBLISHERS

BOULDER
LONDON

Published in the United States of America in 1998 by
Lynne Rienner Publishers, Inc.
1800 30th Street, Boulder, Colorado 80301

and in the United Kingdom by
Lynne Rienner Publishers, Inc.
3 Henrietta Street, Covent Garden, London WC2E 8LU

Library of Congress Cataloging-in-Publication Data
The expanding European Union :   past, present, future   /   edited by John
  Redmond and Glenda G. Rosenthal.
      p. cm.
    Includes bibliographical references and index.
    ISBN 1-55587-623-4 (hardcover :   alk. paper)
    1. European Union.   2. European Community.   3. European
  communities.   4. European federation.   I. Redmond, John, 1953–
  II. Rosenthal, Glenda G. (Glenda Goldstone)
  JN30.E95   1997
  341.242'2'09—DC21   97-15802
                                                                             CIP

British Cataloguing in Publication Data
A Cataloguing in Publication record for this book
is available from the British Library.

Printed and bound in the United States of America

    5 4 3 2 1

Contents

Tables

vii

Greenland
(Denmark)

*Greenland
Sea*

Jan Mayen
(Norway)

Iceland

*Norwegian
Sea*

Faroe Islands
(Denmark)

Sweden

Finland

*White
Sea*

Russia

Norway

Gulf of Bothnia

Atlantic

Gulf of Finland

Estonia

Ocean

North

Latvia

*Baltic
Sea*

Lithuania

Denmark

Russ

Ireland

Sea

Belarus

*Irish
Sea*

U.K.

Neth.

Poland

Ukraine

English Channel

Belgium

Germany

Czech
Rep.

Slovakia

Moldova

Lux.

Switz.

Liech.

Austria

Hungary

Romania

*Bay
of
Biscay*

France

Slovenia

Croatia

Bos.&
Herz.

Serbia

Black

Adriatic Sea

Mont.

Bulgaria

Sea

Italy

Mace.

Spain

Alb.

*Tyrrhenian
Sea*

Greece

*Aegean
Sea*

Turkey

Portugal

Mediterranean Sea

*Ionian
Sea*

Malta

The European Union, 1997

1

Introduction

John Redmond & Glenda G. Rosenthal

The European Union (EU) has never been an exclusive club. From its very start, the possibility of more members was not only expected but actually anticipated. Article 237 of the treaty establishing the European Economic Community, signed in Rome on 25 March 1957, by France, Italy, the Federal Republic of Germany, Belgium, the Netherlands, and Luxembourg (the original six members of the European Community [EC]),[1] states quite explicitly: "Any European State may apply to become a member of the Community." Thus, the way was opened up for three enlargements of its membership to include Denmark, Ireland, and the United Kingdom in 1973, Greece in 1981, and Spain and Portugal in 1986. The fourth enlargement took place on 1 January 1995, under the provisions of Article 238 of the Treaty on European Union signed in Maastricht in February 1992.[2] Accession by Austria, Finland, and Sweden took the EU to its current membership of fifteen states.

The enlargement story by no means stops there. Recent rhetoric frequently mentions the possibility of a future EU composed of twenty, twenty-four, twenty-seven, even thirty members. German chancellor Helmut Kohl declared in an April 1994 speech that the "Baltic Sea is just as much a European one as the Mediterranean. It is quite simply intolerable for us to adopt the attitude that we want to create some sort of closed shop."[3] The fall of the Berlin Wall and the disintegration of the Soviet Union have radically changed the architecture of Europe. As Rose and Haerpfer point out, "The 1995 expansion of the European Union (EU) plus German unification have moved the Union's center of gravity well to the east of Brussels."[4] In addition to outstanding membership applications by Turkey, Malta,[5] and Cyprus, post–Cold War changes in Europe have prompted many former Soviet bloc members to make a bid for membership or start positioning themselves to apply. The four Visegrad countries (Czech Republic, Hungary, Poland, and Slovakia); Romania and Bulgaria; Slovenia; and the

1

three Baltics (Estonia, Latvia, and Lithuania) have all been given special status as applicants for membership and, as Redmond indicates, "the potential membership queue becomes even longer as a whole range of newly established and often small nations may well see joining the EC as an obvious step . . . [O]ther former Soviet republics, Albania, whatever emerges from the tragedy of Yugoslavia—all of these and others may seek EC membership in due course."[6]

Although there has been much scholarly writing about what has come to be known as "enlargement" since the inception of the EC,[7] comparative studies of the four enlargements that have already taken place and their impact on policymaking, institutional structures, and decisionmaking processes and styles are practically nonexistent. Nowhere can one find the kind of broad-based, multifaceted comparative study undertaken in this book. There is no detailed and systematic analysis of similarities and dissimilarities between the enlargements that have already taken place and those that are likely to occur in the not too distant future. Only in the last year or so, a few studies of particular aspects of enlargement have adopted a comparative approach, and one or two broader comparisons have sought to draw limited lessons from past enlargements to instruct the future.[8] Despite the fact, as Rose and Haerpfer maintain, that "it [the EU] has greatly increased its cultural, social and economic heterogeneity,"[9] we dispute Nugent's contention that "it is . . . questionable whether useful lessons can be drawn from the past about present possible relationships between deepening and widening. The situation today is, after all, unique in at least two respects: there is a much larger and heterogeneous queue of potential applicants then [*sic*] previously; the Community is more integrated than it was, and so the expectations required of new members are now all the greater."[10] The existence of greater expectations of new members, which is very clearly the case, in no way negates the usefulness of a comparative study of enlargements. Indeed, it can even help to shed more light on the subject, since old members may well be interacting and negotiating with applicants on the basis of past (and often bitter) experience. As Preston aptly points out, once dispute is internalized into the system, it can create lingering resentments.[11]

Criteria, Methodologies, and Rationales for Enlargement

The original criterion for membership, "Europeanness," has been extended as a result of changing circumstances in the European and international arenas, and also as a result of experiences derived from protracted negotiations with applicants in all the enlargements to date and with the current applicants. Although there have been no treaty-based modifications in the membership criteria, additions to the list have been based on two principal sources: paragraph 2 of Article 237 of the Treaty of Rome and Article 0 of the Maastricht Treaty both lay down that "the conditions of admission . . . shall be the subject of an agreement between the Member States and the applicant State." In addition, and more recently, meetings of the European Council and intergovernmental conferences have more or less officially added three, possibly four, more conditions. In addition to being European, a state must have a liberal democratic system in which the rule of law and respect for human rights prevail; it must have a market-based economy; and it must be prepared to accept the *acquis communautaire* (all the legislation and provisions under the Treaties) as it exists at the time of accession. The fifth, implied, condition is that an applicant must not pose major distributive or budgetary problems for the Union.[12]

The Lisbon summit of 26–27 June 1992, and the Copenhagen summit of 21–22 June 1993, not only rendered the basic conditions more precise but also chose not to define "Europe." A Commission report submitted to the Lisbon Council specifically stated:

> The term "European" has not been officially defined. It combines geographical, historical and cultural elements which all contribute to the European identity. The shared experience of proximity, ideas, values, and historical interaction cannot be condensed into a simple formula, and is subject to review by each succeeding generation. The Commission believes that it is neither possible nor opportune to establish the frontiers of the European Union, whose contours will be shaped over many years to come.[13]

Nevertheless, these summits went on to add four conditions to the basic four of being European, having a democratic system, respecting human rights, and accepting the *acquis communautaire*. First, applicants must accept the emerging *acquis politique* (the declarations under European Political Cooperation)—in other words, the Common Foreign and Security Policy (CFSP) and related provisions as defined in the Maastricht Treaty. Second, applicants must subscribe to the *finalités politiques* (the long-term objectives of the European Union). Third, they must have a "functioning and competitive market economy," although it was not specified to what extent prospective members must fulfill the conditions relating to inflation, interest rates, budget deficits, and national debt that are required to join fully in Economic and Monetary Union (EMU). Finally, new members must be able to implement European Union policies through an adequate legal and administrative system in the public and private sector. However, while this may superficially clarify what an applicant country has to do to ensure its eligibility for membership, it obviously remains true that "there is scope for different interpretations of many of these conditions, and it is not possible to give a clear definition of an acceptable applicant country. . . . [Moreover] . . . it is evident that some aspiring members will have difficulties. . . . It may also be the case that the Community's criteria may be interpreted more generously for some applicants than others, with consequent political implications."[14]

Preston, in a recent article, argues that "the four enlargement rounds to date have all conformed to the 'classical Community method,' with an exclusive focus on the applicant's acceptance of the *acquis communautaire* and negotiations focusing solely on transition periods." The "classical" Community method is based on five key principles "derived from a number of explicit and implicit assumptions about both the rights and duties of both existing members and applicant states."[15] What is interesting for us is Preston's clear recognition of the comparability of enlargement negotiations. The "classical method," he asserts, "has proved remarkably robust," which leads him to draw lessons "as to how far the experience of previous enlargements might be a guide to the future."[16]

There is a widespread view that the most recent enlargement to include Austria, Finland, and Sweden (January 1995) will be the last "classical" enlargement and that in the future a more radical approach will have to be adopted. This is based on the view that post-1995 enlargements will be both qualitatively and quantitatively more extreme than previous ones. In short, the Treaty of Rome structures have reached their limits, and the EU can accommodate new members only if it makes major internal changes. "Classical" enlargement will therefore be superseded by "adaptive" enlargement.[17] Moreover, this cuts both ways: not only will the EU have to adapt, but new members will have to cope with more change. As András Inotai points out in Chapter 8, aspiring members face not only a rapidly changing and less predictable European Union, but also a more integrated one—there is much more *acquis communautaire* to adopt. Future enlargements will take place against a background of fluidity and uncertainty.

However, while the distinction between "classical" and "adaptive" enlargement is clearly important, the transformation from one to the other will not be discontinuous. Because the change in the nature of enlargement will be a gradual process, post-1995 enlargements will continue to exhibit some elements of the "classical" approach; indeed, much of the present EU membership will do their utmost to ensure this. For example, both Desmond Dinan (Chapter 2) and Geoffrey Edwards (Chapter 3) argue that radical change in the Commission and the Council of Ministers will not come easily. Thus, our emphasis is different from that of Preston, who concludes that although the EU is unlikely to abandon all aspects of the "classical method" despite the complexity of the issues raised by further enlargement, 1995 witnessed the last "classical" enlargement and that in the future a more radical approach will have to be adopted. While not disagreeing, we would stress the continuity and evolutionary elements of the enlargement process and argue that much can still be learned from an analysis of the 1995 and earlier enlargements.

It is not only the criteria and framework for enlargement that are important but also the motivation. The rationale for countries seeking EU membership is varied, but only in the degree of importance given to the different elements. The fundamental factors are essentially the pursuit of political, strategic, and, in particular, economic advantage. For example:

- Britain was driven by the realization that its rate of economic growth was lagging behind that of the original EU-6, whereas Ireland and Denmark pursued EU membership because of their close trade links with the UK (and, in the Danish case, West Germany, which was its other major export market).
- Greece, Spain, and Portugal perceived EU accession (and access to the EU's structural funds) as a means of accelerating their economic development.
- Austria, Sweden, and Finland joined the EU because, ultimately, they saw full membership as the only way of participating fully in the EU's single market.
- The post-1995 prospective members see EU membership as contributing to their economic development and offering a means by which to become part of the single market.

The political aspects are also felt strongly on the EU's side and mainly relate to strengthening the restoration of "Western" democracy in countries emerging from periods of nondemocratic regimes, be it from dictatorship (Greece, Spain, and Portugal) or communism (the Central and Eastern European Countries). The security dimension was always there during the Cold War period and right up to 1989, but it has taken a more complex (and important) form since the collapse of the Soviet bloc.

What motivates new members to join is potentially very important. Most specifically, although every new member state has its share of federalists and other Euroenthusiasts, it is debatable as to what, if any, role can be assigned to a belief in the objectives of Jean Monnet and his followers in the late 1940s and 1950s. Instead, countries pursue EU membership because of the advantages of membership and/or the disadvantages of nonmembership. This has been characterized as creating an "integration dilemma."[18] In short, countries join the European Union for the "wrong" reasons—that is, not because they wish to take part in the integration process, but because they fear the negative impact of being excluded from it (the costs of nonmembership). This raises the specter of some of the newer member states not wanting to pursue integration beyond a certain point

and/or in certain areas; from here it is but a short step to "variable geometry." This issue is taken up in a number of the chapters that follow, particularly Chapter 3, on the Council of Ministers.

A Historical Survey of the EU's Enlargements

Although the openness of the European Union to new members is clearly
expressed in the Treaty of Rome (Article 237), the events of the 1960s may
seem to indicate otherwise. Consequently, despite the fact that the United
Kingdom had refused to join the European Coal and Steel Community or to
participate in the preparation of the Rome treaties, and even though France
under de Gaulle's presidency was opposed to British membership, the other
five members retained their enthusiasm for the inclusion of Britain. Even
after organizing the formation of the European Free Trade Association
(EFTA) in 1960,[19] a move particularly provocative to the French, Britain
reversed itself on EC membership in 1961 with a formal application from
the Macmillan government. Two vetoes by de Gaulle, in 1963 and 1967,
did not preclude the reactivation and eventual success of the United
Kingdom's application in 1972.

The reasons for the UK's volte-face were complex and by no means
accepted by all Britons. Some believed that the economic benefits of membership far outweighed the objections of farm interests, Commonwealth
advocates, and those opposed to any organization with federal and supranational goals; others were driven by political motivations. However, there
remains in Britain strong opposition to some aspects of EU membership.
Meanwhile, Ireland, Denmark, and Norway, also convinced that the market
opportunities afforded by quick entry were substantial, and driven by
their close economic ties to Britain, had joined the latter in its bid for
membership. All except Norway, which rejected membership in a referendum in the last phase of the negotiations, became EC members in January
1973.

As a number of authors have observed, all subsequent enlargements
would be affected by the decision to apply existing EC conditions to its
first enlargement.[20] Preston develops this point even further in his discussion of what he calls the five principles of the "classical" Community
method of enlargement. According to him, the principle that applicants
accept the *acquis communautaire* in full with no permanent opt-outs goes
right back to de Gaulle's first rejection of the UK's application in January
1963. The French were afraid that the UK's commitments to the
Commonwealth and its EFTA partners could not be squared with EC membership. "This first, unsuccessful attempt at enlargement," he writes,
"established ground rules which have been adhered to ever since."[21]

The second and third enlargements saw the accessions of Greece (in 1981) and Spain and Portugal (in 1986). All three applied to join the EC in the mid to late 1970s and shared three key characteristics: they were all southern, recently freed of authoritarian rule,[22] and relatively less developed economically than the EU's existing members. The 1981 and 1986 enlargements are in fact frequently grouped under the heading "Mediterranean enlargement." Indeed, the five-year gap between the Greek and the Iberian accessions was largely due to problems relating to the existing EU membership rather than to the three aspiring members. In the Greek case, although the European Commission issued a cautious opinion on the Greek application and recommended an extended preaccession period, the Council of Ministers chose to ignore it in the interest of locking Greece's new democracy into the Community as soon as possible. In the case of Spain and Portugal, the interplay of political and economic problems— French and Italian farm interests and the British budget contribution controversy—blocked negotiations until 1984. In all, therefore, it took Greece six years from the time of application to its actual entry and Spain and Portugal nine, but neither set of negotiations compares with the twelve years it took Britain to achieve membership. As Laurent indicates, with the six, eight, and ten years it took the new members to move from accession to full integration, "enlargement, defined as joining and truly adhering to the integrated conditions of the member states, has been a painfully slow and internally combative process."[23]

The most recent enlargement, in which Austria, Finland, and Sweden took the EU's membership from twelve to fifteen in 1995, has been the quickest and the most complex to date. Initially, there were five "EFTA" applicants: Austria applied for membership in 1989; Sweden followed in 1991; and Finland, Switzerland, and Norway completed the group in 1992, although the Swiss application was dropped after a negative result in the referendum on the European Economic Area (EEA) in December 1992. Just over a year after the last application was received, negotiations opened in February 1993, agreement was reached in March 1994, and the accession treaties were signed the following June. Membership referendums were held in the summer and fall of 1994 in Austria, Sweden, and Finland, but on 28 November 1994, the Norwegians once again rejected EU membership, and by a similar margin—52.4 percent.[24]

Turning now to future enlargement, the EU's agenda is even more crowded than it has been in the past. Applications from non-EFTA states for membership have been received from thirteen states: Turkey (April 1987), Cyprus (July 1990), Malta (July 1990), Poland (April 1994), Hungary (March 1994), the Czech Republic (January 1996), Slovakia (June 1995), Slovenia (June 1996), Bulgaria (December 1995), Romania (June 1995), Estonia (November 1995), Latvia (October 1995), and Lithuania

(December 1995). These potential new members could be divided into three groups: the Mediterraneans, the Visegrad Four, and the remaining central and eastern Europeans. Since Albania, Moldova, and Ukraine have been admitted to the Council of Europe, membership of which is regarded by some as a "significant staging post to European integration,"[25] there is also a possibility that they too will apply for membership in the EU. This leaves two other groups: the rest of the former Yugoslavia, parts of which will certainly apply for EU membership; and what remains of EFTA—Iceland, Liechtenstein, Norway, and Switzerland—none of which has so far decided to pursue EU accession.

Turkey has an association agreement (which includes a provision for eventual membership[26]) dating back to 1963 and has been implementing a customs union with the EU since January 1996. It applied for full membership in 1987. The EC delayed the Commission's opinion until December 1989 and then rejected it—but with an offer of enhanced association. Although a customs union finally started to be implemented in January 1996 after much debate and many threats, there has been little progress toward actual membership, largely because of doubts about Turkey's democratic credentials and reports of widespread human rights violations, especially with respect to the Kurdish minority. There are also fears, as the Federal Trust points out in a recent monograph, about the "economic consequences of Turkish accession in terms of trade, the budget and labor market, an uneasy awareness of the strength of Islamic fundamentalism, and a wide scepticism about its European identity."[27] On this latter point, the Turkish case has not been strengthened by the entry of the pro-Islamic Welfare Party into (a coalition) government in mid-1996, following their electoral victory in the December 1995 general election; they were the party with the largest share of the vote. Moreover, the program of foreign visits of the new Turkish prime minister (from the Welfare Party) has done little to help Turkey's profile in the EU.

The European Commission has taken a different stance on the 1990 applications of the other two Mediterraneans, Cyprus and Malta, and issued moderately favorable (but conditional) opinions in 1993.[28] The Corfu summit in June 1994 went one step further and assured Malta and Cyprus that they would be included in the next phase of EU enlargement.[29] This was confirmed at the Essen summit at the end of that year, and in March 1995, Malta and Cyprus were assured by the Council that membership negotiations would begin within six months after the end of the 1996 Intergovernmental Conference. "Structured dialogue" with the two island states then began to prepare them for membership. It is unclear to what extent the main difficulty in the Cypriot case—the lack of some satisfactory settlement of the Cypriot partition problem—is still an obstacle to accession. This issue is addressed in Chapter 9 by Birol Yesilada, who is ultimately pessimistic. However, while prospects for Cyprus are perhaps now better than they have ever been, this is no longer true of Malta.

The election of a Labour government committed in its manifesto to withdrawing the Maltese membership bid has led to confusion. The new government immediately withdrew from the Partnership for Peace initiative and is committed to abolishing Malta's recently introduced value-added tax (VAT) system, which is an essential requirement for EU membership. Whether the Maltese Labour Party will ultimately follow the reluctant but acquiescent paths of their counterparts in Britain and Greece, which reversed their opposition to EU membership after coming to power, remains to be seen. However, the Maltese membership bid now seems to be frozen, and in early 1997, Malta was no longer participating in structured dialogue with the EU, but the Maltese government was preparing new proposals for EU-Malta relations. Even leaving Turkey aside, another Mediterranean enlargement would undoubtedly raise numerous political, institutional, and economic problems. The neutrality/nonalignment of Cyprus and Malta and, especially, their microstate status create a whole range of difficulties, some of which were addressed at the 1996–1997 Intergovernmental Conference.

However, these are arguably insignificant in comparison with the changes that will have to be made on all sides to cope with inclusion of the Central and Eastern European Countries (CEECs) as members of the European Union.[30] A new form of association, the so-called Europe Agreements, has been negotiated with many of the CEECs, and more are likely to follow. These agreements provide for association institutions, political dialogue, a free trade area in industrial goods and more limited concessions in agriculture, economic and financial cooperation, and cultural cooperation. In other words, a framework is being established for the gradual political and economic integration of the CEECs into the EU.

The mention of Europe Agreements raises the question of alternatives to EU membership, which is examined in detail in relation to the CEECs by Inotai in Chapter 8. This has always been a contentious issue—even in the 1960s, when de Gaulle, on vetoing the first British application for EC membership, offered association as an alternative (which was completely unacceptable to the UK). Association or associate membership in the EU has always been available, originally through Article 238 of the Treaty of Rome, where it is somewhat vaguely defined. It has been defined by practice, having been taken up first by Greece and Turkey, then by Cyprus and Malta, and more recently, in a slightly extended form, by the CEECs. A later alternative has been the EEA, which is a rather closer relationship with the EU than association, involving membership in the single market. The EEA has also been reserved for the EU's "economic equals," whereas association is for economically weaker European states—hence the British outrage at de Gaulle's offer. Both the EEA and association[31] have been made available only to countries potentially eligible for full EU membership.

Unfortunately, the problem with both these alternatives is precisely the fact that they are not full EU membership and, in practice, they involve much of the pain of membership with only part of the gain. In particular, they exclude a seat at the EU's decisionmaking table. They also exclude access to the EU's structural funds and participation in EU policies (such as the common agricultural policy) and often allow the EU to suspend some of its concessions unilaterally, through safeguard clauses. Both association and EEA membership are therefore regarded by any country seriously pursuing membership as only stepping-stones to joining the EU.

This finally has been accepted by the EU, and statements made at almost every summit are steadily advancing EU members' commitment to full membership for the CEECs. The process was begun at the Copenhagen summit in June 1993, when the EU promised that the "associated countries of central and eastern Europe that so desire shall become members of the European Union. Accession will take place as soon as an associated country is able to assume the obligations of membership by satisfying the economic and political conditions required." These requirements were discussed earlier.[32] The Corfu European Council in June 1994 invited the European Commission to make specific proposals regarding the implementation of the Copenhagen proposals. This was followed by approval in December 1994 at the Essen European Council of the Commission's White Paper setting out the requirements for the candidate countries to integrate themselves in the internal market and plans for a "structured dialogue" with the CEECs on a wide range of policy issues. This Essen package has been called a "route plan for the associated countries as they prepare for accession" and constitutes what amounts to an ambitious preaccession transitional period.[33] The Madrid European Council, held at the end of the Spanish presidency in December 1995, called on the Commission to prepare a composite report on individual applications as soon as possible after the end of the 1996–1997 Intergovernmental Conference. "Enlargement," it said, "is both a political necessity and a historic opportunity for Europe. It will ensure the stability and security of the continent and will thus offer both the applicant States and the current members of the Union new prospects for economic growth and general well-being."[34]

Outline of the Book

The origins of this book go back to the Fourth Biennial International Conference of the European Community Studies Association held in

Charleston, South Carolina, in May 1995. Each of the coeditors organized and chaired panels at the conference. John Redmond's panel was entitled "Enlarging the European Union: Theories, Issues and Themes," and Glenda Rosenthal centered her panel on the topic "EU Enlargements—Past, Present and Future—Institutions and Decision-Making." After the conference, Lynne Rienner proposed the current book. We asked our contributors, most of whom gave papers on our conference panels, to focus particularly on the elements of comparability in successive enlargements to see if we can draw lessons from the past as we confront the problems associated with the applications for membership being considered by the European Union from the Mediterranean and the CEECs.

The book is divided into three main parts. In Part I, "The Institutional Impact of Enlargement," we look at the European Commission, the Council of Ministers, and the European Parliament. In Chapter 2, Dinan examines the effect of enlargement on the Commission; he argues that the enlargement, despite providing a wealth of possibilities, has tended to lead to adjustment of the Commission rather than to radical restructuring, and that this is also likely to be the case with post-1995 enlargement. Similarly, Edwards (Chapter 3) is doubtful if the pressures of enlargement will force any changes in the Council in the immediate future; he believes that enlargement to a membership of twenty-five or so members will ultimately force reform, but that resistance to (probably inevitable) change will be strong. Karlheinz Neunreither (Chapter 4) is less sanguine about the ability of the Parliament to resist change. He argues that the impact on the Parliament of enlargement in the past has been, as with the Commission, fairly minimal; but he does not think that this can continue in the future. In particular, he observes that any shift toward "variable geometry" will be highly problematical for the Parliament and its procedures.

Part 2, "Policy Perspectives," examines the Common Agricultural Policy (CAP), the Common Foreign and Security Policy, and trade and industrial policy. In Chapter 5, Tim Josling shows that while previous enlargements have posed problems for the CAP, the accession of the CEECs will provide a challenge of a much higher order. He concludes that the forthcoming enlargement of the EU to the east will provide an opportunity to make needed reforms in the CAP, but if the opportunity is not grasped, discord and renationalization of the CAP are the most likely outcome. However, David Allen (Chapter 6) is much more optimistic about the impact of enlargement on the CFSP, but arguably for unfortunate reasons. He contends that past enlargements have had little effect on the CFSP and its forerunner, European Political Cooperation (EPC), but mainly because they have never amounted to much; he then concludes that as long as this continues to be the case, future enlargements will be similarly unimportant. (The development of the CFSP is driven by other factors.) To some extent,

Heather Grabbe and Kirsty Hughes, in their examination of trade and industrial policy (Chapter 7), take the opposite view: they conclude that enlargement has influenced and will continue to influence policy development in both these areas.

Part III, "Looking Forward," takes a regional perspective, with chapters on the two regions that will provide the future new EU members. Inotai (Chapter 8) considers the position of the CEECs. In a wide-ranging contribution, he examines the development of adjustment criteria, the sensitive issues, the financial transfers required, and transitional arrangements. He argues powerfully in favor of a rapid accession of the CEECs. Yesilada (Chapter 9) examines the prospects for the Mediterranean trio of Turkey, Cyprus, and Malta and sets their applications within the broader sphere of EU policy toward the Mediterranean in general. In the concluding section, Roy Ginsberg (Chapter 10) considers the impact of enlargement on the EU's role in the world. More specifically, he examines the relationship between enlargement and EU foreign policy and foreign policy decision-making and the effects of enlargement on the EU's position in Europe and the world. He concludes that enlargement does indeed enhance the EU's role in the world but warns against neglecting further integration. This focus on the "widening versus deepening" question, also taken up among other key issues in a short conclusion (Chapter 11), is a highly appropriate note on which to end. It is a conflict the EU has had to face throughout its existence, as both widening and deepening have been permanently on its agenda. It has become perhaps the greatest dilemma and policy issue that faces the European Union as it approaches the millennium.

Notes

1. The abbreviation EC (European Community) is used throughout this introduction when referring to developments ending before the creation of the European Union (EU) on 11 November 1993. EU is used for developments from then on.

2. Article 237 of the Treaty of Rome was repealed by the Maastricht Treaty and replaced by Article 0 in Title VII, which also stipulated that "any European State may apply to become a member of the Union."

3. Cited in "New Phase for EU as Hungary Asks to Join," *Independent,* 2 April 1994.

4. Rose, Richard, and Haerpfer, Christian, "Democracy and Enlarging the European Union Eastwards," *Journal of Common Market Studies* 33, no. 3 (September 1995), p. 428.

5. The Maltese position has become unclear following the election, in October 1996, of a Labour government committed to withdrawing Malta's application for full EU membership.

6. Redmond, John, *The Next Mediterranean Enlargement of the European Community: Turkey, Cyprus and Malta?* (Aldershot, Eng.: Dartmouth, 1993), p. 4.

7. A very partial list would include Camps, Miriam, *Britain and the European Community, 1955–63* (Princeton: Princeton University Press, 1965); George, Stephen, *An Awkward Partner* (Oxford: Oxford University Press, 1990); Wallace, Helen, ed., *The Wider Western Europe* (London: Royal Institute of International Affairs, 1991); Pinder, John, *The European Community and Eastern Europe* (New York: Council on Foreign Relations Press, 1991); and Michalski, Anne, and Wallace, Helen, *The European Community: The Challenge of Enlargement* (London: Royal Institute of International Affairs, 1992).

8. Preston, Christopher, "Obstacles to EU Enlargement: The Classical Community Method and Prospects for a Wider Europe," *Journal of Common Market Studies* 33, no. 3 (September 1995), and *Enlarging the Union,* Federal Trust Papers, No. 5 (London: Federal Trust, 1996).

9. Rose and Haerpfer, "Democracy and Enlarging the European Union Eastwards."

10. Nugent, Neill, "The Deepening and Widening of the European Community: Recent Evolution, Maastricht and Beyond," *Journal of Common Market Studies* 30, no. 3 (September 1992), p. 317.

11. Preston, "Obstacles to EU Enlargement," p. 457.

12. Nugent, "The Deepening and Widening of the European Community," p. 322.

13. *The European Council: Conclusions of the Presidency 1992–1994* (Luxembourg: Office for Official Publications of the European Communities, 1995), pp. 24–25.

14. Redmond, John, "The Wider Europe: Extending the Membership of the EC," in Cafruny, Alan, and Rosenthal, Glenda, eds., *The State of the European Community, Vol. 2* (Boulder: Lynne Rienner, 1993), p. 210.

15. Preston, "Obstacles to EU Enlargement," p. 451.

16. Ibid.

17. For an analysis of the concept of "adaptive" enlargement, see Redmond, John, "Mediterranean Enlargement of the European Union," in Xuereb, P., and Pace, R., eds., *The State of the European Union* (University of Malta Press, 1996).

18. For an exposition of this argument, see Kelstrup, M., "Small States and European Political Integration," in Tiilikainen, T., and Petersen, I., eds., *The Nordic Countries and the European Community* (Copenhagen: Copenhagen Political Studies Press, 1993), pp. 136–162.

19. Laurent, Pierre-Henri, "Widening Europe: The Dilemma of Community Success," *Annals of the American Academy of Political and Social Science,* special issue, "The European Community: To Maastricht and Beyond" (January 1994).

20. Preston, "Obstacles to EU Enlargement," p. 452.

21. Ibid.

22. Greece was ruled by a military junta from 1967 to 1974; Salazar was ousted in Portugal in 1974; and the death of Franco in Spain in 1975 opened up the way for the institution of democratic government there.

23. Laurent, "Widening Europe," p. 128.

24. There are excellent and detailed accounts of the fourth enlargement negotiations in Laurent, "Widening Europe," Cameron, Fraser, "Keynote Article: The European Union and the Fourth Enlargement," *Journal of Common Market Studies,* Annual Review of Activities (1994), pp. 17–34; Miles, Lee, "Enlargement of the EU and the Nordic Model," *Revue d'Intégration Européenne/Journal of European Integration* 19, no. 1 (fall 1995), pp. 43–69. See also Redmond, John, ed., *The 1995*

Enlargement of the EU: Negotiations, Issues, Accessions and Rejections (Aldershot, Eng.: Dartmouth, 1997).

25. *Enlarging the Union.*

26. There is some debate between the EU and the Turkish sides over how "automatic" this provision is. For a full discussion, see Redmond, *The Next Mediterranean Enlargement,* p. 26.

27. *Enlarging the Union.*

28. For a detailed analysis of the Commission's opinions, see Redmond, John, "Cyprus and Malta: Still the Mediterranean Orphans?" in Redmond, John, ed., *Prospective Europeans: New Members for the European Community?* (Hemel Hempstead, Eng.: Harvester Wheatsheaf, 1994), pp. 141–144.

29. *The European Council.*

30. Excellent and up-to-date accounts of the situation with respect to the current applicants may be found in *Enlarging the Union,* and in Rose and Haerpfer, "Democracy and Enlarging the European Union Eastwards."

31. The association agreements made with the ACP (African, Caribbean, and Pacific) countries are originally through Part IV of the Treaty of Rome. This is a different form of association made available to former colonies of EU member states.

32. See "Criteria, Methodologies, and Rationales for Enlargement," this chapter.

33. *The European Council.*

34. *Bulletin of the European Union,* no. 12 (1995), Office for Official Publications of the European Communities, Luxembourg.

Part 1

The Institutional Impact of Enlargement

2

The Commission and Enlargement

Desmond Dinan

The institutional history of the European Commission is one of almost continuous adjustment—but not of radical restructuring or reform—in response to successive enlargements. Today's European Union (EU) has double the population, more than double the membership, nearly three times the number of official languages, and an immensely greater range of responsibilities than the original European Economic Community. Yet, as the late Émile Noël, secretary-general of the Commission from 1958 to 1987, observed, "While the Community . . . may have undergone a root-and-branch transformation regarding its sphere of action, the extent of its operations and the size of its membership, the Commission's role and structure remain unchanged."[1] Indeed, apart from a larger college of commissioners and a threefold increase in the size of its permanent staff, today's Commission looks remarkably like the original model.

Such continuity is especially striking because reformers—both inside and outside the Commission—have repeatedly attempted to overhaul the institution on the basis of impending enlargement. Their efforts have focused on reducing the use of official languages; strengthening the Commission's cohesiveness and collegiality by ending the right of each member state to appoint a commissioner; curbing the growing power of commissioners' *Cabinets* or private offices; rationalizing the Commission's departments; strengthening the authority of the directors-general; and enhancing the Commission's power, notably in the area of implementation. On each occasion, member state inertia or outright opposition resulted in a maintenance of the status quo. Under these circumstances, it is surprising not that the Commission is unwieldy and somewhat inefficient, but that it functions as well as it does.

The institutional history of enlargement therefore suggests that the Commission will muddle through future rounds of accession agreements. After all, the same points being made now about the institutional impact of

enlargement to the east were made at the time about the EU's first enlargement (1973), and especially about its double Mediterranean enlargement
(1981 and 1986). Yet the Union's future enlargements are likely to differ
qualitatively and quantitatively from those of the past. Specifically, the
small size of the new Mediterranean applicants, the varying size and seemingly unlimited number of potential eastern European applicants, and the
hugely varying levels of administrative values and competence of both sets
of prospective members will severely test the Commission's cohesiveness,
quasi-collegiality, and character. So great is the likely impact of enlargement that it looms over the agenda of the ongoing Intergovernmental
Conference (IGC), which in any case would have addressed the
Commission's structure, role, and responsibilities.

Like previous enlargements, previous IGCs have left the Commission
relatively unchanged. For the current exercise, however, the fundamentally
different nature of the EU's next enlargements, together with a post-
Maastricht legacy of intense public skepticism about the Union's policies
and institutions, exerts enormous pressure on member states to alter the
Commission. The outcome, however, may not be what traditional reformers
have advocated. Indeed, instead of emerging from the IGC with a streamlined structure and enhanced power, the Commission may remain outward-
ly the same but have its authority and responsibilities severely curtailed.
Thus, for the Commission, the challenge of the next enlargement has come
early—at the IGC. It is to convince skeptical populations and jealous
national governments that the Commission should remain at the center of
the Union's institutional structure, not least because of its essential role in
expanding the Union eastward.

This chapter describes the Commission's role in the enlargement
process, examines the effects of successive enlargements on the
Commission's college and civil service, and analyzes the Commission's
response to the challenges and opportunities that enlargement has presented
to the EU's institutional and political development. Using an understanding
of these procedural, administrative, and political factors as a basis, the
chapter then draws some conclusions about the Commission's likely
involvement in the next rounds of enlargement. First, however, the chapter
puts enlargement in historical perspective by pointing out how, virtually
since the beginning, the Union has been preoccupied with the accession of
new member states and related issues.

The Ubiquity of Enlargement

At the outset, the European Community (EC) seemed forever limited to a
"Little Europe" of the Six. To the east, the Iron Curtain rigidly, and appar-

ently permanently, limited the Community's expansion. To the south, Spain was still an international pariah, a legacy of its wartime sympathy and support for the Axis. To the north, the Scandinavian countries had demonstrated an unwillingness, during the negotiations in 1948 that led to the launch of the Council of Europe, to share national sovereignty. Finally, to the west, Britain had not only shown a great dislike of supranationalism but had also, in the run-up to the Treaty of Rome, tried to abort the Community by proposing instead a broader, looser, European Free Trade Area (EFTA).

Yet in 1961, only three years after the EC was launched, Britain applied for membership. The reason for Britain's application was not only economic—there was a marked redirection of trade toward the European continent in the late 1950s and early 1960s—but also strategic, corresponding to an awareness of the growing importance of the Community within the Western Cold War system. It was the latter point, and especially the United States' advocacy of it, that motivated French president Charles de Gaulle to keep Britain out. De Gaulle's 1963 and 1967 vetoes of British membership delayed the Community's first enlargement until after his resignation in 1969. Britain, Denmark, and Ireland finally joined in 1973. Thus, between the time of Britain's application and eventual membership, enlargement had been a major item on the EU's agenda for eight of its fifteen years of existence.

Moreover, the Commission's first enlargement predated the Community's, as it took place in 1967, when the 1965 treaty merging the three Communities' institutions was finally implemented. Although the Merger treaty did not increase the size of the EC, it nevertheless affected the Commission in many of the ways that subsequent accession treaties would. Including negotiation and implementation of the Merger treaty in the mid-1960s, therefore, enlargement and related issues occupied the Commission for more than ten of its first fifteen years of existence.

Even while the new member states were being assimilated, enlargement quickly returned to the top of the EC's agenda when Greece (1975), Portugal (1977), and Spain (1977) applied for membership. Having just emerged from right-wing dictatorships, all three countries saw EC accession as the key to economic development and political stability. Greece played the trump card of cultural affinity and cultural heritage, and its relatively swift accession, in 1981, was strikingly disproportionate to the length of its assimilation, which arguably is ongoing. By contrast, Spain and Portugal entered the EC in 1986 after difficult and protracted negotiations, but they quickly became model members, notwithstanding their tenacious advocacy of special interests.

Throughout that time, the remaining EFTA countries were content to stay outside the Community. All were democratically sound, economically prosperous, and, with the exception of Iceland and Norway (which had narrowly voted against EC membership in 1972), strategically neutral. After Britain and Denmark joined the EC, the remaining EFTA members negotiated individual trade agreements with Brussels. The success of the EC's single market program, however, prompted these countries to estab-lish with the Community the European Economic Area (EEA), while the end of the Cold War supposedly removed the strategic obstacle to EC mem-bership. Dissatisfied with the EEA and unhindered by neutrality, Austria, Finland, and Sweden applied to join the EC in the late 1980s and early 1990s; Norway soon followed suit. Negotiation and ratification of the EU's fourth enlargement were swift: Austria, Finland, and Sweden joined in 1995; the Norwegians again voted by a narrow margin to stay out.

Thus, enlargement has been a central and quasi-permanent element of the EU's history. The first set of new members (Britain, Denmark, and Ireland) had hardly been assimilated when the second set (Greece, Portugal, and Spain) applied to join. Similarly, the Union was still assimi-lating the second set when the third set of ultimately successful applicants (Austria, Finland, and Sweden) requested accession. Moreover, while the final applications were being lodged, the EU effectively enlarged for the fourth time, by absorbing the former German Democratic Republic (GDR) in October 1990. Given its impact on the Commission's operations and responsibilities, the GDR's absorption, like the 1965 Merger treaty, deserves to be examined as though it were an actual enlargement. Finally, while the Community is in the process of assimilating its most recent new members, it has already begun preparatory work for the accession of Cyprus, Malta, and a growing number of east European countries.

The Commission's Role in the Negotiating Process

Enlargement is a protracted and variable process, entailing five stages: preapplication, application, negotiation, ratification, and implementation. The length of each stage differs from case to case, depending on the appli-cant country's particular economic, political, and administrative circum-stances, and on general circumstances within the EU itself. The Commission is formally and/or informally involved in each stage of the enlargement process, to a greater or lesser extent. The Commission's infor-mal involvement may not necessarily begin at the same stage of each enlargement, but it continues through a number of successive stages.

The preapplication stage is the least definite of the five. It relates to the period during which an application is considered inevitable or imminent, thus allowing or obliging the Commission to make some preparations, including preliminary, unofficial estimates of the political and economic impact of the expected enlargement on the EU, and its administrative impact on the Commission itself.

The length of the application stage—the time between receipt of a membership application and the opening of accession negotiations—varies from case to case. The Commission's formal involvement at this time—and its most conspicuous contribution to the enlargement process—is to prepare and present an opinion on the applicant's suitability for membership and on the likely impact of enlargement on the Union.

The negotiation stage of enlargement has ranged from less than one year (in the case of the last enlargement—largely because of the applicants' earlier negotiation of the EEA) to more than six years (in the case of Spain and Portugal). As the Commission itself observed during the negotiation stage of the first enlargement, its main role during this stage is "to reflect and to take action."[2] Thus, the Commission submits compromise solutions that usually become the basis for joint positions of the existing member states and then for an agreement between them and the candidates. Although East Germany did not accede to the EU under Article 237 of the EEC treaty, but joined instead through the West German government's use of Article 23 of the Basic Law, the short prelude to East Germany's absorption into the Union amounted to an accelerated negotiation stage.

During the subsequent ratification stage, the Commission president allocates portfolios to the new member states' Commission nominees, a process that not only involves the usual amount of lobbying by member states but also offers an opportunity for the Commission president, existing member states, and acceding member states to assuage public opinion in their various constituencies. Thus, new commissioners, especially from large member states or from member states in which negotiation and ratification of the Accession treaty proved unusually contentious, inevitably receive portfolios that are especially relevant to their countries' special interests and concerns.

Finally, in the implementation stage of enlargement, after the applicant countries have joined, the Commission has numerous responsibilities with regard to putting the Accession treaties into effect and extending the EU regime to the new members.

Effects of Enlargement on the Commission

Enlargement has had an immediate and obvious effect on the size and collegiality of the Commission, on the role and influence of the commissioners' *Cabinets,* and on the composition, character, and effectiveness of the Brussels civil service. As a result, enlargement has become synonymous with a widely accepted, but largely unfulfilled, need for administrative and organizational reform. Such reform is generally understood to mean reducing the number of commissioners and Commission departments, improving the Commission's collegiality, curbing the power of the commissioners' *Cabinets,* streamlining and restructuring the civil service, and coping with the proliferation of official languages. As early as 1979, during the negotiation stage of the Mediterranean enlargement, Commission president Roy Jenkins asked Dirk Spierenburg, a former commissioner, to recommend improvements in the Commission's structure and operations, not least because of impending enlargement. Spierenburg identified a number of problems inside the Commission that are as familiar now as they were then: a lack of cohesion within the college; an imbalance between portfolios; insufficient coordination between senior officials; poor distribution of staff between departments; shortcomings in the career structure of the civil service; and a growing emphasis on the roles of the *Cabinets.*[3] The failure of the Commission and the member states to implement the most important of Spierenburg's proposed reforms, due to inertia and a reluctance to cede national influence over the Commission's operations, testifies in part to the frailty of enlargement as a spur to EU reform.

The Proliferation of Commissioners and Departments

The formula for the number of commissioners was, and remains, one commissioner per small member state and two per large member state. Thus, the first Commission comprised nine members. Although from diverse backgrounds (politics, government service, academia), the first Commission, under Walter Hallstein, was particularly tight-knit and, at least until the crisis provoked in 1963 by de Gaulle's first veto of Britain's application, strikingly successful. Under Hallstein's dynamic leadership, and in the benign political circumstances of the EU's "pioneering period of integration," the Commission fared exceptionally well.[4]

The success of the first Commission contributed to a warm and fuzzy feeling that nine commissioners, or close to it, was the optimum number, not least because of the relatively even distribution of portfolios in the early 1960s. The Union's first enlargement, therefore, seemed to threaten the Commission's cohesion by raising the specter of too many commissioners chasing too few portfolios. Here the Commission's experience of the Merger treaty is instructive. Article 32 of the Merger treaty stipulated that the new, unified Commission would have fourteen members until such time as a treaty establishing a single Community entered into force, but in any case for a period not exceeding three years from 1 July 1967, after which time the Commission would revert to nine members. Accordingly, between July 1967 and July 1970, at a time when the EU had only six member states, the Commission had fourteen members (three each from Germany, France, and Italy; two each from Belgium and the Netherlands; and one from Luxembourg).

The first postmerger Commission tackled the problem of too few portfolios for too many members by dividing the Commission's responsibilities into fourteen or more parts, thereby giving each commissioner at least one specific responsibility, and by organizing the commissioners into groups, ostensibly "to ensure internal coordination and to facilitate the preparation of its work" under the politically most influential commissioners.[5] The seven groups corresponded to the Commission's main areas of responsibility: general economy, industrial affairs, agriculture, external relations and development aid, social affairs, enlargement and association, and administration. It was with considerable relief that the Commission reverted to nine members in 1970, after the expiry of the Merger treaty stipulation of an interim fourteen-member Commission. As the Commission's 1970 General Report noted dryly, the new Malfatti Commission allocated portfolios "bearing in mind in its discussions that with a smaller membership, its decisions would be the more essentially corporate in character."[6] Significantly, the Malfatti Commission portfolios corresponded closely to the groupings of portfolios under the previous, larger Commission.

By that time, the Commission was preparing for the EU's first enlargement and for a postenlargement Commission of fourteen members. In 1973, when the first enlargement took place, the Commission again increased in size, but only to thirteen members (as in 1994, Norway signed an accession treaty in 1972 but did not, in fact, join). Indeed, the Council of Ministers adopted a Commission proposal for a complete renewal of the Commission on the date when the Accession treaty came into force. Thus, instead of joining the existing Commission, the four commissioners from the acceding states joined an entirely new Commission.[7]

Finding meaningful jobs for all thirteen commissioners was once again a problem, which the Commission resolved by allocating the five most important portfolios (agriculture, economic and financial affairs, the internal market, competition, and external relations) to the five politically most important members, who by definition included at least one commissioner from each of the larger member states. This was the relatively simple stratagem by which the Commission continued to resolve the problem of too many commissioners and too few good jobs, a problem that arose during each successive enlargement. In effect, it created a first- and second-class Commission, conveniently masked by what had become the fig leaf of collegiality—the illusion that all commissioners were equal and that collective responsibility leveled out the disequilibrium between portfolios.

Perhaps because of the romantic lure of the first Commission, or because a Commission of more than ten or twelve was so obviously out of proportion to the amount of work to be done, the Commission itself used the opportunity of successive enlargements to advocate a permanent restriction on its growth. Nevertheless, early in the Mediterranean enlargement, the Commission advocated upholding the rule, defined when the institutions merged in 1967 and confirmed at the time of the first enlargement, that all member states be represented in every Community institution, including the college of the Commission itself.[8] Thus, any curtailment in the Commission's size, at least until the number of member states exceeded twelve, would have to be at the expense of the larger member states' second commissioner.

One of the Spierenburg Report's main recommendations was to reduce the number of commissioners to ten when Greece joined, rising to twelve when Spain and Portugal joined. The number of portfolios would be amended to eight and then ten, corresponding to the changes in the number of commissioners. Moreover, Spierenburg recommended that the content of those portfolios remain as stable as possible and not be subject to negotiation each time the Commission was renewed. A strengthened presidency—comprising the president and a single vice-president—would control all the horizontal departments, while the other members would each hold one vertical portfolio.

Aside from Spierenburg's recommendations, French president Giscard d'Estaing prevailed upon his fellow heads of state and government, in December 1978, to convene a committee of prominent personalities to consider adjustments to the EU's institutions and procedures "if the enlarged Community is to function properly." Although concerned with much broader issues than merely Commission reform, the report of the "Three Wise Men" recommended, among other things, that "the number of Commissioners in the enlarged Community should be limited to 12: one per member state," and that "the number of Directorates-General should be reduced and brought in line with that of the Commissioners."[9] Clearly, the need for a smaller college of commissioners was high on the Community agenda.

Roy Jenkins, who solicited the Spierenburg Report in 1979, experienced firsthand the difficulty of finding jobs for thirteen commissioners. He managed to allocate portfolios only after four days of arduous negotiations, involving commissioners in direct contact with their national governments.[10] Successive Commission presidents, who also went through the painful exercise of distributing portfolios in an oversized Commission, strongly supported the idea of reducing the Commission's size. Not only did Jacques Delors have to find work for fourteen commissioners in 1985, but the following year, when Spain and Portugal joined the EU, he had to rejuggle portfolios and find work for the three new Iberian commissioners.

At least Spain's and Portugal's accession had suggested to Delors a new Commission portfolio. Because Spain and Portugal brought to the EU a greater interest in Mediterranean and Latin American affairs, Delors decided to create a new portfolio of Mediterranean policy and north-south relations, which he assigned to Claude Cheysson, who worked closely with the commissioners responsible for external relations and development. This was an example of how enlargement sometimes suggests a new portfolio that can be distributed among a larger Commission, without necessarily being given to a commissioner from an acceding state.

Despite near unanimity among Commission presidents that the number of commissioners should be reduced, and recommendations to the same effect by Spierenburg and the Three Wise Men, the heads of state and government have consistently declined to do so. Even a commitment in the Maastricht Treaty to review the Commission's size in 1992 went unheeded. In reality, not only are most large member states unwilling to give up the perceived status and political advantage of a second commissioner, but no member state is willing to forsake appointing at least one commissioner. Thus, despite the apparent logic and urgency of restricting the number of commissioners to nine, ten, or twelve members, national governments have repeatedly refused to sanction such a change.

The number of Commission departments—directorates-general and other services—grew over the years at a far larger rate than did the number of commissioners. This reflected both the growing complexity of the EU's policies and programs and the fissiparous impact on the Commission's administrative structure of successive enlargements. In theory, enlargements provided an opportunity to try to streamline the Commission's departments. Yet in every case, the member states' determination to preserve as many senior civil service posts as possible, which they jealously hoarded as national sinecures and as a means of exercising national influence in the Commission, prevented reform.

The Myth of Collegiality

As already noted, the Commission's size is perceived as having a direct bearing on its collegiality. According to Spierenburg, fewer commissioners would result in better coordination of the Commission's work, a better discussion of items on the Commission's agenda, clearer conclusions, a better image of the Commission, better Commission teamwork, and a better collegiate spirit. The Commission's modus operandi, first worked out under Walter Hallstein, was a combination of individual responsibility for the management of a particular portfolio and collective responsibility for the Commission's activities. Genuinely shared responsibility, based on camaraderie, relatively equal ability, an equitable sharing of the Commission's burden, and a thorough examination and discussion of important issues, is the essence of collegiality. But collegiality is an ideal that rarely exists in any walk of life. Moreover, although collegiality does not preclude strong leadership—the Hallstein Commission was as close to being collegial as any Commission is ever likely to be—it tends to inhibit decisive action and bold initiative.

Partly because of its size, and partly because of the disequilibrium between portfolios, the Commission, with the possible exception of its earliest years, has never really been a collegial body. Instead, there has always been an unstated but clearly understood hierarchy of commissioners, corresponding to country of origin (at least in the case of one of the two commissioners from large countries), to the allocation of portfolios (this is related to a commissioner's country of origin), and to ability. Usually one or two smaller country commissioners are allocated important portfolios (invariably agriculture), and some smaller country commissioners, regardless of the importance of their portfolio, show exceptional ability and commitment. Thus, the "core group" of commissioners usually includes those who hold key portfolios, plus a small number of others who have exceptional talent, experience, or charm. The remaining commissioners, although nominally equal, are peripheral to the Commission's major initiatives and activities.

The Commission's progressively larger size may have resulted in a reduction of collegiality, but not necessarily in a decline of efficiency. Most observers agree that Delors's first Commission, which after Spanish and Portuguese accession numbered seventeen commissioners, was the most successful in the EU's history. Apart from the prevailing political climate, which gave the Commission far greater leeway to promote deeper integration, the Commission's success owed much to Delors's disregard for the concept of collegiality and his practice of working exclusively with a small number of commissioners.

Collegiality may therefore be an ideal state but one which, given the political constraints on the Commission's size, is no longer attainable. Its real meaning now is to help disguise the disequilibrium between portfolios and the imbalance in power and influence between commissioners. In that regard, collegiality serves a useful purpose. But the lesson of the Delors decade is that a strong presidency, allied with a small number of strong commissioners, holds the key to advancing the interest of the Commission and the Union—if the political and economic circumstances are propitious. Therefore, the Three Wise Men's recommendation that "the college of Commissioners should be more homogeneous and should act more as a collective body" is laudable but unrealistic.[11]

The Power of Private Offices

As George Ross has observed, "It is the collegial essence of the Commission which has necessitated the *Cabinet* system."[12] Spierenburg identified one of the *Cabinet*'s tasks as ensuring "that the Member is fully briefed on matters covered by his colleagues' portfolios to enable him to meet the demands of collective responsibility."[13] Yet, paradoxically, those who idealize collegiality see in the current *Cabinet* system the root of all evil. That is because, as the Commission grew and as a greater number of commissioners needed to be kept informed of a greater number of issues, the *Cabinets* correspondingly grew in size and authority. Core commissioners' *chefs de Cabinet* became especially powerful, often exercising more influence than peripheral commissioners, and accentuating the divide between influential and uninfluential commissioners.

At the same time, the *chefs de Cabinet* rode roughshod over the directors-general and other senior officials, thus subverting the Commission's administrative system. The increasing political and administrative power of *Cabinets,* and especially their *chefs,* reached its zenith under Delors. Indeed, Delors could not have succeeded without using his *Cabinet* to cut through the bureaucracy, expedite policy formulation, and force rapid decisionmaking. As Ross has argued, it was not really Delors, but Delors and Lamy, his powerful *chef de Cabinet,* who were responsible for the Commission's metamorphosis in the late 1980s.[14]

As early as 1979, Spierenburg had urged that *Cabinets* revert to their original function of promoting, rather than undermining, the Commission's collegiality. Subsequent enlargements, however, contributed to the Commission's unwieldiness and, accordingly, to the growth of *Cabinet* power. Yet the current backlash against powerful *Cabinets* is clearly a reaction against the Delors/Lamy ascendancy. Although that team demonstrated that powerful *Cabinets* are essential for a strong presidency and for the Commission's political success, Delors/Lamy nonetheless further marginalized peripheral commissioners and the upper echelons of the civil service. Perhaps the greatest challenge facing the present Santer Commission is coping with Delors's legacy: the growth of presidential and of *Cabinet* power; the increasingly obvious gap between core and peripheral commissioners; a renewed attachment to an idealized and romanticized view of collegiality; and a restive and resentful civil service.

The Creaking Civil Service

Both the obligations of making enlargement possible and the need to absorb large numbers of new officials from countries with markedly different administrative practices and traditions have greatly added to the stresses and strains in the Commission's civil service. In the final stage of enlargement, after the applicant countries finally join, the Commission must bear the administrative burden of implementing the Accession treaties and assimilating the new members. The task of extending the Community's rules and regulations into new member states is arduous for the Commission, despite temporary derogations and transition periods for acceding countries. Greece posed a particular problem by submitting to the EU, in March 1982, a memorandum on the economic and social problems posed by membership, requesting exemptions from EU rules. The March 1982 European Council asked the Commission to study the memorandum and to report to the Council. As Commissioner Burke, who was given responsibility for dealing with the Greek memorandum, observed, "the problems of Greece posed a challenge to the Community and in the first instance to the Commission."[15] Accordingly, the Commission became directly involved in the Greek government's efforts to modernize its administration and train qualified officials. Over 200 Commission officials went on mission to Greece over a six-month period, putting an unexpected and costly strain on the Commission's resources. The Commission's preaccession strategy for the Mediterranean and eastern European prospective members is based in part on the lessons of the Greek enlargement.

Once enlargement takes place, the rapid recruitment of staff from the acceding countries involves temporary derogations from the staff regulations so that the Commission can discriminate by recruiting only nationals of the new member states. Moreover, in the EU's first three enlargements, the Commission proposed to the Council a special regulation to facilitate the early retirement of senior officials whose posts were needed for officials from the new member states. That explains why, despite an influx of new officials immediately after each enlargement, the size of the Commission's staff at that time shows no more than the usual annual increase. In the latest enlargement, however, for budgetary reasons, the Commission decided not to opt for early retirement but instead to depend on natural retirements at a rate of approximately 300 to 350 annually, although more than 1,000 Austrian, Finnish, and Swedish officials were earmarked to join. The drawbacks of this decision are twofold: it extends the period of transition before the new member states' officials are totally integrated into the bureaucracy; and it means that the recruitment of civil servants from the EU-12 will come to a virtual standstill for at least the next three years.

Absorbing large numbers of new officials into the Commission often poses serious problems. The Commission's experience of the Merger treaty was an example of how difficult assimilation can be. Although no new countries were involved, the amalgamation into a single Commission of the three administrations, with their different organizational structures, proved difficult and time-consuming. As a result, the Commission lost valuable time that could have been spent on other, more important, tasks.

In the case of conventional enlargements, the civil service needs not only to absorb new officials, but also to digest different national administrative traditions and practices. With some Mediterranean countries—both current and probable future members—and some of the eastern European prospective members, that means dealing with lower levels of administrative competence and probity. The impact of enlargement on the EU's administrative culture has hitherto been largely positive, however. For instance, some of the attitudes and assumptions that new Union officials brought with them to Brussels enlivened and improved the Commission's ethos and operating procedures. This was especially so after the 1995 enlargement, as Swedish and Finnish officials, renowned for their integrity and openness, begin to permeate the bureaucracy.

In general, however, enlargement has contributed to the Commission's administrative shortcomings. Indeed, the process of negotiating particular enlargements has overtaxed the Commission's resources and put additional strain on an already frayed bureaucratic structure. For example, the demands of facilitating East Germany's rapid absorption into the EU put the Commission under enormous administrative pressure. Of course, the Commission's response to impending German reunification was essentially Delors's response, resulting in ad hoc arrangements that bypassed established lines of command and sidestepped numerous senior officials. Arguably the Commission could not otherwise have responded adequately to the challenge of incorporating East Germany quickly into the EU, but the adverse impact on the Commission's already overburdened administration was considerable.

Inevitably, over the years, enlargement has fueled calls for radical reform of the Commission. Many civil service reforms do not require the Council's consent and can be undertaken unilaterally by the Commission, but the Commission's reform record is poor. Successive enlargements have provided an opportunity to reorganize departments, not least because of the need to redistribute portfolios among members of the enlarged Commission. On the other hand, the influx of officials from new member states, sometimes bringing with them dubious or unacceptable administrative practices and traditions, has militated against fundamental reform.

The Commission adopted some of Spierenburg's recommendations regarding the decentralization and delegation of responsibilities, the improvement of interdepartmental consultation and of decisionmaking procedures, and the adoption of training seminars and staff policy measures. Staff mobility, long regarded as seriously inadequate in the Commission, remained susceptible to member state sensitivities regarding the power and prerogatives of what they consider to be their own, "national" units inside the Commission's departments. The Commission finally introduced greater internal mobility in the early 1990s as a response not to enlargement, but to the growing strain on the Commission's resources as a result of internal EU initiatives and external developments, notably in central and eastern Europe.

The Proliferation of Official Languages

The increase in the number of official languages, with its associated costs and administrative difficulties, has been a constant concern for the Commission. It made the case against the proliferation of official languages in 1978, at the time of the Mediterranean enlargement. A year later, observing that the enlarged Community would have nine official languages, the Three Wise Men remarked that "the costs and implications will be on a scale to make it essential that pragmatic arrangements are found allowing the number of interpreters to be reduced according to the nature of each meeting." Yet the Three Wise Men were well aware that "any attempt to limit systematically and by compulsion the use of any official language would be unjust as well as politically impractical."[16] Indeed, political sensitivities have prevented a reduction in the number of official languages, thereby obliging the Commission to meet the high costs of interpreting, translating, and printing. On a daily basis, however, English and French established themselves early on as the Commission's two working languages. Successive enlargements strengthened the position of English and German, although French remains central to the Commission's day-to-day operations.

The Commission's Response to Enlargement

The Commission has repeatedly warned that enlargement would overburden not only the Commission itself, but also the EU's institutional and decisionmaking system. The Commission has therefore sought to leverage enlargement not only to restructure and reform itself administratively, but also to strengthen its power vis-à-vis the Council, notably in the vexed and complex area of implementation, to strengthen the European Parliament's (EP) legislative powers, and to promote greater use of qualified majority voting in the Council. Thus, the Commission's informal but important role as a lobby for deeper integration and institutional reform accelerates during enlargement and continues during several stages of the process.

The 1965 Merger treaty provided the first opportunity for the Commission to advocate institutional reform. When the European Economic Community (EEC) and the European Atomic Energy Community (EURATOM) were launched in 1958, the two organizations shared a legal service, a statistics office, and an information service with the High Authority of the European Coal and Steel Community. This was an effort to reduce overlap resulting from the decision to have three separate Communities, with three separate executive bodies. From the outset, however, Commission president Hallstein, imbued with a strong "political" mission, lobbied to end this institutional anomaly by merging the three Communities or, as a preliminary measure, merging the three executives. As the largest of the three executives, the EEC Commission was especially vociferous in advocating a merger. Apart from administrative streamlining, the Commission anticipated that merging the three Communities would strengthen its power by incorporating a common energy policy and a common steel policy into the EC's overall economic policy. The Commission hoped that such increased power, together with direct elections to the EP (which did not happen until 1979), would "give the integration process a vigorous impulse in the direction of economic union and political union."[17]

In the event, merger proposals became an early victim of France's refusal to cede any more power to the Union. After four years of laborious negotiations, the member states agreed in April 1965 only to take the administrative step of merging the three executives. Ratification of the Merger treaty became, in turn, a victim of the "empty chair" crisis and its aftermath, notably de Gaulle's refusal to reappoint Hallstein as Commission president. As a result, the treaty was implemented only in July 1967, after Hallstein withdrew his candidacy.

The Commission's failure to achieve institutional reform and deeper integration at the time of the Merger treaty was the harbinger of a similar outcome five years later, on the occasion of the EU's first enlargement. According to President Malfatti, the first enlargement became "the main-spring of [the Commission's] political action."[18] The Commission lobbied in the early 1970s to strengthen the Commission and the EP and to revitalize the Community. In a speech at the signing of the Accession treaties in 1972, Malfatti urged that the Community's unique institutional structure be "safeguarded and enhanced to prevent the downgrading of the Community to a mere intergovernmental agreement and ensure for it the full executive competence, streamlined decision-making, and essentially political character of the independent institution that acts as a watchdog of the treaty and discharges the vital function of initiating proposals."[19] Earlier, Malfatti had expressed the hope that the forthcoming summit of EU leaders would tackle, among other pressing problems, "the functioning and reinforcement of the institutions of the enlarged Community."[20]

Like Hallstein, however, Malfatti failed to win greater power for the Commission and for the EU, despite the improved political climate of post–de Gaulle Europe. Not only did the member states remain unwilling to link enlargement to a further loss of sovereignty, but they refused to allow the Commission to sign the final act of the enlargement negotiations. This led an embittered Malfatti to observe, in a telling comment on the Commission's impotence and on the state of Commission-Council relations, that "there are times when prejudice replaces judgement, when an academic, legalistic approach replaces considerations of what is politically desirable. Sometimes, too, there is uncertainty where there should be clarity."[21]

By contrast, during the Mediterranean enlargement, the Commission eventually succeeded in linking accession to far-reaching reform and deeper integration. In February 1976, six months after Greece applied to join the EU and six months before entry negotiations began, Commission president Ortoli again linked deeper integration, institutional reform, and direct elections when he asked how the member states could not think "in terms of more radical change," given that direct elections would "recast the structure of the Community at a time when it must again tackle the problem of enlargement."[22] In a series of reports in early 1978, published even before Spain and Portugal lodged their applications, the Commission declared its "profound conviction that the challenge of [Mediterranean] enlargement can and must be the start of a new Community thrust towards the objectives set by the authors of the Treaties."[23] A Community twice its original size, the Commission warned, and far less homogeneous as a result of the different political, economic, and social structures of the new member states, would have greater difficulty reaching decisions and implementing them properly.[24] The Commission's exaggerated fear was that enlargement would destroy the EU by reducing it to a customs union or even a free trade area. Indeed, the Commission warned, enlargement "might . . . weaken [the Union] to such an extent that its fundamental objectives would be called into question."[25]

The report of the Three Wise Men, which came out in 1979, generally shared the Commission's concerns about the potential negative impact of Mediterranean enlargement on integration and decisionmaking. However, most member states, not least France, were unwilling at that time to take any action to limit intergovernmentalism and to share additional sovereignty. The heads of state and government listened politely to the conclusions of the Three Wise Men at the December 1979 European Council, but refused to implement virtually any of their recommendations.

Thus, during the application and early negotiation stages of the Mediterranean enlargement, the Commission—coincidentally allied with the Three Wise Men—failed to convince member states to deepen integration or to reform the Community's decisionmaking system. By the ratification stage of the Iberian accession, however, a profound change in the member states' perception of the EU's economic and political circumstances resulted in a renewed commitment to complete the internal market. Eager to implement the single market program by 1992, yet fearful of the institutional implications of enlargement without decisionmaking reform, the member states convened an ad hoc Committee on Institutional Affairs to suggest ways of strengthening Community policies and decisionmaking procedures. At the June 1985 Milan summit, where the heads of state and government discussed the committee's report, the Commission tried to force the issue by proposing that, as a short-term measure and without prejudice to general reform, the Treaty of Rome should be amended at the same time as the Accession treaties for Spain and Portugal were ratified. The Commission's suggested amendments focused on making decisionmaking more efficient and democratic and on increasing the Commission's executive powers. Because the European Council favored an IGC, however, the Commission decided not to pursue its effort to achieve an immediate decision in the context of enlargement.[26]

Instead, the Commission participated actively in the IGC, which was dominated by the implicit linkage between enlargement, deeper integration, and institutional reform. The ensuing Single European Act (SEA) was testimony to the Commission's persistence in advocating far-reaching reform and to the need for favorable political circumstances—the goal being to gain the member state support necessary for the Commission to succeed. The Commission's most conspicuous contribution to the SEA, and one specifically linked to enlargement, was a commitment to economic and social cohesion. Although the SEA was not as comprehensive as the Commission had hoped, the SEA's policy and procedural provisions presaged a significant improvement in the EU's fortunes. In most respects, the SEA was to confound its early critics—including the Commission—and lead to a significant deepening of European integration. In one respect, however, the SEA had a disappointing sequel: the member states never made good on the proposal to delegate to the Commission greater implementing powers.

The Commission's use of German reunification as leverage to achieve deeper integration can be considered to some extent in the context of enlargement. Once again, however, it was not the Commission but key member states—notably France and Germany—that determined the timing and agenda of the pre-Maastricht IGCs. The Commission is justifiably proud of both its immediate and sincere support for German reunification and the indispensable part it played in expediting East Germany's EU membership. But the Commission's success came at a high political price: it coincided with a number of major Commission initiatives, notably on monetary and political union, that combined to fuel the member states' perception and growing resentment of the Commission as overweening and too ambitious. Such resentment accounts in part for the Commission's relatively minor role in the 1991 IGC and its political demise during the Maastricht Treaty ratification crisis.

Having repeatedly attempted to exploit enlargement and related IGCs in order to increase its limited implementing powers, the Commission sought at the time of the Scandinavian and Austrian enlargement to press the member states to make good on their SEA undertaking in that regard. The preliminary stages of the Union's first accession, however, coincided with the Maastricht Treaty ratification debacle, when the Commission's political leverage was greatly reduced. In the post-Maastricht climate of rampant Europhobia, the Commission did not attempt to link the Scandinavian and Austrian enlargement to further deepening integration or reforming the decisionmaking process.

In conclusion, the links between enlargement, deeper integration, and institutional reform are clear. The Commission consistently argued that a wider Union would be a weaker Union unless the member states agreed to integrate further on the occasion of enlargement. But the logic of that argument, and the Commission's powers of persuasion, were never sufficient by themselves to impel the member states to act. It was other factors, such as the changing political and economic circumstances of the early 1980s, that led the member states to renew their commitment to the single market and to adopt the necessary institutional reforms, thereby launching the only appreciable deepening of European integration concurrent with enlargement.

Current and Future Enlargements

The EU has already embarked on a new series of enlargements. The European Council confirmed at its meetings in Copenhagen and Corfu that the associated countries of central and eastern Europe could join when they have met the necessary political and economic conditions. Ten of those countries have now applied for membership: Hungary and Poland (in 1994); Romania, Slovakia, Latvia, Estonia, Lithuania, and Bulgaria (all in 1995); and the Czech Republic and Slovenia (in 1996). In addition, three Mediterranean countries—Turkey, Cyprus, and Malta—have applications on the table, although those of Turkey and Malta have been sidelined (the former by the EU, the latter by the new Maltese government).

In some respects, the Commission's role in the new enlargements will be identical to its role in previous enlargements. Already, it has prepared opinions on the applications of Turkey, Cyprus, and Malta and is expected to do so before the end of 1997 on the central European applicants. Yet the new enlargements are likely to differ radically from earlier ones, thereby presenting the Commission with unique challenges and responsibilities. First, the exceptionally small size of the two Mediterranean applicants will affect their representation and involvement in the EU's institutions.

Moreover, Cyprus is bitterly divided between the Greek south and Turkish north.

Second, the large number and varying size of the central and eastern European potential members, and their relatively low level of economic development, have implications for the enlargement process, and especially for the future functioning of the EU's institutions and policies. As a result, the Union has adopted a new approach to the earlier stages of the Central and Eastern European Countries' (CEECs) enlargement, modifying the Commission's role accordingly. At the same time, the fortuitous convening of an IGC in 1996 gave the member states an opportunity to embark on wide-ranging institutional reform in the light of impending enlargement.

The Commission has assumed much greater responsibility than in any previous enlargement for helping to prepare the new applicants for membership. Of course, most countries from previous accessions had levels of economic and administrative development similar to that of the existing member states. Greece, Portugal, and Spain are the obvious exceptions. Understandably, the Union's approach to the eastern European accession is dictated in part by lessons from the Mediterranean enlargement, and especially by the problems of Greece's assimilation. Also, the EU's *acquis* and policies have developed greatly since the Mediterranean enlargements. In particular, the implementation of the single market program opened up an even greater gap between the member states and the Europe Agreement countries.

Accordingly, at the request of the heads of state and government at the Corfu summit, the Commission, along with the Council, drafted a comprehensive strategy for preparing the Europe Agreement countries to join the Union. The essential element of the strategy approved at the subsequent December 1994 Essen summit was to facilitate the countries' progressive integration into the internal market, through their phased adoption of the EU's expanded *acquis*. To get the process going, the Commission undertook at the Essen summit to present to the next European Council a White Paper outlining the measures the CEECs will need to adopt to participate in the single market. At the same time, the Commission would propose policies to promote integration through the development of infrastructure; cooperation in the framework of trans-European networks; and the promotion of intraregional cooperation, environmental cooperation, and cooperation in pillars II and III of the Maastricht Treaty.

Although onerous, the Commission's reporting requirements and its obligation to prepare the applicant countries for membership are proportionate to the probable impact of the next enlargements on the Commission's and the Union's character and structure. The opening of EU membership to the east, together with the new Mediterranean applications, raises the prospect of a Union of at least twenty members within the next ten to twenty years. The likely size and diversity of such a Union make it imperative for the existing members to devise in advance a workable institutional system and a durable policy framework.

The 1996–1997 IGC represented a useful opportunity for doing so. Indeed, the prospect of eastward enlargement has given the IGC the raison d'être it otherwise patently lacked. The 1996 IGC was mandated by the Maastricht Treaty to review the Treaty's institutional arrangements and its provisions for a Common Foreign and Security Policy (CFSP). In the aftermath of the ratification debacle, however, there is no enthusiasm among either the peoples or governments of the member states for a follow-up conference only three years after the Treaty was finally implemented. Now, enlargement may rescue the IGC and allow it to reform the treaties in a way that would not only facilitate enlargement but also make the EU's institutions and decisionmaking procedures more relevant and comprehensible to ordinary people. Thus, the Essen European Council endorsed the accession preparation strategy "in the knowledge that the institutional conditions for ensuring the proper functioning of the Union must be created at the 1996 IGC, which for that reason must take place before accession negotiations begin."[27]

At the 1985 IGC, the EU's impending enlargement was relevant but not central; at the 1996–1997 IGC, enlargement is dominant. Also, at the 1985 and 1991 IGCs, there was a concerted effort to deepen integration; in 1996–1997, there is not. Instead, the IGC focuses almost exclusively on institutional issues with a view to improving the existing Union's functioning, completing the Maastricht agenda, and facilitating EU expansion to the east.

The Commission's internal structure and working methods are not on the IGC's agenda, but the Commission's poor public image and declining political fortunes and the demands of enlargement make it imperative for the Commission to address those problems immediately. The Santer Commission is already attempting to improve administrative efficiency and, within the limits of the Commission's own freedom of action, to restructure its services. Yet it is difficult to foresee far-reaching reform. Here the lessons of previous enlargements are most instructive and to some extent reassuring. Future enlargements will result in more official languages but will not add to the existing three working languages (English, French, German); and future enlargements will bring into the Commission officials from many more countries, further encumbering the institution's bureaucracy but not necessarily to the point of collapse.

As for the size of the college, radical change is both unlikely and undesirable. Although the question of "national representation" on the Commission undoubtedly consumed a lot of time and energy at the IGC, radical reform is not necessarily in the Commission's interest. Indeed, it is arguably more important for the member states, their citizens, and the Commission to have direct, high-level channels of communication via "national" commissioners than to go through the politically painful and essentially unrewarding exercise of reducing the Commission's size. In the event, despite dire warnings about the unmanageability of a college of more than the existing number of commissioners, and about imaginative proposals to limit the college to ten or twelve, national governments are unlikely to surrender their right to appoint one commissioner each. In the end, with the exception of tiny Cyprus and Malta—which doubtless will be obliged to forgo the appointment of a commissioner—and the larger member states, which may, after a struggle, give up their second commissioners, the current system of selecting commissioners could well remain the same. Thus, in a Union of twenty-five states, the Commission would have twenty-three members, only three more than at present. Most important, the Commission is likely to retain sufficient flexibility to excel politically when favorable external circumstances coincide with an inspired presidency, as happened a decade ago.

As a result, the Commission will function much as it does now, with a group of undeclared but easily identifiable "core" commissioners, supported by powerful *Cabinets,* setting the Commission's agenda and launching major initiatives. In such a quasi-collegial system, the president will play an increasingly important role. The practice of EP approval of the Commission's president-designate, introduced in the Maastricht Treaty and first used at the time of Jacques Santer's nomination (with near disastrous consequences when he won only slim support), has the potential to strengthen the presidential office. An institutionally stronger presidency, a forceful presidential *Cabinet,* and a small group of powerful commissioners are essential for the Commission's survival and success in the post-IGC, postenlargement period.

Politically, the 1996–1997 IGC should enable the Commission to do what it has tried to do during previous enlargements: leverage the impending accessions in an effort to achieve greater power for itself, institutional reform for itself and for the Union, and deeper European integration. But prevailing circumstances will severely limit the Commission's options for the foreseeable future. Although Santer claims that the present Commission is politically influential because it contains more than the usual number of former senior ministers (including prime ministers), it was unlikely to make the kinds of demands or launch the kinds of initiatives at the 1996–1997 IGC that characterized the Delors Commission's contributions to either the 1985 or 1991 IGCs. Undoubtedly, the Commission would like to see Maastricht's three pillars replaced by a unitary structure, and wants at least to become centrally involved in more effective pillars II and III. However, given the current backlash against supranationalism and against the Commission, Santer surely realizes the political and public relations danger of making such proposals, for which there is little support in national capitals.

Instead, it is likely that the Commission will focus in the coming years on making the most of the Maastricht Treaty, including using its right of initiative in CFSP and, following the IGC, trying to achieve important but unglamorous objectives in the sphere of openness and transparency, such as reducing the number of legislative procedures (currently an astonishing twenty-three) and simplifying the Treaties' impenetrable language. Acutely aware of its vulnerability to charges of elitism and technocracy, the Commission will also strive to strengthen its indirect accountability to the public, something Santer feels his commissioners' high political profiles in their own countries are already helping to do. Finally, in the name of efficiency, the Commission will reassert its right to full implementation powers, originally conferred on it by the SEA but never granted by the Council.

Far from taking bold policy and institutional initiatives, the Commission was likely to be on the defensive during the IGC. One of the Commission's greatest challenges was to deflect some member states' demands, first made during the 1991 IGC, that the Commission be shorn of its exclusive right to initiate EU legislation. In 1991, the Commission successfully argued that a unique "European" perspective, free of excessive national influence, warranted the continued exclusivity of its right of initiative, which largely defines the Commission's position in the EU's institutional system. Six years later, however, with national governments more resentful of the Commission's position and eager to maximize their influence over the legislative process, the Commission may not be so fortunate.

The European Parliament's efforts to exert greater influence over the Commission's appointment and greater oversight of its operations will also worry the Commission. For much of the Community's history, Parliament and the Commission were cast as allies against the Council. Although they still have more in common with each other than with the Council, they are increasingly at odds, substantively and procedurally. The EP's investiture of the Commission, granted under the Maastricht Treaty and first exercised in 1995, generated unnecessary tension between the institutions. With the EP now pushing for an independent approval procedure for each commissioner, politically if not constitutionally, the Commission is in danger of ceding institutional primacy to the EP and the Council. As things now stand, Delors's pugnacious approach toward the EP in 1985 was in striking contrast to Santer's timidity in 1995.

In response to these challenges and, in some cases, outright assaults, the Commission could make a constitutional argument in favor of preserving the integrity of the EU's unique institutional structure. This will be all the more pressing in view of possible pressure at the IGC to go beyond the

Maastricht Treaty's institutionalization of variable geometry with respect to monetary union and social policy. Acutely aware of the risks to European integration and to European institutions of such a development, the Commission is deliberately playing down the prospect of radical change. Should it happen, however, the Commission, supported by Germany and some other states, will advocate preservation of the EU's single institutional structure.

Apart from constitutional and institutional principles, the IGC is likely to judge the Commission on its mixed record of administrative ability, legislative initiation, treaty protection, and budgetary management. Aware of these political realities, and eager to allay public criticism, Santer is striving to improve the Commission's performance and to develop close connections with national parliaments and regional authorities and bodies. Citing the subsidiarity principle, the Commission is more selective than ever before in its choice of legislative proposals, and more thorough in its preparation. At the same time, Commissioners Gradin and Liikanen, who share responsibility for the Commission's financial management, have set about putting the institution's financial house in order. Significantly, both commissioners come from the new Scandinavian member states. As for some of its new responsibilities under the Maastricht Treaty, the Commission is playing a crucial and deliberately understated role in the move toward monetary union. Proud and protective of its reporting and surveillance responsibilities under the Treaty's monetary union provisions, the Commission did not want the debate reopened at the IGC.

Finally, the Commission could use its indispensable role in the EU's current and future enlargements to strengthen its position. Already, the preapplication and application stages of those enlargements have involved the Commission in extensive preparatory work, culminating in the 1995 White Paper.[28] After the IGC, during the negotiation stage of enlargement, the Commission's skills as a broker and facilitator of compromise agreements will be essential for a successful outcome, as was the case with past enlargements. The Commission's independence of other institutions and of the member states, and its espousal of genuinely European interests, are vital for its mediatory role. As much as any other factor, the imminence and importance of future enlargements strengthen the Commission's claim to remaining at the center of the EU's institutional system, in full possession of its existing powers and prerogatives.

Notes

1. Noël, Émile, "Towards a New Institutional Balance of Powers," in Davignon, E., Ersboll, N., Lamers, K., Martin, D., Noël, É., and Viaber, F., eds.,

What Future for the European Commission? (Brussels: Philip Morris Institute for Public Policy Research, 1995), p. 63.

2. Commission of the European Communities, *Fifth General Report (1971)* (Luxembourg: Office of Official Publications [OOP], 1972), p. 21.

3. Commission of the European Communities, *Proposals for the Reform of the Commission of the European Communities and its Services* (Spierenburg Report) (Luxembourg: OOP, 1979).

4. Von der Groeben, Hans, *The European Community: The Formative Years: The Struggle to Establish the Common Market and the Political Community (1958–1966)* (Luxembourg: OOP), p. 25.

5. Commission, *Eighth General Report (1967)*, p. 448.

6. Commission, *Fourth General Report (1970)*, p. 361.

7. Commission, *Fifth General Report (1971)*, p. 395.

8. Commission, *Bulletin,* S1/78, p. 15.

9. Commission, *Bulletin,* 11/1979, p. 27.

10. Jenkins, R., *European Diary, 1977–1981* (London: Collins, 1989), p. 667.

11. Commission, *Thirteenth General Report (1979)*, p. 8.

12. Ross, G., "Inside the Delors *Cabinet," Journal of Common Market Studies* 32, no. 4 (December 1994), p. 500.

13. Commission, *Spierenburg Report,* p. 22.

14. Ross, "Inside the Delors Cabinet"; and Ross, G., *Jacques Delors and European Integration* (Oxford: Oxford University Press, 1995).

15. Commission, *Bulletin,* 3/1983, p. 17.

16. Commission, *Bulletin,* 11/1979, p. 28.

17. Von der Groeben, *The European Community,* p. 175.

18. Speech to the European Parliament, 8 February 1972, reprinted in Commission, *Fifth General Report (1971)*, p. x.

19. Quoted in Commission, *Sixth General Report (1972)*, p. xii.

20. Speech to the European Parliament, p. xi.

21. Speech to the European Parliament, p. xii.

22. Speech to the European Parliament, 10 February 1976, reprinted in Commission, *Ninth General Report (1975)*, p. xvi.

23. Commission, *Bulletin,* S1/78, p. 26.

24. Commission, *Bulletin,* S2/78, p. 14.

25. Commission, *Bulletin,* S1/78, p. 18.

26. Commission, *Nineteenth General Report (1985)*, pp. 27–28.

27. Essen summit communiqué, reprinted in Commission, *Bulletin,* 12/94, p. 13.

28. Commission, "Preparation of the Associated Countries of Central and Eastern Europe for Integration into the Internal Market of the European Union," Brussels, 3 May 1995.

3

The Council of Ministers and Enlargement: A Search for Efficiency, Effectiveness, and Accountability?

Geoffrey Edwards

Concern that enlargement would change the nature of the European Union (EU) and its institutions has been a source of debate ever since the British first applied for membership in 1961. Any widening has tended to be set against deepening; there has been a concern that the Community would be endangered and the closer union many seek would become impossible in the face of increased numbers and the greater challenge of diversity. But not only has there been a steady increase in numbers, from six to nine, to ten, to twelve, to fifteen in 1995, but the queue of those waiting at the door has steadily lengthened since 1989. It now stretches well beyond the Mediterranean states (such as Turkey), which have long declared their "European" vocation, and includes the countries of central and eastern Europe; the Union could expand to twenty-five, even thirty, states. The challenge of such a Union to the institutional structure of a Community designed for six states is obviously profound.

Enlargement, in giving rise to fears about the continued ability to maintain the dynamism of the integration process, has been an important factor in all the major treaty revisions so far. It may not always have been the primary factor but has certainly hovered in the background. As Keohane and Hoffmann put it in relation to the negotiation of the Single European Act (SEA) in 1985: "In a dialectical manner, the enlargement of the six to twelve first appearing as an antithesis to effective decision-making, became a decisive element in decision-making reform."[1] The same process was apparent in the negotiation of the Treaty on European Union (TEU) in 1991, including the consequences of the absorption of East Germany into the Federal Republic in 1989–1990—a case of accession without enlargement.[2] In each case, the often posed dichotomy of widening versus deepening played an important part in reinforcing some positions or in exacerbating problems. This was the case even if the outcome was usually a carefully, though not necessarily tidily, negotiated compromise that sidestepped the issue, so that deepening went together with widening. The dichotomy has so far proved to be somewhat false because all member states—as well as the central institutions of the EU—have had vested interests to promote or protect in the larger Union. These interests have required either constitutional reform, which has modified the institutional arrangements between national governments and the EU, or policy development—or, more usually, both.

Enlargement and treaty revision have frequently raised concerns over the effectiveness of the new order. Article B of the Maastricht Treaty, for example, refers to the aim of ensuring effectiveness of the TEU's new measures through the 1996 Intergovernmental Conference (IGC). Heads of state and government, at the 1994 Corfu European Council, established a Reflection Group on the 1996 IGC and called on it to consider further enlargement as part of the context for that conference. As a result, the group regarded improving the functioning of the EU and meeting the challenge of enlargement as fundamentals and devoted a whole chapter of a draft report to the need for greater effectiveness and democracy.[3] A key element in focusing the group's attention closely was the growing disillusionment of Europe's electorates with the EU, which the tortuous ratification of the TEU had only too clearly revealed, and which had been powerfully itemized by the CDU/CSU Fraktion in the German Bundestag in their report of September 1994.[4]

Widening Versus Deepening

The fear that widening and deepening were mutually exclusive was apparent even during the 1960s, when the EU faced the possibility of enlargement to include the British. The 1969 Hague summit sought to ensure the maintenance of core values (or rather the return to core values after the Gaullist challenge to them) by positing the triptych of "completion, deepening and enlargement." But the early experiences of an enlarged EU were not particularly happy: the British, for example, sought to renegotiate their accession terms almost immediately. That coincided with the 1974 oil crisis and then economic stagnation and inflation, so that the prospect of a second (Mediterranean) round of enlargement reinforced a general concern. As Emanuele Gazzo put it:

> After the first enthusiastic reactions [to the applications of the newly emerged democratic states of Greece, Spain, and Portugal], everyone in Europe felt some sort of uneasiness and a feeling that we were going to enter into a new political phase which would probably lead to the creation of a "different Europe."[5]

That "different Europe" was generally assumed to be a less firmly struc-tured Europe, one suggestion being that "an enlarged Community could thus resemble more the free trade area proposed by Mr. Maudling in 1957 than the European Union envisaged by the founders of the EEC."[6]

Such concerns need to be set against a background of several reports and articles in the 1970s that suggested that uniformity was not necessarily the overall medium- or even longer-term goal. Ralf Dahrendorf, the former commissioner, appeared to advocate a Europe à la carte, where cooperation should occur only in those areas where it was useful and realizable.[7] In November 1974, Willy Brandt suggested a Europe of different classes or tiers,[8] while in December 1975, the former Belgian prime minister, Leo Tindemans, published his *Report on European Union,* which included sup-port for different speeds of integration among different EU member states, especially toward Economic and Monetary Union (EMU). The aim, for Tindemans at least, was to safeguard the possibility and desirability of moving toward EMU, without being held back by those whose levels of development might prohibit it.[9]

The accession of Greece, and the ultimate prospect of enlargement to include the two Iberian states, led to such ideas being developed further in the 1980s. Helen Wallace, who saw the focus of the debate as being on the rules governing decisionmaking and the identification of new tasks within a Community of greater diversity, listed the different strategies under discus-sion.[10] At one extreme was the continued development of the Communities on the basis of the uniform application of all policies—whatever the dispar-ities in economic and political systems—and at the other extreme was a Europe à la carte. In between lay ideas of tiers and speeds, graduation (*abgestüfte*), concentric circles, and variable geometry. The primary dis-tinction for most of these was to what extent all the member states had to agree with the ultimate goals and at what pace and in what manner states were willing or able to reach those goals. Orthodoxy held that, the experi-ence of the European Monetary System (EMS) notwithstanding, everyone should pursue the same goals at the same speed, with derogations allowed only to new member states—and those would usually be negotiated on the basis of reciprocal restrictions on other issues, such as the free movement of labor into the existing member states. But even if not all member states fully participated in the EMS, common goals were agreed on and all were involved in decisionmaking. Variable geometry, however, raised the possi-bility that not all member states would pursue common goals and, beyond a core group of policies (the single market, say, and other closely related policies), that they would decide themselves in which policy areas they would participate.

It was really only with Maastricht that the veil of conformity was dropped, with the British and Danish opting out on social policy and stage

III of EMU, and on defense. When decisions have been taken within the EU on the basis of the social protocol, to which Britain is not a party, the British have not participated in the decisionmaking process.[11] Yet, despite the precedent they seemed to have established, all the member states remained determined to restrict opting out to existing members; they were not about to allow opt-outs or opt-ins to be taken up by the European Free Trade Association (EFTA) applicants in their membership negotiations prompted by the TEU. Each applicant was obliged to accept not only the *acquis communautaire* and provisions and the *acquis politique,* but also the *finalité politique.* Moreover, the Copenhagen European Council of June 1993 laid down that the accession of the Central and Eastern European Countries (CEECs) "will take place" as soon as they are able to assume the obligations of membership—reiterating the point that "membership presupposes the candidate's ability to take on the obligations of membership including adherence to the aims of political, economic and monetary union."[12]

However, given the prospect of the EU's expansion to more than twenty-five members, it has become less a question of whether the same conditions will be demanded of all new applicants than a question of whether, in the face of such numbers and the greater diversity of interests they bring, the EU can actually meet the demands for uniformity of policy within a single institutional framework. Effective decisionmaking in such circumstances becomes ever more problematic. As the 1993 Copenhagen European Council conclusions put it, "The Union's capacity to absorb new members, while maintaining the momentum of integration, is also an important consideration in the general interest of both the Union and the candidate countries."[13] In the dichotomy between enlarging and deepening, Metcalfe has suggested that the latter has tended to revolve around furthering federalist ambitions rather than improving the management of European integration.[14]

Efficiency and Democracy

Many of the concepts of efficiency and effectiveness in public policymaking and administration commonly used at the national level may sometimes be difficult to transfer to the international (European) level. This is especially the case, of course, for those concepts derived from practice in unitary systems where considerable efforts have been made to divorce administration and management from political decisionmaking and responsibility. The EU, after all, remains a constitutional hybrid, neither classically federal nor confederal—nor is it even a coincidence of sovereign states where bargaining remains exclusively interstate. The EU also includes supranational and intergovernmental, even transnational, procedures within a single institutional framework. In keeping with the principle of subsidiarity, policy complementarity and approximation tend to be valued more highly than harmonization and centralization. And while rationality in decisionmaking may be prized, it has, by most accounts, rarely been achieved in the Council of Ministers. The practice of resolving conflicts of interest through bargaining and compromise is supposedly common to all levels of government, but the negotiation of package deals within the EU has become almost an art form, because of the need to avoid institutional paralysis. But, as Scharpf suggested in his highly pertinent analogy with the German federal system, the outcome is likely to be decidedly suboptimal for both those participating and the EU itself.[15] Moreover, effective decisionmaking, in the sense of legislation uniformly decided and implemented so that outcomes match objectives, also remains just an aspiration. As the Court of Auditors regularly discovers, member states may pay lip service to effective implementation but do not always have the capacity or the inclination to ensure it (and then they tend to use the Commission as a scapegoat for their own failings). In the circumstances, a determination to avoid too much transparency and accountability might have been expected, and results so far suggest that despite pressure from a number of governments, the majority remain convinced of the practicality and desirability of only limited steps toward greater openness in EU governance.

The attempt to balance efficiency in decisionmaking with the protection of national prerogatives, whether real or symbolic, necessarily focuses attention not only on the institutional balance in Europe but specifically on the Council. Whatever one's theoretical (or even ideological) approach to integration, the Council is at the heart of decisionmaking in the EU.[16] From the beginning, the formula was that the Commission proposed and the Council disposed, even if that has become marginally more complicated with the still limited moves toward codecision with the European Parliament (EP). Clearly, because the Council remains the forum where national interests are represented, it is often held to epitomize an integration process that leaves the political order in Europe essentially one of states.[17] And yet, even from an early stage, an alternative view was possible. Ernst Haas, for example, wondered why it was that the Council of the European Coal and Steel Community (ECSC) was different from other organizations in Europe, such as the Organization for European Economic Cooperation (OEEC, later OECD). He also wondered why such a clearly intergovernmental body continuously produced decisions that endorsed progress toward economic integration.[18]

Haas's answer of "engagement"—by which he meant the process of identification with decisionmaking procedures that led member governments to consider themselves completely "engaged" by the results even if they did not fully concur with them[19]—seemed somewhat optimistic once General Charles de Gaulle adopted his "empty chair" policy and insisted on the "Luxembourg compromise." And yet, even during the worst period of "Eurosclerosis" in the late 1970s, Christoph Sasse could write of the Community: "Its institutions are, for all the inadequacies, something more than mere forums for intergovernmental coordination exercises."[20] With the reforms introduced (or in some cases, codified) by the 1987 SEA and extended by the 1993 TEU, especially those relating to qualified majority voting (QMV), the nature of the Council becomes much more ambiguous. Despite the post-Maastricht reemphasis on the state and the questioning of decisionmaking procedures, few member governments have consistently challenged the decisionmaking process. The Council remains key for what Bulmer and Wessels have termed "transnational" negotiations:

> On the one hand, governments see the need to enlarge the scope of EC activities in order better to fulfil the needs of national welfare states, on the other, they are reluctant to give up control of their policies. As a result of this, government and national bureaucracies are in a permanent process of "transnational" negotiations.[21]

The Council (especially if one includes the European Council in addition to the Council of the Union, or Council of Ministers) is both the arbiter of policy and an integral part of a supranational decisionmaking process.

The continued tension between integrationist and cooperatist ideas is seen clearly in the Maastricht decision to move toward a single institutional framework that makes its decisions by different procedures. The renamed Council of the Union thus became the body responsible for decisions within the EU, the Common Foreign and Security Policy (CFSP, the so-called second pillar of Maastricht), and the Justice and Home Affairs (JHA and pillar III) frameworks. The changes had at least a potential importance. On the one hand, QMV was extended to new areas within pillar I and, although unanimity remains the norm in pillars II and III, there is provision, albeit under heavily circumscribed conditions (the European Council has to decide unanimously to allow it), for majority voting within the CFSP and for decisions to be taken under the so-called *passerelle* of J.9 of the JHA within the EU framework. Similarly, although it is not the only right it enjoys under the Treaty of Rome, the Commission under Maastricht is entitled to make initiatives in the second and third pillars. Since Maastricht allows the Commission to be associated with all aspects of the CFSP, this includes initiatives relating to security and, perhaps in time, even to defense. On the other hand, the European Council has been given a very much higher profile.

The Maastricht compromise package was much criticized, and there probably have been efforts to tidy up certain elements of it at the 1996 IGC.

What the Treaty reflected, though, was compromise among the member states on ways to bring about more efficient and effective decisionmaking that was also more democratic in the radically different political and economic circumstances in Europe after 1989. Efficiency, effectiveness, and the lack of democratic accountability within the EU have frequently been decried. And yet, even if not all member states agree on such values, there are real and potential costs if these are neglected. Whether individually or as a bundle, they have been sufficiently important to enough member states to have played a vital role in the creation of a package of measures that has deepened the integration process—whatever the rhetoric deployed by governments to explain the results. After all, a basic requirement of any package is that decisions regarding its elements be timely and appropriate in terms of the instruments deployed. Furthermore, while the policies themselves need to be adequate to meet the purpose for which they were designed, they must also be able to be implemented effectively and enforced uniformly (unless, of course, they are not meant to be). For most governments, the pursuit of efficiency and effectiveness thereby becomes a part of the package deal itself.

Given the UK's political culture of bureaucratic efficiency and political effectiveness (actual political practice being a different matter), such values have been given a particularly high priority by the British. This has been clear, for example, in the UK's approach to its council presidencies.[22] At a more popular level, there has been much hype about fraud and inefficiency, usually about other people's fraudulent or evasive action. During the discussions that led to the SEA, the point was accepted by Margaret Thatcher that, in the interests of more efficient decisionmaking on preferred policies—above all the completion of the single market—QMV would be necessary.[23] This is not to suggest that efficiency has been made a principle above others. The willingness of successive British governments to support any other member state invoking the Luxembourg compromise, whatever the issue involved and the relevant British interests, is revealing. In the example, too, of the Social Chapter opt-out, given its limited development of social provisions beyond those of the Treaty of Rome, dogma appeared to be emphasized at the expense of rationality. And yet, there is a deep-seated concern for efficiency and effectiveness, a sense of being potentially disadvantaged if such values were not strengthened within the Council and the other institutions. In emphasizing such values and the need for practicable policies, the British might well appear cautious and reluctant partners. They would, of course, prefer to see themselves, almost paradoxically in some instances, as ensuring greater unity through the effective implementation and enforcement of agreed policy decisions—hence the dislike of the CDU/CSU and French proposals on core groupings and concentric circles.

In terms of future enlargement, the British government has, as in the past, been confident that there can be a wider and looser Union, and that the efficient and effective implementation of its preferred policies can be maintained in conditions of greater diversity. Elsewhere, however, there are signs of increasing doubt that such core interests as the single European market can be easily maintained without further strengthening the institutions. The dilemma may not yet be perceived as acute, but the concern to maintain effective policies in Europe to ensure the gains of membership, not least the single market, will inevitably have to be set against the political difficulties of British governments with regard to Europe and British membership in the EU.

Other member states have tended to place greater store on other values. Germany, for example, has frequently been at the forefront of moves toward strengthening the role of the EP—as much for reducing popular concern over the so-called democratic deficit within the Community as for longer-term European federalist motives. It may not always have been an overriding concern, and in the face of others' reluctance to develop codecision too far, the German government has been content to accept limited moves. So long as the EU remained concerned largely with technicalities, such modest improvements caused no great problems. Maastricht, however, provided a salutary lesson, not only in terms of popular hostility to further integration in Denmark and in France, but also in the extent of the disenchantment and disillusionment within Germany, whether among *länder* governments or the population at large. Despite the extension of the cooperation procedures and codecision under Maastricht, the EU had simply not achieved the democratic legitimacy those within its decisionmaking processes had assumed it had. Such a miscalculation was perhaps not surprising in view of the growing gap between government and governed discernible in many western European states and the "crisis of the nation state."[24]

The different dimensions of democratic accountability and legitimacy are dealt with in the Maastricht Treaty. Foremost, of course, were the role, responsibilities, and powers of the EP with the extension of the cooperation procedures and the development of codecision to include compulsory conciliation and—in addition to issues such as new members and association agreements—Parliament's positive assent to Council decisions in areas such as citizenship and the structural and cohesion funds. But Maastricht also mentions national democratic practices, recognizing the need, with the extension of QMV, for national parliaments to be more closely involved in the legislative process. One aspect of particular importance has been timely access to full information so that the parliaments can effectively scrutinize their government's actions even if, on most issues within the EU's competence, they had long lost the inclination or the ability to hold governments accountable.

One element, seized upon perhaps because of the long-standing criticism of the secrecy, complexity, and opaqueness of the EU's decisionmaking process, was that of transparency; Declaration 17 of Maastricht points to the linkage between transparency and democratic values. The EP, for example, had been a consistent critic of the Council's role as a legislature that met behind closed doors; national parliaments (with the exception, perhaps, of the Danish Folketing) had been increasingly vocal in their criticisms of national governments as being uninformative and unresponsive, especially after the SEA. Opening up Council meetings and providing easier access to official information, reporting to the EP more fully, and explaining common positions all formed part of a much discussed package within the Council machinery.

But even if member governments recognized the importance of transparency to democratic accountability, they continued to have differences on precisely how both should be developed, especially in view of the fundamental challenges to traditional procedures revealed in the Maastricht ratification debates. There was, for example, considerable reluctance on the part of some member states over the conditions under which the TEU's ombudsman and the public could gain access to Council and Commission documentation: the interinstitutional declaration of October 1993 was subsequently undermined by the Council's later more restrictive code of conduct. The Dutch, in favor of greater access, took the Council to the European Court of Justice on the grounds that these restrictions had been agreed illegally. The idea that the Council, as legislature, should conduct its debates in public was also toned down in 1993 to mean simply television coverage. But coverage was only of the initial *tour de table* in the Council—where set speeches were the norm—or of case presentations by the Commission on issues such as agricultural prices. The success of this coverage has been debatable.[25]

It is perhaps only too obvious that democratic accountability and transparency have played an important part in the past development of the institutional structure of the Union. Certainly they played a significant role in the final compromise packages of the SEA and the TEU. Their importance, in other words, is not new. But with the prospect of further enlargement, they take on an even greater significance and urgency. This is because the means so far used to improve the existing institutional structure and the decisionmaking process look increasingly problematic and difficult. The continued "stretchability" of an institutional system designed for six relatively homogeneous states, reformed only marginally to encompass nine, ten, twelve, and now fifteen rather more diverse states, must be considered doubtful.

Reforms, Past and Present

To assess the possible impact of further enlargement on the institutional structure, it is worth looking back at the way in which the member states and the EU institutions have dealt with these issues within the context of past enlargement. Engel and Welz have summarized a number of discernible patterns in terms of developing methods and procedures already in use; introducing new elements (such as providing for an Ombudsman in the TEU or enabling the Court of Justice to fine member states); and implementing more radical reforms to change the Union's system of governance.[26]

The search for better management and coordination received a particularly strong stimulus with the 1972 and 1974 summits in Paris. These proposed a wide range of new issues to be dealt with at the European level by the newly enlarged Community of Nine. The initial assumption that foreign ministers meeting in the General Affairs Council would be able to exercise an overall responsibility—the so-called La Marlia procedure[27]—soon proved misguided. Foreign ministers, even though they straddled both Community issues and those that came within European Political Cooperation (EPC), were not always in a position, either politically or technically, to coordinate the activities of other ministers. Finance ministers were not always amenable to such management, but neither they nor the foreign ministers were able to rein in the biggest-spending council of all—agriculture. To many, only heads of government (and/or of state) were in a position to exercise sufficient control; this provided a considerable fillip to French president Giscard d'Estaing's ideas of institutionalizing summitry. Nonetheless, despite the growing role of the heads of state and government in the European Council (discussed below), the Reflection Group has suggested that the General Affairs Council regain its coordinating role to ensure consistency over all the areas covered by Maastricht.[28]

But because the fragmentation in decisionmaking was taking place in increasingly adverse economic circumstances, the still extra-Community European Council established, in December 1978, a Committee of Three (known thereafter as the Three Wise Men) to report on institutional arrangements to bring about "the proper operation of the Communities . . . and for progress towards European Union." The report was to take into account the prospect of enlargement to twelve member states.[29] Although the Three Wise Men regarded institutional factors as secondary to economic ones, they did provide a number of suggestions that were acted on over the succeeding decade and that still provide a useful checklist during discussions on the possible enlargement to twenty-four plus.

In broad outline, the Three Wise Men suggested that there was both a vertical dimension to management, which involved political factors and national sensitivities, and a horizontal one, created by the sheer amount of business to transact in different forums. In relation to the Council structure, the Three Wise Men called for a "clearer definition, and the consistently more efficient execution, of responsibilities for the management of business," and suggested that political priorities needed to be established at the highest level, with improved coordination at both the Community and national levels. They also made a number of practical suggestions relating to the presidency of the Council and to the Committee of Permanent Representatives (COREPER) that, despite the changes of the intervening sixteen years, were echoed by the Reflection Group in their report (discussed below). The Three Wise Men—who serve as independents rather than as representatives of governments—also proposed increased use of majority decisions as well as the devolution of decisions to lower levels, including more delegation of management tasks to the Commission.[30]

It is now widely held that more than 80 percent of decisions are taken at or below the level of COREPER, which are then taken by the Council as "A" points.[31] While initially allowed for under the Treaty of Rome, COREPER was first referred to in the Merger treaty as responsible for preparing the work of the Council and carrying out tasks assigned to it. It was initially criticized both as a further manifestation of state dominance in undermining the role of the Commission and as an example of the further technocratization of the EU.[32] However, it gradually became accepted as an essential element in Community decisionmaking. According to Spinelli, this was partly because permanent representatives, en bloc, went "native," caught up in continuous meetings that created "a mandate to contribute to the Community's success"; they became "interpreters and defenders of the points of view of the Commission before their own governments and administrations."[33] The situation would appear to have changed relatively little; Dietrich von Kyaw, the German permanent representative, was reported as saying, only "half in jest," that the permanent representative was known in Bonn not as the *ständiger Vertreter* (permanent representative) but as the *ständiger Verräter* (permanent traitor).[34]

In terms of coordination, both the horizontal and vertical axes meet in COREPER: the permanent representatives are responsible for judging at what point a dossier needs further consideration by the experts in the working groups or the point at which a political decision is required by ministers. Their responsibility (whether as COREPER II, ambassadors, or COREPER I, their deputies) for coordinating across the range of EU activities has grown continuously—in the past limited only by the role of the Special Committee for Agriculture (SCA), the Monetary Committee, and Committee 113 (on external trade matters). Most significantly, the TEU, in the interests of establishing at least a formal unitary decisionmaking process, extended COREPER's mandate to include responsibility for final submissions to ministers on CFSP and JHA issues. This was not established without considerable tension and continuing suspicion on the part of the Political Committee and the K.4 Committee (named after the article in the TEU Title VI establishing the JHA), although, officially, COREPER retains the final say. But it is also clear that COREPER does not have exclusive responsibility over the unitary decisionmaking structure called for under Maastricht. The aim of merging the working groups of the three pillars whose subjects overlapped proved difficult, with several redividing. Although developing further COREPER's coordination and preparatory role remains key, there must be doubts on a practical level about doing so, even if such a course was recommended by the Reflection Group.

While the significance of COREPER has received surprisingly little academic attention to date, the growing role of the Council presidency has been well documented.[35] Initially it had a relatively minor role, responsible for organizing and chairing meetings, assisted by the Council Secretariat and in close liaison with the Commission. From 1970 until 1987, when the Political Secretariat was set up, the presidency was also responsible by itself for organizing meetings of EPC. Organizing meetings, agendas, minutes, or conclusions at all levels of the Council machinery, even with the support of the Council Secretariat and in cooperation with the Commission (practice has varied enormously), has not only placed considerable strains on member state administrations in executing the general responsibility for coordination, but always threatens discontinuity as one presidency replaces another. Contrasts in style can sometimes be marked.[36] Lack of continuity has often been reinforced by the fact that the presidency also allowed member states to seize the opportunity to pursue proposals they particularly favored—at least to the extent that six months in office and an existing momentum of business allowed. This aspect was developed further in the 1980s, when it became a requirement (as recommended by the Three Wise Men) for the incoming presidency to present a program of action to the EP and to answer for its progress at the end of its tenure. In attempting to achieve its program, the presidency came to play a more significant role in mediating among the member states. In some respects, the presidency thereby complemented the role of the Commission; in others, supported by an increasingly active Council Secretariat, it was supplementing, even supplanting, a Commission that, with its own preferred policy proposals, appeared more as an nth state. "Confessionals" and lunchtime and corridor "discussions" conducted by the presidency became the accepted means and opportunities for bringing about compromise.

At the same time, presenting its program to the EP meant that the presidency became even more the focal point of the Council-EP relationship. This too has developed further with the constitutional changes of the SEA and TEU. The presidency not only answers parliamentary questions, takes part in debates on behalf of the Council, and exchanges information in the committees but, with the SEA, its functions have expanded to include reporting and explaining common positions within the Council and organizing conciliation if the EP continues to reject the Council's decisions. It also takes a primary role in attempting to maintain the Council's unity in the conciliation process, not necessarily an easy task given the opportunity the procedure offers member states in the defeated minority to reopen negotiations.

Externally too the role of the presidency became more important. It was not simply a question of the presidency's responsibilities to represent the member states within an EPC context (issuing declarations, delivering *démarches* to third parties, etc.). In addition, the growing number of "mixed" agreements, straddling the EC/EPC divide, has meant the representative role of the Council alongside the Commission has become heavier. Given this increased burden on the administrative resources of the country holding the presidency and the need to ensure continuity between one presidency and the next, the Nine, in the face of enlargement to include Greece, introduced the idea of the troika, whereby the presidency would be assisted by the preceding and succeeding presidencies.[37] While EPC as such was formalized in the SEA, the troika was formally recognized only in the TEU. But even if it has sometimes proved cumbersome and not always the most credible means of projecting a coherent foreign policy on behalf of the Union, the troika has been regarded as particularly useful and necessary. It is not surprising that it has been the subject of serious thought, not least because of the infrequency of any one member state holding the presidency in an enlarged Union and because the Union will contain so many small, even micro, states.

Still, at the more technical end of the Engel-Welz categories (see above), the growing role of the Council Secretariat has also proved highly significant in the continued development of the presidency, especially in its supporting and coordinating role. Insofar as it has been a more traditional, low-key, servicing bureaucracy, it has not been regarded with any great suspicion by member states. That was perhaps the key to its gradual consolidation of influence. The TEU, for example, brought the Political Secretariat within the Council Secretariat, albeit still structured on a distinctive basis (with secretariat officials matched by officials seconded from national foreign ministries) and thereby perhaps being somewhat overstaffed. While the modalities of that incorporation took time to emerge, it was clear that from being "a service organization of note-takers and clock-watchers, the Council secretariat is to become the Union's second executive."[38]

A provision considerably more politically significant to the governance of the EU, even if it appeared in the original Treaties, has been the increased use of majority voting in the Council. The Three Wise Men called for its greater use in dealing with technical issues. It is, of course, not always easy to agree on what is technical—national attitudes differ (not least when brought out of the confines of the working group into the light cast by the mass media), and changes can take place over time. But voting has become increasingly common—with all that has entailed in terms of national strategies and tactics within the Council—and has embraced under both the SEA and the TEU an ever growing number of issues. These have included several introduced during the 1970s or early 1980s under Article 235 of the Treaty of Rome that were subsequently incorporated into the SEA on the basis of unanimity and that, under the TEU, were dealt with on the basis of QMV (environment, education issues, etc.). Some of them (such as visa policy or development cooperation) were also closely interrelated with the other pillars. The extension of QMV has traditionally been regarded as the only way for the Council to avoid immobilization.

QMV might have been regarded as essential for the completion of the single market, but the British especially were considerably reluctant to accept its further extension in the Maastricht Treaty. Uncertainty in the UK over whether the Luxembourg compromise still applied after the SEA—for Douglas Hurd in 1990, for example, it still "hovered over the discussion"[39]—increasingly became outright hostility to any further modification of veto rights. One aspect of this was the Major government's determination to seek to maintain the smallest blocking minority possible during the EFTA enlargement negotiations—that is, no change in the situation that existed in the Union of Twelve, a blocking minority of twenty-three votes out of the total seventy-six. Despite the threat to the enlargement process, John Major was initially supported in his efforts by the Spanish and, perhaps, French. By early spring 1994, however, the British were isolated. A compromise was nonetheless reached in March. Under the so-called Ioannina compromise it was agreed, in words redolent of Luxembourg, that if there were between twenty-three and twenty-six[40] votes opposing adoption by QMV, "the Council will do all in its power to reach, within a reasonable time and without prejudicing time limits laid down in the Treaties and by secondary law . . . a satisfactory solution that could be adopted by at least 68 votes."[41] The procedure was to be reviewed at the 1996 IGC. It was enough to allow enlargement to take place and Major to claim victory, but it was perhaps a preview of a longer-running battle in the next round, not least because of the small size of many of the potential members.

A further recommendation put forward by the Three Wise Men, which several member governments had already determined to pursue, was setting goals at the highest level, that is, at the level of heads of state and government. In its early years, the European Council was, of course, regarded with deep suspicion by many European federalists who saw it very much as a French, or even Giscardian, plot to emphasize still further the role of the French head of state. But there was also a general concern over the trend toward reemphasizing the importance of national governments in an enlarged and, seemingly after the 1974 oil embargo, beleaguered EU. And yet the position of the European Council at the apex of the EU and the determinedly intergovernmental EPC frameworks became increasingly ambiguous.[42] On the one hand, while remaining formally outside the decisionmaking process, the European Council was increasingly referred to by Councils of Ministers unable to reach a political agreement. It gradually became, in other words, a sort of political court of appeals within the EU framework, with issues pushed "upstairs" for heads of state and government to deal with. Moreover, in seeking to set overall guidelines and strategies for the EU, the Council of Ministers tended to reach conclusions, via a variety of reports, that created the framework for further EU action. It then became increasingly the case that European Councils determined much of the subsequent work of the Council of Ministers and the agendas set by the incoming presidency, especially on the bigger, more politically sensitive issues.

In addition, a body conceived very largely as providing leaders of western Europe with the opportunity for a "cozy fireside chat" on the big issues of the day, free from institutional constraints, gradually found that it could not exclude, let alone ignore, the Commission and its president. Within a decade of the European Council's establishment, it had become inconceivable for the Commission president to be excluded from its normal meetings. Indeed, so *communautaire* had the Council become that heads of government also began to include a report from the president of the EP. European Councils, in other words, gradually became an integral part of the EU institutional structure, albeit recognized as such only in the Maastricht Treaty. As the Reflection Group put it, "The Council's role is essential to the Union, as the ultimate political impulse and apex of democratic legitimacy in the Union's policy and decision-making."[43]

Reform and the Future

These, then, have been among the more important ways by which the EU has sought to improve a decisionmaking process that, while not wholly inefficient or ineffective or even wholly undemocratic despite public perceptions, has won little popular legitimacy. The prospect of enlarging the EU to include four EFTA countries began a process both within and outside the institutions to examine the wider implications of a further stretching of that institutional structure. The climate was heavily influenced by the Maastricht debate, in which there had been such suspicion of the EU's institutions that an early draft of an internal Commission paper that suggested a reduced role for smaller member states had been seized on during the Danish referendum to strengthen the "no" campaign. The final "yes" vote in Denmark and the *"petit oui"* in France provided little in the way of complacency, not least when it became increasingly clear, from the European Councils in Lisbon, Edinburgh, Corfu, and Essen that the EFTA enlargement was to be followed far more quickly than could ever have been imagined in 1989–1990 by further waves of acceding states from the east and the Mediterranean.

Any discussion has to take account of the ways in which the 1996 IGC deals with the concerns for efficiency, effectiveness, accountability, and transparency. While Corfu charged the Reflection Group to look at these issues in the light of further enlargement, it is far from certain that the political situation in several member states will allow for any strong or imaginative leadership. Nonetheless, with the Ioannina compromise's call for a review of weighted voting in 1996, and the hierarchy of laws under Declaration 16 to the TEU, which has important implications for efficient decisionmaking, the IGC is required to review such issues. In addition, there is the general mandate of Article N(2) of the TEU, which calls for an examination of the new provisions of the Treaty in light of the objectives of Article B, which refers to "the aim of ensuring the effectiveness of the mechanisms and the institutions of the Community."

Even if the IGC prefers not to focus on further enlargement and its consequences, many recent debates and discussion papers do take account of the possible increase of EU membership to twenty-four and more.[44] Traditional battlelines have in some cases been drawn up between those in favor of further integration and those preferring only cooperation from, say, the out-and-out federalist position of the Bertelsmann Stiftung,[45] in which the Council becomes a second legislative chamber, to the Euroskeptical European Policy Forum, in which the Commission becomes more of a traditional bureaucracy servicing the member states in the Council.[46] But despite the political potential of Euroskeptics in several countries (not least the UK) to disrupt the IGC process as well as further enlargement, there has been less of an ideological debate than one alarmed by the enormity of enlarging to the whole of Europe. At one level, therefore, there have been renewed debates over cores and peripheries, multispeeds, variable geometry, and concentric circles, many of which imply a radical modification of the principles on which the EU has formally been based. Ludlow with Ersboll sum up those principles by stating

> that the weak accept the same goals as the strong and submit themselves
> to the discipline necessary to obtain them and that the strong acknowledge

their solidarity with the weak politically and financially. The reality is what makes both principles feasible, namely the single institutional framework.[47]

But within that single institutional framework, the opportunities available for doing more than modifying or developing methods and procedures already in existence appear relatively limited. Given the interests engaged, and the means by which preferred strategies are pursued and negotiated, the debate seems still to echo the past, with relatively few new embellishments. Perhaps the capacity for inertia on the part of established institutions, including member states, should not be underestimated, especially in circumstances of political uncertainty.

That uncertainty in the face of such a large expansion of membership has tended to focus attention on procedural issues relating to the management of business and the means of reconciling differences. The presidency, especially, has been singled out for reform, as well as the issue of more majority voting to stave off paralysis. It was suggested earlier that the presidency has come to play a key role in the decisionmaking process. Any discontinuities between presidencies have been offset in the eyes of many by the salutary lesson that responsibility for managing the Union belongs to each member government; in any case, lack of continuity has been partially met by the establishment of the troika. But with a Union of twenty-four plus, and the continued rotation of the office every six months, the benefits of renewed energy on the part of each incoming presidency might be offset by administrative incapacity as well as inexperience, loss of efficiency, and external credibility. By itself, the troika does not meet the problem completely, for three small states often follow each other (see Table 3.1); attention has therefore been given to ways in which the troika system might be extended and developed. In the aftermath of the December 1994 Essen European Council, a procedure was agreed on that always ensured the participation of a bigger state in the troika—with the Dutch being given honorary "big" status. The Reflection Group was unable to take this further, however, as there was no consensus on a more permanent, longer-term procedure. Ludlow has suggested team presidencies, in which four or five representative groups would be set up. They would be representative in the sense of geographical spread, length of membership in the Union, and size. The essential functions of the role would remain the same even if the execution of those functions might be radically altered. The group would then hold the presidency for a year to eighteen months.[48] Other suggestions have included delinking the presidency from any rotation by instituting an elective presidency. Most suggest that the resources available to the presidency at the European level be increased.

Table 3.1   The Possible Rotation of the Presidency of the Council in an
             Enlarged EU

België	Lietuva [Lithuania]
Bulgarija	Luxembourg
Cesko [Czech Republic]	Magyarorszag [Hungary]
Danmark	Malta
Deutschland	Nederland
Eesti [Estonia]	Österreich [Austria]
Ellas [Greece]	Polska
España [Spain]	Portugal
France	România
Hrvatska [Croatia]	Slovenija
Ireland	Slovensko [Slovakia]
Italia	Suomi [Finland]
Kypron [Cyprus]	Sverige [Sweden]
Latvija	Turkiye
	United Kingdom

Note: Other possibilities are Albania, Bosnia, Iceland, Liechtenstein, Macedonia, Norway, Serbia, and Switzerland.

The presidency is clearly important—perhaps too important in the future to be left to the vagaries of domestic politics. Moreover, a gap of ten, twelve, or fifteen years between holding the presidency obviously does not lend itself to efficiency. The new proposals, however, have to avoid both the dangers of incoherence—not least during the period when responsibilities are first allocated and tasks learned—and further encouragement to establish a directory of the larger member states. The example in the conflict in the former Yugoslavia of the contact group, comprising three member states (France, Germany, and the UK), together with the United States and Russia, suggests the strength of external pressures toward a directory. The issue would, of course, be made even more complex if a system of variable geometry were formalized; then, perhaps, the presidency could rotate either among those states participating in all elements, or rotate differently in each of the various European organizations, as at present, with considerably stronger institutionalized coordination procedures. Concerns over QMV have been raised already in the context of enlargement to include the EFTA states. The prospect of a large number of new, small member states raises the distinct possibility that three of the larger member states could be outvoted in a Union of nineteen (once the Visegrad Four accede), even if the big four just constitute a blocking minority (if the present ratio is extrapolated) in a Union of twenty-eight (see Table 3.2).

Moreover, although in terms of votes the majority might still be around

Table 3.2   Qualified Majority Voting and Enlargement

If the present weighting system were applied to future EU members, the situation would be as follows:

Present Associates	Population	Weighted Vote
The Visegrad Four		
Poland	38,300,000	8
Czech Republic	10,302,000	5
Slovakia	5,274,335	3
Hungary	10,278,000	5
Other CEECs		
Slovenia	2,020,000	2/3
Bulgaria	8,982,000	4
Romania	22,760,449	6/7
Lithuania	3,724,000	3
Latvia	2,606,000	2/3
Estonia	1,526,177	2
Mediterranean		
Malta	336,541	2
Cyprus	725,000	2

70 percent of the total, in terms of population size, a qualified majority could add up to only 47 percent of the population in a Union of twenty-eight (as against about 60 percent at present). Again, several proposals have been made to meet the problem, including the idea of a double majority, whereby on specified issues there has to be an agreed majority of the votes in the Council, and that majority has to represent the majority of the population of the Union. Under the present system, Germany, France, Italy, and the UK have ten votes; Spain, eight; Belgium, Greece, the Netherlands, and Portugal, five; Austria and Sweden, four; Denmark, Ireland, and Finland, three; and Luxembourg, two.

The qualified majority threshold is sixty-two out of the total of eighty-seven votes, which represents some 70 percent of the vote; the blocking majority is twenty-six though subject to the Ioannina agreement (see Table 3.3). If the double majority proposal sounds democratically unassailable, alternative solutions are possible, including reweighting the votes. Such a proposal was circulated by the French during the EFTA negotiations; it could reappear in the context of the next negotiations. Whether the logic of reducing the bias in favor of smaller states would be taken as far as distinguishing between the four larger states (each of which has ten votes, regardless of population size) is perhaps doubtful.

Any reweighting, however, raises interesting questions about proportionality in the other institutions and their interrelationship. Clearly it

Table 3.3   Qualifed Majority Voting After Enlargement

Enlargement	Total Vote	QM Threshold	Blocking Vote
EU-15 + the Visegrad Four	108	77	32
EU-15 + 4 + Malta/Cyprus	112	80	33
EU-15 + 6 + Slovenia	115	82	34
EU-15 + 7 + Bulgaria/Romania	126	89	38
EU-15 + 9 + Baltic states	134	95	40

Note: The qualified majority falls to just under 66 percent of the vote.

becomes potentially counterproductive to allow the larger member states to be in a position of being continuously outvoted. Any political usefulness in being seen to be outvoted on domestically difficult issues would begin to pall, especially if the voting were too often on financial issues. That raises the possibility of a hierarchy of laws. On some issues, particularly those of constitutional importance, it may be desirable to continue to require unanimity—though that poses the question of whether one state, say, the smallest, Malta, should be able to hold up a constitutional amendment welcomed by the others.

The Institutional Committee of the EP has suggested that perhaps a double majority of four-fifths should be substituted. The Reflection Group, hidebound by the reluctance of one or two governments to envisage any changes, could only suggest the possibility of some flexibility over time for politically important primary legislation. On other issues of political significance, perhaps a less heavily weighted majority might be required; on still others, the double majority might be dispensed with, and so on. But even on secondary legislation, where the majority of the Reflection Group was in favor of extending QMV, there were those who continued to argue "that qualified majority voting does not always mean effective decision-making or unanimity the reverse."[49] Differentiating between the Union's output might be a happy, lucrative hunting ground for lawyers, but it highlights difficult political decisions, not least if all the pillars are included. It raises once again the problems of setting out a coherent and democratically sustainable system in a Europe of variable geometry.

It may be the case that this preoccupation with voting is misguided, at least within the existing Union, because the practice within the Council is always to find the most acceptable compromise.[50] Indeed, much of the literature on negotiation within the EU has stressed the ways in which, as Helen Wallace put it, "cooperative modes can be established and habits of transacting business entrenched."[51] Given the changed nature of the political discourse since Maastricht, however, it is probable that fewer existing member governments are able or content to rely too much on "the rele vance of serial exchanges to the stability and predictability of the [negotiating] process";[52] and it is a moot point whether association or a structured relationship will establish habits early enough for potential members.

In a more coherent and democratic system, much greater responsibility would fall on national parliaments as they attempted to keep abreast of their governments' activities; and the EP's role would be more difficult and conciliation processes even more complicated. Those who take the position that the EU is, and should remain, a Union of states have stressed the need for national parliaments to be more involved. Whether that means, in a Union of twenty-eight, that agreement in Council should in all or certain cases be delayed until all parliaments have been consulted seems less certain. If national parliaments are to be consulted more often, the complexities of the Council's legislative procedures will need to be dealt with in the interest of both efficiency and transparency. At present there are some twenty different Council procedures.

The move toward greater transparency in such a complex system received a huge fillip with the obvious lack of enthusiasm for Maastricht on the part of many electorates. This partially reflected the depth of suspicion of what might be described as the Monnet method of interelite interaction.[53] It may be that with the accession of Sweden and Finland, there will be an even stronger pressure in support of greater openness in the legislative process of the Council. Some other member states regard as inherently problematic the dual function of the Council—as an intergovernmental negotiating forum, in which too much openness might be regarded as potentially counterproductive, and as the Union's chief legislative body. Under its rules of procedure, the Council regards itself as behaving as a legislature when, on the basis of relevant Treaty provisions, it adopts rules that are legally binding on the member states. All the member states have agreed to, though, is that votes should be reported when the Council is acting as a legislature—unless a member state objects.

The complexity of European governance could be increased still further if, in the interest of greater effectiveness rather than transparency, some other proposals are adopted. These would include the establishment of executive agencies to improve implementation over a range of policy areas, whether on the lines of the Court of Auditors or in new areas such as competition policy. Such agencies are perhaps most beloved of UK Conservative governments, whose deregulatory and privatization policies have encompassed the creation of a growing number of them. For the UK, in a European context, agencies might have the added advantage of taking away responsibilities from the Commission. The issue then becomes the extent to which the agency reports only to the Council or is accountable to the EP. The issue, raised here merely for discussion, is one that can be coupled with the whole question of comitology (the numerous management, consultative, and other committees that are involved in the implementation of policy) in pointing to the Union qua Council's ability to obfuscate at the same time as it calls for transparency.

The suspicion is that because of the EU's inherent difficulties, the question of the impact of further rounds of enlargement on the institutional structure of the Union will be delayed until it can no longer be avoided. Despite the growing certainty of all the institutions, including the European Council and the Council of the Union, that they are stretched to the breaking point with fifteen member states, it is likely that with political uncertainty in several member states, whether created by social and economic disquiet over EU policies (including the requirements of EMU) or by other factors, the temptation would have been to do as little as possible at the IGC—to review and repair only where absolutely necessary. Radical change is difficult given the Maastricht debates and the hostility of many electorates and particular governments; it leaves, as usual, the prospect of marginal change at best. But the prospective consequences of once again doubling the size of the EU are so great that it is difficult to reconcile the interests of those same governments with inaction. The dilemma therefore becomes ever more pointed.

Notes

1. Keohane, R. O., and Hoffmann, S., eds., *The New European Community* (Boulder: Westview, 1991), p. 22.

2. The title of David Spence's Discussion Paper (No. 36) for the RIIA: *Enlargement Without Accession: The EC's Response to German Unification* (London: RIIA, 1991).

3. Reflection Group, *Reform of the European Union,* Brussels SN 517/95 (Reflex 18), Madrid, 10 November 1995. The final report made some, but not substantial, changes to this draft.

4. CDU/CSU Fraktion (des Deutschen Bundestages), *Reflections on European Policy* (Bonn: CDU/CSU Fraktion, 1994). The CDU/CSU report of September 1994 pointed not only to institutional "overextension" but also to (1) "a growing differentiation of interests, fuelled by differences in the level of socioeconomic development"; (2) different perceptions of internal and external priorities of the Union given its geographical spread; (3) a process of profound structural economic change with mass unemployment creating "a threat to already overstretched social systems and social stability"; and (4) an "increase in 'regressive nationalism' in (almost) all member countries," which is seen as the product of deep-seated fears and anxieties caused by internal crisis and external threats, "such as migration," and as a result, the debilitating effects of the political demands placed on national governments.

5. Gazzo, E., "Enlargement of the Community: Attitudes of Member States," in Schneider, J. W., ed., *From Nine to Twelve: Europe's Destiny?* (Alphen aan den Rijn: Sijthoff and Noordhoff, 1980), p. 7.

6. Edwards, G., "How Large a Community?" *New Europe* 4, no. 4 (autumn 1976).

7. Dahrendorf, R., *Die Zeit,* 9 July 1971; reprinted in translation in Hodges, M., ed., *European Integration* (Harmondsworth, Eng.: Penguin, 1972).

8. See Wallace, H., with Ridley, A., *Europe: The Challenge of Diversity,* Chatham House Papers No. 29 (London: Routledge Kegan Paul, 1985).

9. Tindemans, L., *Report on European Union,* Bulletin of the European Communities Supplement, Brussels, January 1976.

10. Wallace with Ridley, *Europe: The Challenge of Diversity.*

11. The number of occasions on which the TEU rather than the Treaty of Rome was used as the legal base has been deliberately kept to a minimum by the Commission exercising considerable legal dexterity. There were, however, noises from some parliamentarians that the UK opt-out should extend to UK parliamentarians as well as the government on TEU social policy.

12. *Presidency Conclusions of the Copenhagen European Council,* June 1993.

13. Ibid.

14. Metcalfe, L., *The European Commission as a Network Organization,* Maastricht European Institute of Public Administration, 1995.

15. Scharpf, F. W., "The Joint Decision Trap: Lessons from German Federalism and European Integration," *Public Administration* 66 (1988), pp. 239–278.

16. Wessels, W., "The EC Council: The Community's Decisionmaking Center," in Keohane and Hoffmann, *The New European Community.*

17. Hoffmann, S., "Balance, Concert, Anarchy, or None of the Above," in Treverton, G. F., *The Shape of the New Europe* (New York: Council on Foreign Relations, 1991).

18. Haas, E. B., *The Uniting of Europe* (London: Stevens, 1958).

19. Ibid., p. 522.

20. Sasse, C., et al., *Decision-Making in the European Community* (New York: Praeger, 1977), p. 86.

21. Bulmer, S., and Wessels, W., *The European Council* (London: Macmillan, 1987), pp. 10–11.

22. Edwards, G., "The Case of the United Kingdom," in O'Nuallain, C., *The Presidency of the European Council of Ministers* (London: Croom Helm/EIPA, 1985).

23. Wallace, H., "Britain and Europe," in Dunleavy, P., Gamble, A., and Peele, G., eds., *Developments in British Politics* (London: Macmillan, 1990).

24. "Crisis Of The Nation State?" *Political Studies,* Special Issue, 1994.

25. One Belgian MEP, Madame Dury, declared that she preferred to switch channels to watch Maigret rather than continue to watch the Danish president's conclusions on its period in office (EP Debates No. 3-433/122, 14 July 1993).

26. Engel, C., and Welz, C., "Synergy or Antithesis—The Institutional Dimension," in Wessels, W., and Engel, C., eds., *The European Union in the 1990s: Ever Closer and Larger?* (Bonn: Europa Union Verlag, 1993).

27. Edwards, G., and Wallace, H., *The Council of Ministers of the European Community and the President in Office* (London: Federal Trust, 1977), pp. 27–28.

28. Reflection Group, *Reform Of The European Union,* para. 124.

29. Committee of Three, *Report on European Institutions* (otherwise known as the Report of the Three Wise Men), presented to the European Council, Brussels, 1979.

30. Ibid., p. 92.

31. Rometsch, D., and Wessels, W., "The Commission and the Council of Ministers," in Edwards, G., and Spence, D., *The European Commission* (London: Longmans, 1994), p. 213.

32. Spinelli, A., *The Eurocrats: Crisis and Conflict in the European Community* (Baltimore: Johns Hopkins Press, 1966); Noël, Émile, and Étienne, H., "The Permanent Representatives Committee and the 'Deepening' of the Communities," *Government and Opposition* 6, no. 4 (1971), pp. 422–447.

33. Spinelli, *The Eurocrats,* p. 79.

34. *Financial Times,* 11–12 March 1995.

35. Edwards and Wallace, *The Council of Ministers;* and O'Nuallain, C., and Hoscheit, J. M., eds., *The Impact of European Affairs on National Administrations: the Case of the Presidency* (London: Croom Helm, 1985).

36. Contrasts at least in style between presidencies were shown in, for example, a report of *The European,* 28–30 December 1990: "While some British journalists likened the Italian Presidency to a bus trip with the Marx brothers in the driving seat, the Luxembourg Presidency has all the signs of being driven by a sedate couple who only take to the road on Sundays and then infuriate other motorists by respecting the speed limit."

37. Nuttall, S., *European Political Cooperation* (Oxford: Clarendon Press, 1992).

38. Buchan, D., *Europe: The Strange Superpower* (Aldershot, Eng.: Dartmouth, 1993).

39. Edwards, G., "National Sovereignty Versus Integration: The Council of Ministers," in Richardson, J., ed., *Policy Making in the European Union* (London: Routledge, 1996).

40. The number became twenty-six rather than twenty-seven after the Norwegians rejected membership for the second time in 1992.

41. *Agence Europe,* 14 April 1994.

42. Bulmer and Wessels, *The European Council.*

43. Reflection Group, *Reform Of The European Union,* para. 113.

44. Among other bodies, the Commission set up an information network on the IGC, while nongovernmental bodies such as the Belmont European Policy Centre, the Centre for European Policy Studies (CEPS), and the Philip Morris Institute for Public Policy Research published bulletins, conference proceedings, etc., from 1994 onward. Academic reports began to emerge in ever greater numbers during 1995.

45. Weidenfeld, W., ed., *Europe 96: A Reform Programme for the European Union* (Bonn: Verlag Bertelsmann Stiftung, 1994).

46. Vibert, F., *The Future Role of the European Commission* (London: European Policy Forum, 1994).

47. Ludlow, P., with Ersboll, N., et al., *Preparing for 1996 and a Larger European Union,* Special Report No. 6 (Brussels: CEPS, 1994), p. 9.

48. Ibid.

49. Reflection Group, *Reform Of The European Union,* para. 116.

50. Wessels, "The EC Council."

51. Wallace, H., "Making Multilateral Negotiations Work," in Wallace, W., ed., *The Dynamics of European Integration* (London: Pinter, 1991), p. 225.

52. Ibid.

53. The "Monnet method" being used here as shorthand for the traditional interelite negotiation (that is, among national and European political, administrative, and economic elites) that has characterized decisionmaking in the Community since its inception.

4

The European Parliament
and Enlargement, 1973–2000

Karlheinz Neunreither

From an Informal Parliamentary
Club to an Anonymous Powerful Machine

In the early 1950s, when Jean Monnet sat with a few friends discussing whether or not to include a parliamentary assembly in the new organization that was to become the European Coal and Steel Community (ECSC), he certainly did not imagine what would develop forty years after the small club of delegated national members of Parliament was finally agreed upon. Since a rather large assembly of the Council of Europe already existed, the founding fathers of the new Community thought it might be safer to include a new parliamentary body in their plans, thus excluding all possible attempts from the Council of Europe Assembly to fill the gap and to exercise parliamentary control of the ECSC. What we might consider a tactical move had far-reaching consequences. Out of the original seventy-eight members (which were the same delegates from national parliaments as those sitting in the Council of Europe Assembly), a directly elected Parliament has now emerged composed of no less than 626 members.

The increase in membership, combined with the increase in working languages from four to eleven, has dramatically changed the working methods, the internal structure and coherence, and the possible political impact of the European Parliament (EP). Discussions on its evolution—certainly more profound than that of the Commission or the Council, which in comparison remained much closer to their original concept—are generally held less in terms of size and resulting working methods and more in terms of powers and functions. Increases in the powers of the EP did not in fact coincide with any of the enlargements, which results in a rather complicated picture: the breaking-in period covered the years 1953–1958, during which the parliamentary "club" became established, composed of seventy-eight members delegated from their national parliaments. As the European

65

Economic Community (EEC) and the European Atomic Energy Community (EURATOM) came into force in 1958, three communities with three legal identities were formed. The EP's composition was increased to 142, almost twice its former size. This encouraged the national parliaments to designate special delegations to the new assembly. But during the following years, a substantial number of the members were still delegates to both the Council of Europe Assembly and the EP.

In 1973, the first enlargement took place and the United Kingdom, Ireland, and Denmark joined the Community of the Six; Parliament's membership had increased to 198 members. Direct elections, instituted in June 1979, were the next important landmark in the history of the EP and the event that divided its whole existence into two separate parts. A total of 410 members took up their mandate, again more than doubling the former number.[1] Greece joined at the beginning of 1981, adding 24 members, and Spain and Portugal joined in 1986, adding 84, making a total of 518.

With German reunification, 18 more members were agreed upon, first as observers and then, by modification of the Treaties, as full members starting with the direct elections of June 1994. Since the other member states did not want to have an increase in German members alone, their membership was also changed, resulting in a total increase of 49 members. Finally, in January 1995, Austria, Finland, and Sweden joined the European Union (EU), bringing the membership in the EP to 626.

Where should this evolution lead us? A Parliament of 1,000 or perhaps 1,500 members? The EP said no and adopted a resolution, to the effect that a total of 700 members would be the maximum to ensure efficiency.[2] If this figure were reached, a new distribution of parliamentary mandates would have to be found.

The Northern Enlargement of 1973

During the period of the nondirectly elected EP, only one enlargement occurred, but one of considerable size and political importance: that of the northern countries—the UK, Ireland, and Denmark; Norway shied away at the last minute after a negative referendum.

The most important impact on the activities of the EP was the adhesion of the UK. The UK could have been a founding member of both the ECSC and the EEC, but after participating in preliminary talks, the British government lost interest in joining a continental grouping it considered potentially protectionist and interventionist. When the EEC took off, rather successfully in its first years, the UK wanted to join, but Charles de Gaulle slammed the door; his successor, Georges Pompidou, renewed negotiations, resulting in the enlargement of 1973. In the meantime, it must be noted that the UK had taken the initiative of founding the European Free Trade Association (EFTA), which was clearly designed to be a competitor in organizing a free market in western Europe.

As far as the EP was concerned, it had favored British membership from the beginning and—like the Commission—considered de Gaulle's veto a severe blow to the Community. When the first British members arrived, it was quite a surprise and a major change for the life of the EP. First, English words were heard in EP meetings, which was as uncommon as if a Russian or Chinese delegation had arrived. French was by far the leading language up to then (when a secretary or administrator joined the EP's secretariat, a very good command of French was essential, and knowledge of English was taken into account only as one of many other languages). Both in the plenary and political group meetings or in committees, the influential speaker was one who had a dominant knowledge of French. In addition, formation of political groups was not then as rigid and well established as in later years, especially after direct elections and, even more so, when legislative work became abundant in the mid-1980s. As a result, a good speech could make an impact in parliamentary deliberations. In addition, many issues were new to all participants and not just a repetition of earlier deliberations and votes, as has become the rule in recent years, when relatively few major new issues have been put on the agenda, as compared with the large bulk of amendments of previous legislation.

The arrival of the British had many other consequences, which can only be described in sociological terms.[3] Everyone, including myself, then a relatively young committee secretary, suffered from the high temperatures in committee meeting rooms in the summer during lengthy afternoon meetings with crowds of people moving in and out. Until 1973, there was a strict rule that jackets were never removed. A dark suit, white shirt, and extremely orthodox tie were worn. Then I received one of the major shocks of my professional career. The first meeting started in the Political Affairs Committee, in which a substantial number of British members, including the frontbenchers of the new British delegation, took part. Moreover, since the British Labour Party had boycotted sending members from the British Parliament to Strasbourg (still then in the period of the nondirectly elected Parliament), the Conservatives, who had to take into account the possibility of losing a vote in the Commons during a Strasbourg session, had consequently increased their delegation from the House of Lords.

As a result, the British delegation included a considerable number of lords in the first meetings, which very much impressed the participants from other European countries, both members and staff. In that committee meeting on a hot, sticky July day, in the rue de l'Empereur in Brussels, the lords had been shown to their seats and the chairman had just pronounced a few words of welcome, when the first of the lords looked around uneasily, took off his jacket, and loosened his tie. In a few minutes, the whole British delegation did the same—to the great shock of some of the leading members from other EEC states, to the astonishment of others, and to the great relief of yet others.

Another obvious aspect of British participation was the transfer of British parliamentary procedures and the way of doing business in Parliament, which surprised members of the European parliament (MEPs) from the other eight countries. Those who were not accustomed to life in the British House of Commons were quite taken aback when they were confronted for the first time with the aggressiveness of the two major parties (Labour finally sent a delegation in 1975) in the Strasbourg chamber, who often rudely attacked each other, usually on home matters that were only marginally linked to EU affairs. A lot of shouting, interrupting, and points of order as well as interventions and calls for order from the chair were the result. It must be said that the British members, who did not behave differently from the way they did in London, were for their part somewhat puzzled by the extremely orderly way parliamentary affairs were conducted in the EP. It should be added that, because the majority of participants listen to a speech via an interpreter, spontaneity is considerably reduced. If, for example, a member tries to make a joke, it might be very successful in a national parliament, but in the EP, even in the 1970s with only six languages, the resulting laugh would occur a few seconds or even a minute later, depending on how fast the interpreter was following the speaker. At present, with eleven languages, the effect might be even worse, because some interpretation is not done from one language directly into another but through a pivotal language—for example, Finnish might be translated into English and only then into Portuguese. Thus, for a Portuguese member to understand a Finnish joke, it would take twice the time needed for a member following the English interpretation. In addition, of course, there would be twice the chance to miss the point.

If we look at elements of more direct concern to the activity and structure of the EP, reinforcement of parliamentary control over the executive should be stressed above all. British parliamentary tradition, perhaps more than any other, is based on confrontation between government and opposition. In the absence of written procedures, and of an extensive system of permanent specialized committees as is found in most European countries and the United States, this confrontation traditionally takes place in the plenary chamber. The British Parliament is to some extent a transplant to government of the ideal type of debating society.

In the Community system, a direct confrontation with "the executive" is not possible, and parliamentary supervision had to be adapted. Since the Council did not participate frequently in EP meetings in the 1970s, the Commission was the only possible institution that could even partially fill the classical role of a parliamentary government in this respect. The Treaty itself gave the function of parliamentary supervision to the EP, and it was generally exercised in plenary debates, through written questions, and in parliamentary committees. The main addition resulting from British entry was the introduction of the classical instrument of Question Time in the EP. In the meantime, Question Time has become a standard procedure of EP activities, and the Council has joined the Commission in its willingness to answer questions.

Another interesting aspect of British membership was its influence on the spectrum of political forces. With great difficulty, the major groups in the Parliament—Socialists, Christian Democrats, and Liberals—had started to move toward closer cooperation and the formation of party confederations—and, more recently, so-called European political parties. In doing this, they had to come a long way. For example, in the first years of the EEC, no less than three political parties from the Dutch side sent delegates to the EP, which on the outside were regarded as Christian Democrats; among themselves they considered one another much more foe than friend.[4] After some hesitation, all three parties nevertheless joined the Christian Democratic group and established a working relationship among their members. As a result, there was feedback to the Netherlands, and the three parties established much closer relationships on the national level, leading in due course to their amalgamation.

When the UK joined, everybody assumed that the Labour members would join the Socialist group, as they in fact did after the 1975 referendum, and that the Conservatives might join the Christian Democrats or at least establish a closer relationship with them. This was not the case and, after some hesitation, the British Conservatives, under the leadership of Peter Kirk, chose to set up their own parliamentary group, which promoted their chairman as a group leader into the inner circles of parliamentary decisionmaking and accorded him his own secretariat. Only very much later, in the late 1980s, did the British Conservatives give up their independence and finally join the Christian Democratic group, which in the meantime had been renamed the Group of the European People's Party. This occurred as a result of a broadening of political interests, pressure from Margaret Thatcher seeking closer relationships with other conservative parties across Europe, and the passage of the Single European Act (SEA) with the large parliamentary majorities it required.

The Greek Enlargement of 1981

In the early 1960s, a number of countries became interested in establishing closer links with the Community of the Six. The question was how this could be done and which policy the EC should pursue to that effect. The EEC treaty provided two formulas: one for complete adhesion (Article 237) and one for a looser tie called association (Article 238). What adhesion meant was relatively clear: the candidate country had to sign the treaty and agree to all its obligations. What is now called the *acquis communautaire* was initially of relatively secondary interest except for the Common Agricultural Policy (CAP). In addition to the economic requirement of being able to fulfill the treaty obligations, a number of political fundamentals evolved gradually; these included the respect of human rights and of minorities and the existence of a pluralistic parliamentary democracy. In addition, only "European states"—whatever that meant—were qualified to apply for membership.

As far as association was concerned, matters were far less clear. For example, a country like the UK, which qualified for full membership, might prefer to be an associate member. Should this be accepted? What about other states that might not fully qualify for membership, either on economic or political grounds? In 1962, the EP took the lead and formulated guidelines for a policy of establishing closer links with the Community beyond mere trade agreements.[5] It claimed that association should not be in a category of its own but should be considered with a view to membership; basically, it should be reserved for those countries that did not yet fulfill the conditions for full membership economically but were politically willing to do so. This meant that these countries should also fulfill the democratic conditions.

These guidelines became quite important, since they were followed by the Commission in subsequent opinions on membership or association and had two immediate effects: they opened the way for transitional association agreements for both Greece and Turkey; and they blocked the UK and other interested states from applying merely for association. As far as Greece was concerned, the association agreement, the first one of its kind, was established on the basis of complete legal equality. An Association Council at ministerial level was created and, on the parliamentary side, a joint parliamentary committee was established, which was given the right to examine the annual report of the Association Council on the progress of the association.

The rather weak joint parliamentary committee, composed of an equal number of Greek members delegated from their national parliament and of MEPs, became instrumental when the colonels took over in 1967 and dissolved the Greek parliament and imprisoned many of its members. Clearly, this was a breach of the unspoken rules that associate members should also respect pluralistic parliamentary democracy and human rights. The EP therefore called for an abolition of the association agreement. This was not followed, either by the Commission or by the member states, which claimed that the text of the agreement did not allow for such one-sided action. The Parliament then claimed that Greece prevented the institutions of the association agreement from functioning because it had put an end to the existence of the Greek parliament, and thus the joint committee was not operational. It was this argument, admittedly a rather marginal one, that succeeded in at least freezing the association agreement—to the great concern of the colonels in power. They subsequently tried to install a puppet parliament to nominate deputies to send to the joint committee; this attempt was rejected by the EP. The result was that throughout the seven years of the colonels' junta, the association agreement was frozen and financial aid was stopped.

The restoration of democracy in 1974 also restored the close ties between the Greek parliament and the EP. Consequently, the EP became one of the most ardent advocates of early Greek membership, mainly on political grounds to strengthen democracy. It is quite obvious that on economic grounds alone, membership might have been further delayed.

To sum up, as far as the Greek enlargement is concerned, the period preceding it is more interesting politically. The addition of twenty-two new members had less of an impact compared with the earlier northern enlargement; this was due to the fact that in 1979, the EP had been elected directly for the first time and more than doubled its number to 412. In 1981, it numbered 434 with the Greek members.

The Iberian Enlargement

With the end of the nondemocratic regimes in Spain and Portugal, the question of the membership of these two countries came onto the agenda. The extremely lengthy and difficult negotiations that took place before actual membership were due primarily to the fact that the *acquis communautaire* had been growing in importance over the years and that Spain was trying to get the best possible bargain on a number of economic issues. For Portugal, once the turmoils of its transition to democracy had passed, the main question was the rather poor state of its economy. Should the EC, after taking in Ireland and later Greece more on political grounds than anything else, now add to its members a third country whose economic efficiency was far lower than the average of the existing members? Or was it politically feasible to decide otherwise? The answer is known.

The Spanish parliament in particular was very keen to participate in the activities of the EP before formal adhesion. The question was how this could be done. The Spanish side would have preferred participation by its members of parliament, if not in the plenary, at least in EP committees. Spain wanted to follow subjects that were still in negotiation in the context of adhesion and also familiarize themselves with the *acquis communautaire*.

The EP was very hesitant to give its consent to such a formula, which was not foreseen in its own internal rules. As a consequence, a compromise had to be found. It consisted of a proposal from the EP to set up a specific body to be called the "joint parliamentary committee." Experience was drawn from the existing joint committees with Greece and Turkey in the framework of the association agreements. It is true that the legal situation was not the same, because this ad hoc formula would be applied in a preadhesion phase in the absence of any intergovernmental agreement and, even more important, while negotiations were still going on.

Finally, this formula of a joint parliamentary committee was agreed upon with both Spain and Portugal and worked quite satisfactorily, bridging the time until full adhesion. Incidentally, the same formula was revived recently for central European states looking for closer parliamentary contacts with the EP. In light of its experience with both the classical association agreements and the preadhesion phase with Spain and Portugal, the EP agreed to set up joint parliamentary committees with those Central and Eastern European Countries (CEECs) that have concluded so-called Europe Agreements and look toward future membership. This again shows that a kind of parliamentary tradition is growing, revealing a considerable degree of flexibility in offering formulas for closer cooperation.

Another element that might be mentioned in connection with the Iberian enlargement is that of staffing. The EP has at its disposal a permanent staff of about 3,500 officials, many of whom (40–45 percent) work in language-related positions. This includes interpreters, translators, and staff responsible for handling the documents in the eleven official languages. This staff of the general secretariat of the EP (which does not include the secretariats of the various political groups) have the same legal status as staff of the Commission, the Council, or the other EU institutions. Appointment to the EP secretariat is difficult; candidates have to pass an examination given every few years and taken by several thousand candidates in a given language. Only twenty or thirty of the candidates (1–2 percent) are put on what is called a "reserve list," from which appointments are finally made. This very formal and rigid recruiting procedure, which is based on French administrative traditions, has the advantage within the EP of blocking lobbying by the 626 members to recruit all kinds of people for the EP's staff.

Once a young staffer has been appointed, he or she follows a normal career pattern, based mainly on merit, not nationality. On the other hand, staff rules say that the EU institutions should look for an overall balance of "regions," which means member states. The question then is what to do about this balance and about recruitment in the event of enlargement? The solution generally applied is to organize special entry examinations for nationals of the respective countries.

An additional, rather tricky question arises out of the provision that once a person enters an EU career, promotion should not be based on national criteria. This means that for a new member country to be represented at the various levels of the hierarchy, and not just at the lower levels, entry possibilities are necessary at all levels, because accelerated promotion to fill national gaps in higher career brackets later are not allowed.

But that is exactly what happened in the case of Spain and Portugal. Spaniards who were recruited at the lower levels of the promotion system (A7 and A8) convinced their national authorities, and above all their MEPs, that it would be unfair to organize additional competitions (*concours*) for more senior jobs for which they were not yet qualified. It would be much more logical to acquire the necessary experience within the institutions and then be in a position to apply for senior posts. Unfortunately, the exceptions permitted with new membership are strictly limited in time. This means you may organize a *concours* only for nationals of a country that has just entered the EU, but not later on. Some of the young Spaniards who were recruited by the EP did not accept no for an answer and tried to prove that they were discriminated against insofar as Spain and, to a lesser degree, Portugal initially had a smaller percentage of middle management and senior staff posts. They claimed that they should have access to these by accelerated promotions. Even after almost ten years of membership, background papers on these questions pop up periodically, and parliamentary questions are asked on the subject.

Obviously, with successive waves of enlargement it will be more and more difficult to maintain a national equilibrium of staffing for all EU institutions. There is a real danger that the present system might in future be handled more rigidly and that the most senior staff posts (A1 and A2), but not many others, will be earmarked for a given nationality. This would be a disaster for any public independent service of the EU.

German Unification: A False Enlargement?

When the Berlin Wall came down, questions of closer ties between the still existing German Democratic Republic (GDR) and the EU arose very quickly. The EP had already established a parliamentary delegation with the Volkskammer, the East German parliament. The GDR's transitional government was preparing the first democratic elections, to be held in March 1990, and tried to develop formulas for closer links with the EU. It was obvious that this process would have to be harmonized with the one of establishing a special relationship between the two Germanies. For some months it was felt that the GDR, in line with other countries, could be given an associative status that would provide for a period of transition prior to full membership. This would have corresponded to the rather shaky condition of the East German economy and the environment. Some EC member states favored such a gradual approach.

But all drafts became obsolete when the German government made a bilateral agreement with Gorbachev on a very much accelerated solution providing for a full economic and monetary union between the two Germanies as early as 1 July 1990. In all practical respects, the GDR ceased to be an independent state.

What about the European Community? Would a modification of the existing treaties necessarily be signed by all member states and ratified by all national parliaments? After some hesitation, a rather surprising solution was found. The German government, referring to a secondary text annexed to the EEC treaty, declared that in future its territories would include the former GDR, and this modification of its borders would not require any rat- ification or any change in the treaty itself. To counter any concern over the balance between member states, the German government added that not the slightest modification of the existing balance and of the distribution of influence in the EC institutional system was envisaged. This applied not only to the weighting of votes in the Council and the composition of the Commission, but also to the number of seats in the EP.

The EP did not like this at all and insisted that the new Bundesländer should have parliamentary representatives as well. After difficult talks, a compromise was found by adding eighteen parliamentary "observers" to the total number of seats in the EP. These eighteen members were members of the East German parliament, officially designated by a vote in the Bundestag. They were given the right to sit in the chamber but not to take the floor or vote in plenary session. In parliamentary committees they could participate in discussions but not vote.

This unsatisfactory transitional solution was supposed to come to an end with the Maastricht negotiations, but in the final round, the German government did not manage to have it included in the new treaty. That is why a special round of talks had to be arranged, resulting in an increase in MEPs for a number of member states and giving Germany eighteen new seats (the former "observers") but also adding six new seats for the other "large" countries (France, Italy, and the UK); a few additional corrections were made.[6] As an indirect result of German unification, total membership of the EP increased from 518 members to 569 (total number of MEPs cho- sen in the 1994 elections).

Membership of Austria, Finland, and Sweden

As of 1 January 1995, Austria, Finland, and Sweden became members of the EU, bringing the total number of member states to fifteen. The EP is now composed of 626 members. During a transitional period not to exceed two years, the three new member states are allowed to delegate members from their national parliaments.[7] The immediate result for the EP of this recent enlargement is an increase in the number of official languages from nine to eleven. The impact on interpretation and translation is tremendous: possible combinations between two official languages increase from 72 to 110; the percentage of direct interpretation or translation between two given languages decreases correspondingly.

Initially, MEPs from the three new member countries had to spend some time acquainting themselves with the working methods of the EP. Due to their late arrival in a legislative period already started, they did not immediately take up functions in the official hierarchy of the Parliament as vice-president, chairman of committee, or otherwise; and only a few of them were nominated *rapporteurs* or drafters of opinions for various committees. Instead, they had to wait until the next internal nominations fell, at half-term (the end of 1996), before they could participate more fully in the Parliament's internal power structure. It therefore remains to be seen to what extent typical elements of Nordic democracy in the field of the protection of individual rights, the ombudsman,[8] and others, will find their way into EP practice.

MEPs from the three new member states also participated in the confirmation hearings of the new members of the Commission, held for the first time in 1994, as provided for in the EU treaty. Originally it was planned that after the nomination of Jacques Santer as president of the Commission and the designation by member states of the various candidates for the Commission, Parliament would give its final consent in December 1994, thus allowing the new Commission to assume office during the first days of January 1995. The EP insisted that hearings in parliamentary committees, the final debate, and the vote in the plenary take place in January so that MEPs from the three new member states could participate. In addition, the three candidates for commissioner from these countries could be questioned at the same time. The EP succeeded in this important modification of the agenda and organized a full week of hearings of the nineteen new commissioners (except President Santer, who already had been subject to scrutiny in July 1994); the results were astonishing. The Commission candidates from the three Nordic countries received bad marks from the parliamentary committees; this was mainly because the candidates strictly followed the guidelines given by Commission officials that they should not concede anything that might prejudge future Commission policy and, above all, that they should not promise to take over parliamentary amendments or withdraw Commission proposals if Parliament vetoed them. The new commissioners from Denmark, Finland, and Sweden followed those recommendations very strictly and were not well received. In contrast, the candidate from Austria chose a rather "Mediterranean" approach. Since the conclusions of the various committees were considered as only recommendations to the plenary, the Commission finally received approval as a collegial body. This is an example of how difficult it is to amalgamate political cultures in the EU institutional system.

Another remarkable event in preparation for the latest enlargement occurred in Strasbourg in May 1994. EU governments had promised that to increase efficiency, entry of the EFTA countries would not take place without adjustments in the existing institutional mechanisms. When negotiations with the applicant countries came to an end, it became clear that the existing members were unable to agree on institutional reform for the time being. This was not well received by the EP. Much worse was that the UK made a major issue out of maintaining the blocking minority in the Council. Until then, twenty-three votes had been sufficient to block a majority vote, and it was proposed that the blocking minority should be increased in that event to twenty-seven.[9] The UK threatened to veto any enlargement. Under the Greek presidency, a compromise was agreed upon in Corfu: the Council stated that if member states representing at least twenty-three votes declared that they could not agree to a proposal, the Council would continue its discussions "during a reasonable time" in order to reach an agreement. If that was not possible, it would proceed to majority voting and the final blocking minority would be twenty-seven votes. The EP disliked the so-called Ioannina compromise and insisted on improvements. Failing to achieve satisfaction, the major political groups threatened to veto enlargement. Quite clearly, Parliament found itself in a major dilemma: it had a good case on internal institutional efficiency, but could it actually link this issue with the historic possibility of including three or four countries in the EU that had expressed their wish to join? Enlargement would certainly strengthen democracy in western Europe, present no economic difficulties whatsoever, and marginally improve the budgetary situation of the EU, since the candidates were future net contributors.

It was evident that public opinion in the EU would not understand this rather complicated reasoning if there was a negative vote. But one week before the decisive dates, most observers would have placed their money on that outcome. Only in the final days did the EP's mood change: members of the various governments and political party leaders had vigorously lobbied their political friends in the EP. In addition, Chancellor Kohl addressed a personal letter to EP frontbenchers insisting that Parliament vote yes. Kohl indicated that Germany, which would be exercising the presidency of the Council in the second half of 1994, strongly favored a parliamentary representation in the preparatory group of the 1996 conference—this was another request from the EP—so that the EP would be directly involved in the discussion of the future institutional reform. These initiatives were instrumental in the final positive outcome.

This example shows how tempting it can be to link completely different issues. The EP has done this with success in the past, on "conditionality" in external trade relations and other matters.[10] But in this case it stepped back at the last moment, and some cynical press observers commented that this confirmed the EP's reputation as a dog that often barks but never bites.

The EP and the Challenge of Future Enlargements

If we look at the forty years of the EP's existence, we can conclude that it has dramatically changed both in its internal structure and in its importance as compared with other EC institutions.

Enlargements did certainly contribute to these fundamental changes, though they were only indirectly linked to the increase in the overall role of the Parliament, especially in legislation and other fields. We may refer to Parliament's role in the budgetary procedure, to its new relationship with the Commission and the procedures leading to the nomination of commissioners, and to its engagement in issues like human rights, environmental questions, and many others of concern to the public at large. If, during this process, the EP has changed from an informal club of members of national parliaments to a somewhat anonymous machine, the efficiency of fulfilling its role depended very much on a parallel increase in leadership. This leadership is largely concentrated in the political groups but also, and to a larger extent than is usually understood, in the office of the president of the EP and to some extent in the system of committee chairs.

If we ask what past enlargements have in common, one could say that at least they did not challenge the functioning of the EP as such, and they were not linked to a threat to the institutional system of the EU itself. This may dramatically change in the years to come. The general feeling is that the EU requires a major adaptation of its institutional system before additional members can join. Indeed, the Intergovernmental Conference of 1996–1997 had to deal with two major questions: (1) how to increase the efficiency of the EU institutional system, and (2) which mechanisms to devise to ensure progressive enlargement of the EU mainly toward central and eastern Europe.

A most serious challenge stems from possible forms of differentiated integration. Whatever the possibilities of adaptation for the other institutions, the EP will face increased difficulties. A member of Parliament is a representative of the people.[11] It is against any parliamentary representative tradition to split up the composition of a Parliament into first-grade and second-grade members. In addition, if Parliament wants to increase its legitimacy, it must try to bring to an end two major shortcomings: the differences in the actual electoral procedures and the representativeness of the parliamentary mandate.

On electoral procedures, the EP has put forward a number of proposals[12] but is still blocked by the Council, which is unwilling to force Britain to give up its objections to harmonization (in other words, to allow some form of proportional voting system in the UK). It is not out of the question that the EP will initiate formal action before the European Court to force the Council to act on this important matter.

The second issue is the imbalance of representation in the election of an MEP. A Luxembourg MEP is elected on the basis of roughly 60,000 citizens, while a German member is elected in a theoretical district of about 800,000 citizens. It is extremely difficult to tackle this problem in a unicameral system: in the United States, the principle of equal importance of the composing states is represented in the Senate, while the House of Representatives represents the population in the various states on a roughly proportional basis.

In the EU, all institutions try to reconcile the two conflicting elements within themselves: the Council by having weighted votes (ranging from two to ten), the Commission by according two commissioners to the so-called larger countries and one each to all the others, and the EP by being composed of national groupings between ninety-nine (Germany) and six (Luxembourg) members. But whatever the numbers, the smaller countries get more than their share of representation would be under a strictly proportional distribution. Of course, they could argue that they get less than in an international organization like the UN, where each country has one voice and all states are equal. Accordingly, one could argue too that the present situation reflects the halfway situation of the EU between international organization and a federal state. But concern is growing, and proposals for change are more intensively discussed than ever before.

An even more fundamental question concerns the EU's institutional system. All former enlargements have not questioned the fact that the EU institutions are competent for all EU members. Even the opt-out clause of the Social Chapter in the Maastricht Treaty is linked to the Community system and does not introduce a Europe à la carte. Basically, Community rules will apply and the EU institutions, including the Court of Justice, will be responsible. Much closer to the classical institutional paradigm is the chapter in the EU Treaty on monetary union, where not only the goal but also the prerequisites for reaching it are clearly defined. In this case, all member states agreed on setting objectives and defining the various steps and criteria that would lead from one stage to another.

It is also very important that all member states, when they fulfill the criteria, are obliged to move on to the next phase.[13] This is far from a system where a number of member states would be allowed to arrange common programs among themselves—for example, on high technology, protection of the environment, and common actions outside the Union. Perhaps some of these arrangements would be discussed among a few interested members, while the others would be invited to participate later, when they were capable of doing so. If the EU entered this new dimension of differentiated integration, clearly beyond anything that has happened so far, it would have major repercussions on the institutional system.

The main question here is how the various EU institutions could handle programs or activities that would still be qualified as EU activities, but in which only a limited number of member states actually participated. Could the Commission play its role drafting such programs and administering them? Would the full Commission as a collegial body be responsible, including those commissioners who are citizens of member states not participating?

While an elective composition seems possible for the Council, where respective majorities would have to be fixed and the administrative committees would have to be recomposed accordingly, the general problem is much more acute for the EP. Is it possible to envisage the EP, which meets in Strasbourg for one week a month, starting plenary discussions at the beginning of the week in which only those members from member states participating in a given subject would be present? There would then be other debates with different participation later in the week, and only a number of points on the agenda would be discussed by all. This structure harks back to the Common Assembly of the Council of Europe when the ECSC was created, namely to be a sort of "mother of parliaments." At that time, the parliamentary assembly of the Council of Europe tended to be the common meeting ground—to some extent the embodiment of parliamentarism—in western Europe; and each subregional grouping had its own parliamentary body composed of national delegations of the respective countries of the parliamentary assembly of the Council of Europe itself. The whole structure would be like a chest of drawers, the Council of Europe being the chest and the respective subregional organizations being the drawers.

In the early 1950s, these ideas were rejected by Jean Monnet and his cofounders of the Community of the Six. They insisted that the Common Assembly should be a completely separate parliamentary body. What might have been feasible in the early 1950s, on the understanding that these institutions were not real parliaments but rather assemblies of national parliamentarians (as de Gaulle had always advocated), is rather difficult to imagine now. The EP has become a real working parliament over the last ten to fifteen years, with more obligations for its members to participate in plenary sessions and committee and group meetings than many national parliaments. And it is difficult to see how this highly complex machine could be restructured internally to respond to differentiated integration initiatives.

In addition, the Maastricht Treaty has opened the way for a political union, and important elements of citizenship have been introduced that are likely to be strengthened in the next round of revisions in the coming years. EU citizens can already vote or be elected in the countries of their residence as well as in the countries of their passport. Many initiatives have been taken to strengthen a common feeling among the citizens of member states so that they might in the long term develop a loyalty not only to their region or to their country, but to the EU as well. It is already difficult to get this new dimension going with all the repercussions it will have on the organization of political parties, socioeconomic organizations, the media, and others. Even individual citizens are asked to identify themselves as European citizens as well as citizens of specific countries. It is certainly out of the question to ask for this new dimension to be divided into a general Union citizenship, a specific program citizenship, and so on. Legitimacy is not just a notion connected with the conduct of election. It goes far beyond that and requires the permanent possibility of identification between citizens and decisionmakers. The EP will still have to choose a policy line on its future role if, as is likely, further enlargement includes some kind of differentiated integration.

The EP conducted a major debate on the main issues of the conference in May 1995.[14] As far as differentiated integration is concerned, the EP stated clearly in a resolution that it is firmly against any internal subdivision that would enable it to exercise control over policies that may be pursued by a limited number of member states. On the contrary, it stated that the EP as a whole should be responsible for exercising such control. This is a point of principle and, for the time being, one to be expected. But can it be maintained during the coming years? Above all, it is difficult to envisage a Community of twenty or twenty-five members, with only eight or ten participating in a monetary union, or other advanced union projects, in which representatives from all member states debate and finally vote on these questions. This could be against the principle of parliamentary representation itself. No representation without taxation might be the formula for the future: rights only where obligations exist.

To sum up, it seems to be quite clear that future enlargements will present a much more fundamental challenge to the European Parliament than any previous ones. For the time being, the answers are limited and the constitutional debate is only beginning. The Reflection Group was cautious about raising issues that called into question the overall structure of the present Union. The Intergovernmental Conference itself will certainly have to come up with more basic answers. That is why the next two or three years will be decisive for the overall orientation of the future of the EU.

Appendix

Table 4.1 Enlargements and Increase in Power of the European Parliament

	Name	Treaty	Members	Functions	Languages
1952	(Common) Assembly	European Coal & Steel Community	78 (delegated members from the national parliaments of the Six: France, Germany, Italy, Benelux	Supervisory powers (on "High Authority")	4 official languages (Dutch, French, German, Italian)
1958	Assembly (European Parliament informal name since 1962)	Plus: European Economic Community (EEC) & Euratom (EAEC)	142 (delegated as above)	Supervision of EEC & EAEC Commissions; opinions on legislation (unified Commission since 1967)	
1970				Budgetary powers introduced	
1973			*First enlargement:* Denmark, Ireland, UK; 56 additional members (198 total)		2 more: Danish, English (6 total)
1975				Reinforced budgetary powers	
1979	European Parliament (official name)		First direct elections; 412 members		
1981			*Second enlargement:* Greece; 22 additional members (434 total)		1 more: Greek (7 total)

(continues)

Table 4.1 continued

Name	Treaty	Members	Functions	Languages
1986		*Third enlargement:* Portugal, Spain; 84 additional members (518 total)		2 more: Portuguese, Spanish (9 total)
1987	Single European Act (first major reform of treaties)		Additional legislative powers (cooperation procedure)	
1990	unchanged	German reunification; add 18 "observers"		
1993	European Union Treaty (Maastricht)		Increased legislative powers (codecision procedure); additional functions in other areas (nomination of the Commission, inquiries, etc.)	
1994	Ad hoc Treaty revision	Increased to 567		
1995		*Fourth enlargement:* Austria, Finland, Sweden; 59 additional members (626 total)		2 more: Finnish, Swedish (11 total)
1996–1998	Next treaty revision scheduled (likely to result in differentiated integration)	*Fifth enlargement:* likely to be staggered; principally Central and Eastern Europe (max. 700 MEPs?)	EP will insist on general-ized codecision; increased influence on nomination of Commission	
2000–2005	Possible follow-up conference, if 1996 fails	*Adhesion effective* (possibly total 25–30 members)	Effects of differentiated integration on EP	+/–20 (if not revised)

Table 4.2 Composition of the European Parliament (October 1995)

Member States	Total	PSE	PPE	UPE	ELDR	GUE/NGL	V	ARE	EDN	NI
Austria	21	8	6	—	1	—	1	—	—	5
Belgium	25	6	7	—	6	—	2	1	—	3
Denmark	16	3	3	—	5	1	1	—	4	—
Finland	16	4	4	—	6	1	1	—	—	—
France	87	15	12	15	1	7	—	13	13	11
Germany	99	40	47	—	—	—	12	—	—	—
Greece	25	10	9	2	—	4	—	—	—	—
Ireland	15	1	4	7	1	—	2	—	—	—
Italy	87	18	14	27	6	5	4	2	—	11
Luxembourg	6	2	2	—	1	—	1	—	—	—
Netherlands	31	8	10	—	10	—	1	—	2	—
Portugal	25	10	1	3	8	3	—	—	—	—
Spain	64	22	30	—	2	9	—	1	—	—
Sweden	22	7	5	—	3	3	4	—	—	—
UK	87	63	19	—	2	3	—	2	—	1
Total	626	217	173	54	52	33	28	19	19	31

Notes: Political Groups: PSE, Group of the Party of European Socialists; PPE, Group of the European People's Party (Christian Democrat group); UPE, Union for Europe (from the 1995 merger of the Forza Europa group and the European Democratic alliance); ELDR, Group of the European Liberal Democratic and Reformist Party; GUE/NGL, Confederal group of the European United Left/Nordic Green Left; V, The Green group in the European Parliament; ARE, Group of the European Radical Alliance; EDN, Europe of Nations group (Coordination group); NI, Unattached

Table 4.3 Electoral Participation in European Elections and in Most Recent National Elections: EU and Individual Member Countries (as a percentage total)

	European election 1979	European election 1984	European election 1989	European election 1994	Most recent national election
Overall	62.5	59.0	57.2	56.5	
Belgium (cv)	91.4	92.2	90.7	90.7	92.7
Denmark	47.8	52.4	46.2	52.5	82.8
France	60.7	56.7	48.7	53.5	68.9
Germany	65.7	56.8	62.3	58.0	77.8
Greece (cv)	78.6 (1981)	77.2	79.9	71.9	78.2
Ireland	63.6	47.6	68.3	44.0	68.5
Italy	84.9	83.4	81.0	74.8	76.7
Luxembourg (cv)	88.9	88.8	87.4	90.0	86.6
Netherlands	58.1	50.6	47.2	35.6	78.7
Portugal		72.4 (1987)	51.2	37.5	68.2
Spain		68.9 (1987)	54.6	56.9	77.7
United Kingdom	32.3	32.6	36.2	36.4	77.8

Sources: Jacobs, Corbett, and Shackleton: European Parliament, Bureau Bonn (Harlow, Eng.: Catermill Publishing, 1992); various communications on the 1994 results; ZEUS data-base of national election results.

Notes: Voting is compulsory in (cv) countries. In Luxembourg, first-order national elections were held together with European elections. Most recent national election turnout for France is for the first round of parliamentary elections.

Table 4.4   Influence of National or European Issues on the Vote at European Elections, 1994 (percentage)

	European	National
The Netherlands	53	38
Germany	44	49
France	44	49
Italy	39	54
Luxembourg	38	57
Belgium	37	48
Denmark	34	61
United Kingdom	31	63
Portugal	24	70
Spain	20	65
Ireland	16	77
Greece	11	85
EU-12	37	55

Source: Eurobarometer 41, Figure 1.5.
Note: Figures represent only those intending to vote.

Notes

1. By definition, the inherently double mandate came to an end. But in the directly elected EP of 1979, no fewer than 127 of the 410 members were also members of a national parliament (at the end of 1994, only 21 out of 567). The temporary rules for the 3 new members will be discussed later.

2. See de Gucht Report on uniform electoral procedure, *Official Journal C* 176/72, 13 July 1992. This position (maximum 700 members) was confirmed in the Bourlanges/Martin Report of May 1995.

3. For one of the few sociological or anthropological studies, see Abeles, M., *La Vie Quotidienne au Parlement Européen* (Paris: Hachette, 1992).

4. These were the Catholic People's Party, the Anti-Revolutionary Party, and the Christian-Historical Union.

5. See Birkelbach Report, *Doc. 122/1961–62*, EP.

6. Belgium, Greece, and Portugal each received one additional member; Spain received four and the Netherlands (due to an increase in population) six.

7. In 1995, only Sweden held direct elections to the EP. They resulted in considerable losses for the political groups that had advocated membership, especially the Socialists. This anticlimax added to the inclination of both Austria and Finland to postpone direct elections to the EP as long as possible.

8. In July 1995, the EP elected Jacob Soderman, who had served in the same position in Finland, as the first European Ombudsman.

9. In the EU of Twelve, total votes in the Council were seventy-six. With four new member states (including Norway), they would have gone up to ninety (at present, the number is eighty-seven).

10. Conditionality is the principle of posing conditions before giving parliamentary consent. Especially in trade relations with countries that do not respect human or minority rights, the EP has repeatedly insisted that trade or cooperation

agreements should be signed only if sufficient improvement of conditions were achieved. Needless to say, the Council usually hesitated to follow this approach.

11. Parliamentary tradition insists that members of Parliament represent not only their constituents, which at least in the British tradition they feel they do, but also the people as a whole. Now, according to the EC treaty (Articles 137 and 138), the EP is composed of representatives of the *peoples* of the member states of the EU. Does that mean that a given MEP represents only his or her own people? Or does that MEP represent the plurality of all the peoples of the Union? If in a more traditional way the MEP represents only one of the peoples, why would European political parties (Article 138a) be needed?

12. The most recent one was adopted on 10 March 1993 (de Gucht Report III), *OJ C* 115 (1993).

13. Except the special clauses agreed upon for the UK and Denmark in protocols 11 and 12 of the Maastricht Treaty.

14. See the resolution of the Bourlanges/Martin report of 17 May 1995 (*Doc. PE 190.441*, EP).

Part 2

Policy Perspectives

5

Can the CAP Survive Enlargement to the East?

Tim Josling

Agriculture and the Process of Enlargement

The Common Agricultural Policy (CAP) always seems to be a central issue in the successive enlargements of the European Union (EU). In the early 1970s, when the UK, Denmark, Norway, and Ireland were negotiating accession, the issue of agriculture was important to both the applicants and the existing Union. For the UK, the fear of higher food prices and restricted access for imports from the Commonwealth fueled the opposition to membership, while on the continent the concern was that UK membership would undermine the recently completed CAP. To Denmark and Ireland, the prospect of better access for agricultural exports into markets other than the UK was a significant attraction of membership. For Norway, the prospect of having to reduce prices for agricultural products was a major reason for the popular rejection of the negotiated terms in the 1972 referendum.

In the 1980s, the southern enlargement also caused some agricultural problems, ranging from the challenge to the underdeveloped farm sectors of Greece and Portugal to the impact on the balance of agricultural markets that the entry of a large and relatively efficient producer of Mediterranean goods—Spain—would have. These problems were handled by negotiating long transition periods, over which the agricultural market remained divided. The negotiations leading to the accession of Austria, Finland, and Sweden also revolved around agriculture, mainly because all other sectors had been effectively integrated with the Union over the previous twenty years.

All these agricultural concerns could prove to be minor irritants compared with the problems raised by future enlargements. The EU faces its most daunting political challenge to date in the prospective enlargement that would include up to ten of the Central and Eastern European Countries

89

(Ceecs). It appears that the entry of some of these countries could occur early in the next decade.[1] This gives the EU only five years or so to get ready for the moment of accession. The ease with which the CEECs can be assimilated into the single agricultural market will depend crucially on the development of the CAP over the next few years.

Assimilating New Members into the CAP

The task of incorporating new members into the CAP involves adjustments on the part of both the existing members and the acceding countries. The technical adjustments appear in the agricultural policies and prices of the new members, as they make their law and practice consistent with the common regulations. The adjustments in the existing countries come through the changes in the CAP that occur as a result of the new market situation in the enlarged Union.

Transitional Arrangements in Previous Enlargements

The EU has considerable experience in assimilating countries with different agricultural policies and price levels into the CAP. The accession of the UK in 1973 posed significant problems of a political and economic nature. On the political side, public opinion labeled the European Community (EC) as a bastion of high food prices, in contrast to the price levels in the UK, which for historic reasons had been governed by the state of world markets. The UK had to dispense with the "deficiency payments" farmers had come to accept as the main instrument of agricultural support policy. This system had been considered part of a sound, anti-inflationary food policy that allowed consumers ready access to supplies at low prices, primarily from the British Commonwealth. The reconciliation of this system with the CAP was to result in a transition to the higher CAP prices, along with the step-by-step introduction of import levies and export subsidies. The price gaps over the transition were offset by "accession compensatory amounts," added to or subtracted from the traded price.

In this enlargement, the main burden of adjustment fell on the new members. On reflection, a golden opportunity was lost at that time to radically adjust the EC price level to which the UK farmers and consumers were adapting. Had compensation payments been given to the farmers in the Six, the troubles of the CAP in later years may not have been so great. It would have been difficult to do this, however, in the climate of the time. An extraordinary rise in world prices in the mid-1970s altered conceptions about the long-run state of world markets. As a result, prices rose more slowly in the UK than they would have outside the EC, as they were effectively subsidized by other member states. CAP prices, themselves notched up in lagged response, were left high and dry by the receding world market prices. These price increases led directly to the budget and trade problems of the next ten years.

Transition arrangements had to be negotiated in the second round of enlargements as well. Greece, when it joined in 1981, was given up to seven years to prepare its own markets for competition with EC produce. Portugal was granted an even longer period when it joined the EC in 1986, with a five-year initial phase to allow Portuguese authorities to modify the marketing systems to allow implementation of CAP regulations, followed by a further five years to adopt EC price levels. Portugal had prices that were often higher than the EC's prices, implying some adjustment problem for farmers. A long transition was presumably desirable to allow time for this adjustment in the acceding country. Spain, by contrast, was ready to compete immediately but was deemed to be a threat to the EC market in such areas as wine, olive oil, and fruits and vegetables. As a consequence, Spain also had a transition period, though shorter than that for Portugal, which in effect allowed time for the EU to modify its policies in the area of Mediterranean crops.

The transition arrangements for the European Free Trade Association (EFTA) countries were different again. The EFTA countries had a history of higher price supports than the EU. They also had a history of closed markets and had resisted attempts to open up agriculture among themselves as part of EFTA. Agriculture was kept out of the EU-EFTA bilaterals that were negotiated after the first enlargement; as few agricultural preferences existed within the EFTA, there were few examples of increased trade barriers when the UK and Denmark defected to join the EC. Agricultural goods were also excluded from the free trade provisions of the EEA, which in effect gave EFTA countries economic, though not political, membership in the EU.

When several of the EFTA countries came to apply for membership, the anomaly of agriculture had to be tackled. The normal assumption would have been to negotiate a long transition that would allow farmers in these countries to adjust over time to the considerably lower farm prices. Austria, Finland, and Norway did indeed request such transition periods. Only Sweden, where the farm support prices had been reduced (with the payment of some compensation to farmers) in advance of the membership application as a part of economic restructuring, was prepared for entry without a transition. But the Commission pointed out that the EFTA countries were applying to join the EU, not the EC (that is, under post-Maastricht conditions) and hence had to adhere to the principle and to the practicalities of a borderless EU. Accession compensatory amounts had been traditionally paid or granted at the border. To have preserved borders just to keep farm prices different was seen as unwise. Finally, the new members settled for instantaneous adoption of CAP instruments and policy prices, with an overlay of compensation payments (part national and part EU-financed) based on hectarage and headage.

Enlargement and the Pressures for Changes in the CAP

Though the formal burden of adjustment falls deliberately on the new member, the impact of accession is shared among all members, old and new. The new members change both the political and economic balance in the sector and hence the development of the CAP. The extent of this indirect effect of the incorporation of new members into the agricultural market is conditioned by a number of factors. The most significant of these is the actual or anticipated impact on the market balance for agricultural commodities. This will determine the reaction of producers in the Union and the political impact of their concerns. The market balance will also influence the budget cost and the external trade implications.

The market balance implications of the first enlargement were dominated by the incorporation of the large UK import market for temperate zone agricultural goods. The smaller surpluses of Denmark and Ireland for livestock products did not seriously imbalance the existing markets. Greek accession added an import market for some grains and oilseeds, but it also increased the production of olive oil and Mediterranean crops. The entry of Spain and Portugal a few years later exacerbated the market balance problems in these southern products and led directly to some trade and budgetary problems.

The quantitative impact on European agricultural markets of the accession to the EU of three EFTA members—Austria, Finland, and Sweden—in January 1995 was never expected to be great. The countries themselves are relatively small, in both population and agricultural production; they did not add greatly to the volume of production in the Union. The three new members also negotiated the freedom to pay substantial hectarage and headage payments to farmers in remote areas, which will presumably act to keep those farmers from leaving the land idle. Production will no doubt fall over time, with depopulation and extensification, but one would not expect a major migration in the short run. Moreover, production in some areas could actually increase as a result of the opening up of markets: Swedish sales to Finland, for instance, could expand. Even Finland could find that some parts of the agricultural sector both develop export markets and compete well with imports from the EU: not all sectors in closed markets are necessarily inefficient.

The influences on agricultural policy that can be expected from the accession of the three EFTA countries are more subtle. First, the new members will have some influence on the political balance of the Union with respect to agricultural policy. On the surface, this is likely to show up as strong opposition to further price declines, at least if unaccompanied by compensating headage and hectarage payments. But it is also possible that the experience of the new members with such nonprice payments, and their acceptance as a part of the CAP, will allow price reductions to be continued with less opposition. Nordic and Alpine influence will also be manifest in a stronger interest in the environmental impacts of intensive agriculture and in the pressure to recompense farmers for the scenic and recreational value of their land. Moreover, this interest will show itself in issues of food quality and safety and plant and animal health. The new members are likely to take a more "holistic" view of agriculture, with less concern for individual commodity market conditions and more for the place of rural people in society.

In addition, the accession of the EFTA countries has established precedents for the further enlargements to the east. The new programs for Arctic regions are to be paid for by the individual countries; thus, these payments are an example of further "nationalization" of the CAP. If Finland and Sweden can run "Nordic" agricultural programs, and Austria can maintain its existing small-farmer payments, why not have a special dispensation for national aids for other areas that have special features? The particular needs of the CEECs could presumably be accommodated more easily under this more relaxed view of the role of national policy.

In the case of the prospective enlargement to include the countries of central and eastern Europe, the impact through the budget and trade balance is likely to be dominant. The budget costs of the CAP will continue to be limited by an overall budget constraint that is unlikely to be relaxed. The constraints imposed on the CAP as a result of the Uruguay Round agreement will put strict limits on the price developments under the CAP and help shape the instruments used. As a result, the impact of enlargement is magnified to become a budgetary and trade policy issue.

The prospect of the accession of the central European states with their substantial agricultural production potentials is much more threatening to the stability of the CAP and to its ability to live within financial guidelines than the recent integration of the EFTA countries.[2] The immediate impact of the accession of the Visegrad Four—the Czech Republic, Hungary, Poland, and Slovakia—on the agricultural budget has been estimated at ECU 5–12 billion if current price levels are maintained and if compensation payments are paid to CEEC farmers at the same rate as to farmers in the EU.[3] This jump in budget costs is likely to be enough to force significant policy changes on the EU at that time. The trade impacts will be closely watched by other agricultural exporters to ensure that the process of enlargement does not violate the commitments undertaken in the Uruguay

Round. In addition, the extra net exports of agricultural products from the CEECs will weaken market prices within the EU relative to policy price levels. Such a reduction in the level of price support is likely to foster resentment among existing farmers in the Union.

Constraints on the Expansion of the CAP

The capacity of the CAP to absorb new members is a function of the impact on the Union's budget and trade balance. The entry of the UK in 1973 posed no problems for the common budget, as the incorporation of Britain's large import market for temperate zone agricultural products provided revenue for the EC. Denmark and Ireland as agricultural exporters imposed some extra costs, but not enough to offset the positive budgetary impact of the UK. Indeed, the major budgetary issue at the time of accession and for many years thereafter was the large size of the budget contribution from the UK. One could reasonably argue that the policy continued through the 1980s unreformed, partly because of the relaxation of the budget constraint as a result of the first enlargement.

The impact of external trade considerations on the expansion of the CAP has, until recently, been confined to the indirect constraint through the budget cost. Weakly enforced and ambiguous trade rules prior to the Uruguay Round allowed the EU to raise import restrictions and expand export subsidies without an externally imposed limit. The major exception to this generalization was the impact on U.S. sales of corn and oilseeds to Spain and Portugal. A bilateral agreement eventually guaranteed the United States continued access to these markets for a period of years.

The situation has changed markedly in both budgetary and trade respects in recent years. It is now possible to argue that budget costs and external trade balance are likely to act as effective constraints on the ability of the CAP to absorb new members. This in turn makes it much more likely that the CAP itself will be modified as a result of enlargement. The budget and trade constraints are discussed in the following section.

Budget Limits and the CAP

For the past five years, budget costs for agriculture have been subject to limits, based on the proportion of total spending and EU growth. The extra payments needed for CAP reform have strained these limits. Even without new members influencing the budget, it is likely that current policies will exhaust the budget allocation in the near future. The higher world prices in 1995 may have put off the budget squeeze for a year or two, but no one expects world markets to stay short of supplies for very long.

The response of the Union to these future budget pressures will to a large extent determine the CAP that will be in place at the end of the century. If the response is to reduce support prices, this will add to the chances of the CAP's survival and will be consistent with eventual accession of the CEECs. If the reaction of the Union is to tighten supply control and remove productive capacity, this will tend to make accession more difficult. Any attempt to shift the burden to consumers will run into problems with the General Agreement on Tariffs and Trade (GATT) (see next section), because reduced consumption will increase the amount that has to be exported with subsidies.

One possible way out would be to shift the financial burden back to the individual member states. Without threatening the unity of the market, it should be possible for individual members of the EU to take over some part of the compensation payments, properly disconnected from production incentives, as national obligations.[4] This would not only reduce FEOGA (Fonds Européen d'Orientation et Garantie Agricoles) spending but also make the budget burden easier for new members to accept.

GATT Obligations

Even if the limits on budget shares failed to keep CAP spending within strict limits, there is now for the first time an effective external constraint on the CAP. The Uruguay Round Agreement on Agriculture will have major implications for the CAP until 2000. The agreement calls for a conversion of all nontariff trade barriers (including variable levies) into tariffs, which would then be reduced on a given schedule. Export subsidy expenditure is constrained, and it is also to be reduced on a given schedule. Most significantly, the volume of exports benefiting from subsidies is to be reduced, and export subsidies cannot be introduced on other products. Though the degree of liberalization incorporated in the agreement is not dramatic, there will be additional pressures before the end of the decade to negotiate a continuation to the agreement in order to liberalize agricultural trade further.

The GATT is unlikely to have a marked impact on price support for EU agriculture in the next two years. Agreement was made possible by the slight decline in farm prices (expressed, however, in terms of a strengthening "green" ECU) over the years since the Uruguay Round started, and more particularly by the bold Reform of 1993. As a result, the constraints on export subsidies and total support can be met in the short term without immediate policy change. In the medium term, the constraint on the volume of exports that can be subsidized represents the most binding constraint and is likely to impact CAP price decisions by 1997.

The agreement also mandates a change in the variable levy system for import protection, replacing it with tariffs. This tariff imposition is accompanied by a special safeguard mechanism that can be used in cases of import surge or world price collapse. The new bound tariffs should put little pressure on domestic market prices for the next few years. Moreover, for cereals, a maximum, duty-paid import price has been negotiated as part of the EU's obligations. This implies a continuation of a modified threshold price system, at least as long as world prices do not drop to very low levels.

However, it would be a mistake to think that the impact of the GATT on the CAP is small. Even though it does not mandate many price and policy changes in the immediate future, it effectively constrains future decisions. Specifically, it makes it difficult, if not impossible, to revert to the policy price levels that were obtained before CAP reform. It makes it difficult to increase the level of compensation to farmers under CAP reform, or to relax set-asides, without incurring the risk of challenge under the GATT. It makes it impossible to expand the use of export subsidies beyond the limits agreed in the schedules. And it obliges the EU to maintain current access for specified agricultural products. In effect, it locks in the policy changes of the past few years and makes any deviation from that path both politically and economically costly.

Options for the CAP During the Preaccession Period

The ease with which the CEECs can be assimilated into the EU will depend crucially on how the CAP reacts to these budgetary and trade pressures over the next five to ten years. In the following discussion, three medium-term policy options will be evaluated: minimal changes to the present CAP; continuation of CAP reform through extended commodity coverage and adjusted policy instruments; and completion of the reform process to create an agricultural sector that is competitive under world market conditions.

Option One: Minimal Changes to the CAP

One reaction to all the different factors affecting the CAP is to try to preserve the policy as it exists, adapting to pressures in an ad hoc way. Such a strategy would avoid taking action to forestall crises. This reactive approach to policy developments has the ring of reality: the CAP has usually required a crisis to force change. However, such a passive drift toward the next crisis is not necessarily good policy. Changes in policy that would in any case be in the interest of the EU would be delayed. These changes include the promotion of a competitive agricultural industry that can sell goods on world markets without the need for subsidies, the provision of raw materials for a food industry that is also competitive, and the removal of the artificial incentives to keep land in inefficient activities for the sake of benefiting from support payments. Governments pay lip service to such objectives, but they seem reluctant to take action to bring them about.

The undesirability of the present state of affairs is easily demonstrated. European agriculture now appears to add little or nothing to the GNP of the Union. Net value added in the sector as a whole was about ECU 110 billion in 1991, or 49 percent of the value of final output. For the same year, the Organization for Economic Cooperation and Development (OECD) calculated that ECU 68 billion had been transferred to the sector through the CAP for a number of the major commodities, a sum equal to 49 percent of the value of sales of those products.[5] The transfers through policy are therefore of the same order of magnitude as the excess of revenue over costs of inputs from other sectors (that is, value added). This means that the cost of inputs must be roughly the same as the market value (without policy intervention) of output. In other words, no value is being added to the inputs purchased from other sectors, and the industry as a whole contributes nothing to GDP. It is this total waste of good agricultural resources and the skills of the farming community that constitutes the biggest reason not to continue with current policies.

In addition to internal economic considerations, there are other reasons to change policies before being forced to do so by crisis. A strategy of waiting for further crises to develop will inevitably increase the likelihood of conflict with GATT obligations. It will also maximize the likely political cost of enlargement and of conforming with GATT obligations. Those who support the continuation of the CAP as it stands will always be seen to be at odds with those who are arguing for EU enlargement, for good trade relations with other OECD countries and with the developing world, and for a competitive EU agriculture that can support a competitive food industry and contribute to the economy.

Casual observation of the political process suggests that the option most likely to be followed is indeed that of relative inaction until provoked by crisis. However, that time may not be far away: if yield increases for the major crops continue at 1.5–2.0 percent a year, the inaction strategy will soon prove untenable. Similarly, if world prices are seriously depressed following an expansion of output in response to the current high prices, export subsidy expenditure as allowed under the GATT will be inadequate to remove surpluses from the domestic market. Changes in the CAP will be forced by both the GATT and the budget. The changes will be either of the type outlined below—in which case the delay will just have been costly— or of a much less desirable nature.

Option Two: A Modest Continuation of CAP Reform

An alternative approach is to attempt to continue in a modest way the reform process started in 1992. This means at least two further stages in the reform process. The first is to complete the reform of sectors other than the cereals and oilseeds complex. Reform of the dairy industry was shelved at the last minute in 1992 to get agreement on the cereals sector. At that time, further dairy quota cuts were contemplated, along with price cuts for dairy products. Some price cuts survived, but the dairy sector is still operating with prices far above world market levels. Reform of the dairy sector needs to be restarted. Price reductions could be compensated for by issuing certificates to farmers, as suggested in the original MacSharry reform paper.[6] The cereal and dairy sectors are not the only ones in need of policy modification to become more efficient. The sugar sector, long neglected in reform discussions because of its small budget cost, along with the wine sector and fruits and vegetables, could also be improved by inclusion in the reform process.

The second step in this modest completion of CAP reform is to reduce the incentive that currently exists for farmers to continue to farm hectares just to get compensation payments. If the farmer cannot make a profit from producing cereals and oilseeds at the market price, as supported by the threshold price (or maximum duty-paid price under GATT rules, in the case of cereals) and the intervention price, it is clearly a waste of resources to insist that the land be used in this way.[7] One might wish to suggest other criteria for receiving the payments, but use of the land in an inefficient way should not be one of them.

This apparently modest option of a continuation of CAP reform is inherently more costly in political capital than inaction, but it has certain advantages. First, the reduction in the market price for dairy, sugar, and other newly reformed commodities offers to those sectors the advantages the first stage of reform offered to grains and oilseeds. Lower consumer prices and lower prices for the processing industry would in effect remove a tax that currently holds back consumption and reduces competitiveness. Compensation payments would preserve for some time the income streams to producers until they were able to switch to alternative commodities. GATT constraints would be more easily met, and the improved international climate would have beneficial consequences for exporters of other products.

Nevertheless, there is a problem with this strategy: it may prove inadequate when faced with the challenge of CEEC membership, as price levels would still be higher than is sustainable in the long run. It would require a long transition period to avoid the overstimulation of production in the new members. The question is whether such a transition period is desirable or feasible as the Union is enlarged.

Option Three: Completion of the Reform
Process to Make Agriculture Competitive

The third strategy is more proactive, anticipating changes and adapting before a crisis occurs. It involves going considerably further than the present reform in lowering market prices and in compensating only those that are severely disadvantaged.

In the case of the cereal sector, the next step would be to lower the market price by some significant amount until close to expected medium-run world market price levels are reached. The extra compensation payments would be made in a different way from the current payments for the CAP reform price drop. First, no further use of land would be necessary to receive the payments. They should carry a termination date, say, ten years, with a declining payment value, but they should be fully portable and transferable. Set-asides would be discontinued, as they would be unnecessary if market prices are close to world market levels. Because export subsidies would fall with the drop in market price, the level of exports need not be constrained by set-asides. Farmers would make planting decisions based on the best use of their land rather than on the need to satisfy program requirements.

In the case of the dairy sector, this option could include a commitment to move support prices toward those on world markets, compensated where necessary by payments not tied to continued milk production. In any case, the system of dairy quotas itself needs to be overhauled to allow the sale of quota rights across member states. Production of without-quota milk should be allowed by producers who wish to compete with overseas producers. Products made from this without-quota milk would not receive an export subsidy. Over time, such milk could replace quota milk on the domestic market as the quantity of quota milk is reduced by the purchase of quotas from farmers. These quotas would not be reissued, and the effect would be to give compensation to the farmer for loss of the quota rents inherent in the supported market.

The more positive policy change would not only complete the MacSharry reforms, but would also lay the foundation for a competitive agriculture for a Union of about twenty countries. This would include a truly single market over the area of the current Union, which would be offered to new members from the start. It would provide for payments to farmers based on their past production of supported commodities, as an ex gratia compensation for being misled by government promises. It would allow farmers to make their own planting and livestock-raising decisions. It would remove the artificial incentive to maintain high use of chemical inputs that jeopardize the environment.

The benefits of taking CAP reform to its logical limit would be considerable. First, the wastage of resources that currently go to produce goods that have no commercial markets would be reduced. Second, the food industry could develop on a pan-European basis with the lowest raw material costs possible. Third, it would give the EU a position in world trade it has not had for years, in the forefront of those seeking to improve world markets. Fourth, and most important, the assimilation of the CEECs would be made both easier for the EU and less costly to the entrants. Such a comprehensive and thorough reform cannot be implemented immediately. It would have to be phased in over the medium term.[8] The rewards of starting early would be considerable, though, since the benefits of a competitive, decentralized, and equitable agriculture could be reaped sooner.

The Task of Assimilating New Members into the CAP

The assimilation of the CEECs into the EU will be the most ambitious project so far undertaken by the EU (or the EC before it). There are, however, lessons from previous enlargement activities that can be useful. This section looks at the task of incorporation of the CEECs into the CAP in the light of previous enlargements. The changes in the CAP discussed above are put in the context of the timescale of transition. Decisions made on the development of policy in the EU-15 will have implications for the CEECs, and vice versa. In effect, the transition has started. The CAP is already being shaped by the need to effect a smooth docking with the CEECs.

Options for the CEECs over the Transition Period

Transition arrangements for the CEECs could follow one of the models described in the previous section. Should the CAP undergo the completed reform of option three above, the best strategy for the CEECs would be to keep prices low. This would eliminate any false expectations of highly protected markets. It would also avoid the preaccession costs of increased price support. And it would reduce tensions arising from GATT obligations that might otherwise constrain policy in the medium term. As important, it would minimize the potential threat, as seen by the EU, of the disruption of markets following accession.

If the EU does not manage to reform its agricultural policy completely until the time of CEEC accession, arrangements for the timing of price and policy adjustments in the CEECs will have to be made. Policy proposals of this type aim to keep the agricultural markets of the EU and the CEECs separate.[9] The advantages and disadvantages of these different transition policies can again be illustrated by looking at three representative options.

First, one could imagine an agreement for membership that so circumscribed agricultural trade flows that it constituted a de facto exclusion of the sector from the internal market between the existing EU and the new members. The analogy is with the treatment of agriculture within the European Economic Area (EEA). This virtual exclusion could take the form of strict quantitative restrictions on imports from the CEECs, or semipermanent taxes on imports from (and subsidies on imports to) the CEECs. The implication would be that the price levels need not converge and that the policies need not be harmonized. The internal agricultural market in the EU would be protected from competition from the CEECs. Such a situation is more likely to obtain if the CAP has not been reformed further (option one for the EU, above) and if the CEECs have not made a move to EU price levels. Under such circumstances, the price gap could be wide. The temptation to exclude agriculture from the process would be considerable.

This would have a number of serious economic and political implications. It would perpetuate the current imperfect market access of CEECs into the EU. As a result, the CEEC states would be denied benefits other members enjoyed in the internal market. Politically, this would constitute "second-class citizenship" for the CEECs. From the point of view of European integration, it would imply a breach in the principle that single market legislation applies to all members. It would in effect represent a move to Europe à la carte: other countries may be tempted to have their own separate agricultural markets and policies. Last, it would postpone the removal of border posts between the current EU and the CEECs and hence represent a further departure from the free internal market.

On the other hand, the situation would have potential offsetting benefits for the CEECs: they would not be under any obligation to distort their economies by setting high border taxes for agricultural products and encouraging the production of unwanted surpluses. Indeed, if foods and processed agricultural goods were allowed access into the EU, the CEECs could make use of their cheaper raw materials to develop competitive export industries in these areas. And the CEECs would be better able to establish export markets in other parts of the world, including the states of the former Soviet Union, Asia, and the Americas.

As a way of avoiding the political problems of excluding agriculture from the free circulation of goods within the Union, though not obviating the need for border posts, one could imagine a long transition period, say, fifteen years, that would have a similar economic effect. This again denies the new members immediate market access, and also gives them the option of keeping prices low in the meantime. A long transition period would inevitably postpone adjustments in CEEC agriculture. The problem with postponing adjustment is that necessary changes are delayed, and the costs of being out of adjustment are borne for a longer period. There is a cost to keeping two different price levels for agricultural goods in the EU (or more, if the CEECs have not harmonized their own prices). This cost is a misallocation of resources within the agricultural sector of the enlarged EU, leading to higher production costs and ultimately to lower farm incomes. But there would be benefits to a delayed adjustment if the end point were itself unsatisfactory. Adjustment to farm prices that are too high has its own costs. Too many resources are kept in agriculture, to the detriment of other sectors and the economy as a whole, so any delay in imposing these costs on the economy need not be a bad strategy.

The economic cost of this strategy may well revolve around the budgetary arrangements. If the CEECs are relieved of paying agricultural levies to the EU and are denied access to export subsidy funds, the appropriate price level for agricultural products will be close to the expected level on world markets. Higher price levels impose taxes on consumers and necessitate export subsidies. If, however, the EC does collect revenue, over the long transition period, from the (lower) level of tariffs applied in the CEECs; if the CEECs receive export subsidies from the EU for their third-country exports; and if there is no artificial ceiling on budget transfers from and to the new members, this makes the world market price in effect irrelevant. In that case, the economic benefits will depend crucially on the market balance for agricultural products: for export products, a rapid shift to higher EU prices will be advantageous; for imports it will impose an economic cost. On balance, it would seem that a long transition is likely to be against the interests of the CEECs if they have a predominant export interest in agriculture and if they are immediately drawn into the budget process.

The issue of the speed of transition is therefore closely tied to that of the medium-term development of the CAP and to the strategy of the CEECs prior to accession. Put simply, if the CAP is not reformed, much of the urgency to move to full market integration in agriculture is lost. If the CEECs raise their prices before entry, they will then pay a high financial and economic cost for anticipating membership. However, a rapid rise in prices would have the advantage of shortening any transition period, and if they prove to be net exporters of farm products, they will benefit after membership from the high internal prices and the availability of export subsidies. A modification of a "rapid price rise" strategy would therefore be to keep prices low until either the CAP is further reformed or until full membership (including open-ended budget participation) is imminent. At that stage, rapid harmonization of prices is the most sensible policy.

If, by the time of accession, the CAP does undergo further reform, the strategy of not rapidly moving to CAP prices will have been proved beneficial, as there would be a cost in adopting a price level too high to be maintained. The new members would risk building the expectations of farmers and incurring obligations for compensation if prices had to come down. The strategy of maintaining current price levels below those of the Union until membership is imminent would reduce this risk. In practice, this implies a cautious policy of preparing CEEC agricultural sectors for membership, without overstimulating those sectors that would be profitable only with CAP membership.

Trade and Budgetary Arrangements for the Transition

Intra-EU flows after enlargement would be governed by the choice of transition period. If price levels are still different at accession, border tax adjustments such as have been used in the past would seem to be needed. If the decision has been made to keep quantitative controls on CEEC imports, more extensive monitoring will be necessary. This raises the question as to whether there will be commercial borders between the EU and the new members. If the only reason to have such borders is to regulate agricultural markets, there will be considerable pressure to speed up the process of policy and price harmonization. Given the tendency of border controls, especially those of a quantitative nature, to be used as a hidden form of protectionism, there is much to be said for removing such borders as a priority within the enlarged Union. This suggests that any price level differences at the time of accession should be compensated by making payments directly to farmers (if the price level is higher in the acceding country) to avoid interference with cross-border commerce. The other aspect of this is that CEEC farmers would benefit immediately from higher prices in the Union.

Trade flows from without the EU would, under such arrangements, be immediately subject to the same tariffs as charged on imports into other member states. CEEC goods would be eligible for the same export subsidies as those of other members. The EU might under these circumstances consider negotiating an increase in the allowed expenditure on export subsidies under the GATT schedule and the allowable quantities that can benefit from a subsidy. But as the CEECs did not have significant export subsidies in the base period, other countries may take the view that enlargement of the EU is not a reason to create more problems for other exporters. In this case, the EU may have to absorb the extra exportable surpluses on the domestic market.

The budget arrangements for new members will no doubt be a matter for negotiation and compromise. The new members will be expected to contribute their tariff revenue on imports to the budget and be reimbursed for intervention and export subsidy costs. They should be eligible for full participation in EU structural programs. How much additional funding will be forthcoming is a political decision. If there is an effective agreement on the net transfer to the new members, at the margin they will pay for their own export subsidies and keep their own tariff receipts. They will therefore need to calculate the benefits and costs of price policies at world market prices, the marginal cost of imports, and the marginal value of exports. If there is no effective limit on the net financial contribution or disbursement, the marginal cost of imports and value of exports are the internal policy prices. Under such circumstances, the acceding countries (as with existing members) have no incentive to keep production in check, because the Union membership as a whole underwrites the disposal of surpluses and taxes any imports that might otherwise be available at world prices.

Policy Toward Agricultural Trade with the CEECs

Financial support and technical advice from the EU can help the CEECs in their internal transformation process. But more important, the EU could contribute most by providing an economic environment in which these countries can develop a functioning market economy. This would ideally involve the offer of free exchange of goods and services on open markets, in particular free trade with the EU. Given the geographical proximity with the EU, and the political and economic attractiveness of being more intensively integrated in EU markets, an expansion of trade relationships with the EU is one of the central ingredients of the process of strengthening the CEEC economies. Unfortunately, some of the agricultural subsectors in the CEECs that are most capable of exporting and earning much-needed foreign exchange are also the ones that are the most "sensitive" and regulated within the EU. The internal political resistance to liberalizing these sectors stands in direct conflict with the broader policy objective of stabilizing the emerging market economies in central and eastern Europe.

To adhere to the foreign policy and security goal of stabilizing the CEECs and integrating them into the west, the EU has to give the CEECs the chance to participate in the benefits of international trade. This would mean both the reduction of import barriers and the reduction of EU-subsidized exports to the CEECs. The former would allow the CEECs to specialize in the production of goods for which they have a comparative advantage, while the latter would avoid detrimental price distortions on their domestic markets.

The Europe Agreements between the EC and the CEECs could provide a framework for the liberalization of agricultural trade in Europe. The agreements called for the establishment of a free trade area over a maximum period of ten years. But special arrangements limit the degree of EU agricultural market access for the CEECs. For most agricultural products, the import duties and levies were reduced; but this reduction applies only to limited quantities of exports. The base periods for the determination of the reduced levy quotas were generally chosen to be periods of low EC-CEEC trade. So even substantial increases in percentage terms of these quotas over time do not correspond to the true export potential in the CEECs.

Furthermore, increased exports of the products that are most severely restricted in terms of EU market access (beef, dairy products, cereals, sugar) would most greatly benefit the CEECs. A revision of the Europe Agreements in accordance with the original free trade spirit of these agreements might therefore be the most promising form of assistance for the ongoing economic reforms in central and eastern Europe.

Conclusion

Previous enlargements have posed problems for agriculture and challenged the continuity of the Common Agricultural Policy. The enlargement to include the CEEC countries may prove to be the greatest threat to the policy. The accession of some of the countries of central and eastern Europe, with their substantial agricultural production potentials, would inflict severe budgetary and trade policy strains on the current EU policy regime. The basic principles of the CAP—market unity, community preference, and financial solidarity—are in jeopardy unless further reforms toward a less regulated common agricultural market are undertaken. Such reforms would improve economic efficiency, distributional equity, and international trade relations. The prospect of eastward enlargement might in the end turn out to be the trigger to overcome internal political resistance against another round of CAP reform that is in the interest of the Union anyway.

A reformed CAP would also facilitate the current transformation process from centrally planned to market-based economies in the CEECs, as well as their later integration into the EU. No expectations about high policy prices would be raised among farmers in the CEECs, thereby avoiding either the substantial financial and economic costs of agricultural support for the CEECs or discomforting political reactions from disappointed eastern European farmers. Moreover, a more market-oriented CAP would allow for expanded trade in agricultural products between the EU and the CEECs during the preaccession period already, because the differences in commodity prices and market organization would no longer be that substantial. The later integration of the CEECs into the Union could then take place much more quickly and smoothly, avoiding a two-tier Europe and making the CEECs immediately into equal partners.

The CAP as a common sectoral policy can survive the decade, including budgetary pressures, the GATT, and enlargement to the east, but it has to be slimmed down to be fit for the challenges that lie ahead. If politicians cannot be persuaded to take such action, the prospects are for a dismal decade of discord and divisiveness on the agricultural front and the likely renationalization of the CAP.

Notes

I would like to thank Peter Walkenhorst, a graduate student in the Food Research Institute, Stanford University, for research assistance and comments on this chapter.

1. Several other countries are likely to join over this time period, including Malta and Cyprus. Neither of these countries would have a marked impact on the CAP and are not discussed here. The accession of Turkey would have a much more significant impact, but this is unlikely in the foreseeable future. Of the other European countries, Norway may feel the need to reapply to avoid economic and political isolation, as might Switzerland if it were to begin to lose the benefits of being "different." One would assume that the special measures designed for Finland and Austria would be applied to Norwegian and Swiss agriculture.

2. Jackson, M., and Swinnen, J., "A Survey and Evaluation of the Current Situation and Prospects of Agriculture in the Central and Eastern European Countries with Emphasis on Six States with Europe Agreements," report prepared for Directorate-General I of the European Commission, Leuven, 1994.

3. Tangermann, S., and Josling, T., "Pre-Accession Agricultural Policies for Central Europe and the European Union," report prepared for Directorate-General I of the European Commission, Göttingen/Stanford, 1994.

4. Larsen, A., Anderson, R., Frohberg, M., Keyzer, M., Koester, U., Mahe, L., Merlo, M., Molander, P., Sarris, A., and van der Mensbrugghe, D., "EC Agricultural Policy for the 21st Century," *European Economy* (December 1994).

5. Organization for Economic Cooperation and Development (OECD), *Agricultural Policies, Markets and Trade* (Paris: OECD, 1993); and OECD, *Economic Accounts for Agriculture* (Paris: OECD, 1994).

6. Tangermann, S., "A Bond Scheme for Supporting Farm Incomes," in Marsh, J., Green, B., Kearney, B., Mahe, L., Tangermann, S., and Tarditi, S., eds., *The Changing Role of the Common Agricultural Policy: The Future of Farming in Europe* (London and New York: Belhaven Press, 1991), pp. 95–96.

7. Josling, T., "The Reformed CAP and the Industrialized World," *European Review of Agricultural Economics* (1995), pp. 513–527.

8. Josling, T., and Tangermann, S., *Toward a CAP for the Next Century* (London: European Policy Forum, 1995).

9. Nallet, H., and Van Stolk, A., "Relations Between the European Union and the Central and Eastern European Countries in Matters Concerning Agriculture and Food Production," report prepared for Directorate-General VI of the European Commission, Brussels, 1994.

6

Wider but Weaker or the More the Merrier? Enlargement and Foreign Policy Cooperation in the EC/EU

David Allen

General Issues

In 1969, the six member states of the European Community (EC) decided at the Hague to both initiate enlargement negotiations with the four applicants (UK, Ireland, Denmark, and Norway) and begin the process of foreign policy cooperation known as European Political Cooperation (EPC). There has always been a certain ambiguity about this decision, which can be seen either as a determination to match enlargement (widening) with a parallel decision to enhance integration (deepening), or as an intergovernmentalist challenge to the Community method along the lines initially proposed by de Gaulle and Fouchet in the early 1960s.[1]

The idea that enlarging the EC might be accompanied by its deepening (including progress in the foreign policy sphere) has been regularly repeated over the years, and many would see the establishment of the Common Foreign and Security Policy (CFSP) in the Treaty on European Union (TEU) as part of the Twelve's preparation for the European Free Trade Area (EFTA) enlargement. Similarly, there were those who argued that one of the tasks of the 1996 Intergovernmental Conference (IGC) would be to reform the CFSP procedures to prepare the European Union (EU) for the planned further enlargement that would include the Central and Eastern European Countries (CEECs) as well as Cyprus, Malta, the Baltic states, and the former Yugoslavian state of Slovenia.

Widening and Deepening

The relationship between widening and deepening has always been a contentious one that has divided, in particular, Britain, France, and Germany. The British have always appeared to believe, most vociferously during Margaret Thatcher's premiership, that any enlargement is attractive because it will lead to a weakening of the Union's supranational elements and federal ambitions. The British calculation has always been a quantitative one, based on the erroneous assumption, to date at any rate, that the achievements of the Community (the *acquis communautaire*) could not be stretched to include new members without being watered down. On the other hand, it would also seem to be the British belief that the achievements and practices of EPC/CFSP (the *acquis politique*) are infinitely stretchable—that is, any number of member states may participate—and that those achievements are in no way endangered by the prospect of further enlargement.

The French have always shared the British view of the relationship between widening and deepening but have usually come to the opposite conclusion about the attractiveness of EC enlargement. It was de Gaulle, essentially for his own foreign policy reasons, who unilaterally terminated enlargement negotiations in 1963 and 1967; it was France that was most hesitant about both the Mediterranean and EFTA enlargements; and it is France that is least enthusiastic about bringing in the CEECs. Thus, despite their closeness on so much to do with the evolution of the EU, France and Germany have often found themselves in disagreement over the question of enlargement. Germany has never accepted the notion that wider means weaker and has always perceived the twin processes of enlargement and deepening to be compatible, indeed mutually reinforcing. It was clearly a desire to maintain the special relationship with Germany and to ensure continued German interest in the EU that persuaded France to eventually accept the inevitability of further EU enlargement.

However, even if the establishment of the EPC process can be said to support the view that EC/EU enlargement will encourage further integration, the nature of EPC might be said to move things in the opposite direction. From the outset, EPC[2] was to be an intergovernmental procedure, initially without a treaty base of any kind and designed for the exclusive participation of the member states, with both the European Commission and the European Parliament (EP) firmly excluded. Thus, while enlargement may well stimulate further cooperation in the foreign policy sphere, that very cooperation was originally inspired by a desire to undermine or at best restrict the development of the Community system and to replace it with something that seemed less threatening to the sovereignty of the participant states.

Although the CFSP provisions in the TEU can be seen as an attempt, partly in response to a prospective enlargement, to develop procedures to promote integration by enhancing the collective international effectiveness of the EU's member states, they can also be seen as a consolidation of intergovernmentalism and a rejection of further supranationality. If the TEU was designed to deepen the EU before enlargement, it is clear that the member states remained undecided about how best to achieve this in the area of foreign policy. Maintaining a separate pillar for the CFSP kept things much as they had been under EPC (with the addition of a defense dimension a potential major advance), but the linking of the three pillars in a "common institutional framework,"[3] along with specific recommendations about how the CFSP and the Justice and Home Affairs (JHA) pillars might be more effectively coordinated, suggested some doubts about the efficacy of preserving the distinction between them. It is not that clear from the TEU itself, or from the subsequent operation of the second pillar, that the Twelve in fact gave much attention to enlargement considerations in reaching their specific agreement on the CFSP arrangements.

Reform

It will be one of the contentions of this chapter that the difficulties the EU has experienced in the foreign policy area in recent years cannot be explained by the impact of recent enlargements on a process that was designed from the outset with just ten states (the founding six plus the UK, Ireland, Denmark, and Norway) in mind. Enlargement from the original six to nine (UK, Ireland, and Denmark—Norway rejected membership at the last moment in 1972 after a negative referendum result), to ten (Greece), to twelve (Spain and Portugal), and to fifteen (Austria, Sweden, and Finland) states may have served to highlight some of the problems with the EPC/CFSP process; but increased numbers alone cannot account for its failure to produce progress toward a coherent foreign policy for the Union. Similarly, while the prospect of further enlargement to include the CEECs has already led for calls to reform the CFSP process at the 1996–1997 IGC in preparation for a significant increase in participants, it is argued here that the problems are more fundamental and apply to the present membership regardless of any future enlargement.

In any case, many people would argue that the present calls for reform are somewhat premature, given the very short time since the Maastricht Treaty was finally ratified (November 1993) and the CFSP arrangements came into effect. Although the EU has indeed enlarged since then, and although recent developments (most notably at the Essen European Council in 1994 and the Madrid European Council in 1995) would seem to suggest that further enlargement is imminent, this is not in fact likely to be the case.

At most, probably only five or six states will join the EU over the next ten years, and while this may well require major changes to a number of aspects of the EC pillar (most obviously the Common Agricultural Policy [CAP] and the structural funds), it is argued here that the CFSP pillar, as it is presently constituted, could probably easily accommodate a few more members without seriously affecting the apparently limited aspirations of its members.

Indeed, former UK foreign secretary Geoffrey Howe has recently argued that enlargement delays caused by difficulties in negotiating pillar I (EC) arrangements could be bypassed by allowing the CEECs immediate involvement in the CFSP in advance of full membership in the Union. One way would be to make the applicants associate members (as in the Western European Union [WEU], where they have been made associate partners) of the CFSP, able to speak in the Council but not vote; another would be to go the whole way and enlarge the CFSP pillar to give the CEECs full membership with full voting rights immediately. Howe also discusses the possibility of creating a European Political Area (rather like the European Economic Area that Jacques Delors devised to give the EFTA applicants effective membership in the EC without involvement in EPC), which he suggests might be "based on a formal treaty and underpinned by joint decision-making in certain fields of mutual interest."[4]

Finally, there is the suggestion that a collective security guarantee might be extended to the CEECs and Baltic applicants. This would require the relationship between the WEU and the EU to be more clearly established. This could prove a difficult task, given that the implications of the last enlargement have not yet been fully dealt with. New members Austria, Sweden, and Finland have opted for observer status in the WEU along with Denmark and Ireland, but the question of their neutrality is clearly not yet fully resolved.

If, on the other hand, some or all of the present member states were to seek to move beyond the present—essentially diplomatic—arrangements toward a serious attempt to create a common foreign and security policy with central institutions, the prospect of future enlargement to include the CEECs would indeed be significant and would present a much more fundamental challenge. Even here, though, some of the potential CEEC applicants, particularly those with small, inexperienced, and underdeveloped foreign policy machinery, might be more willing to participate in a full-fledged European foreign policy than some of the present member states.

Foreign Policy

If the member states decide that they do wish to make a major federal leap in this area, an enlarged EU may well face problems in reconciling the foreign policy interests of a growing number of small states with those of an essentially static number of large states, particularly if one of the ways forward is seen to be the extension of majority voting to all aspects of CFSP. It should be recognized that the successful trick of the old EPC process was a flexibility and an informality that enabled states with varying foreign policy experience and ambitions to attempt to exploit jointly their collective strength at a time when their ability to exert influence unilaterally was either waning or nonexistent. It may well be that an increase in numbers will lead to calls for an extension of majority voting (from the very limited provisions of the Maastricht Treaty) within the CFSP. The problem caused by the small states' ability to exercise their veto in the CFSP—best illustrated recently by the lengthy Greek refusal to allow the EU member states to collectively recognize the former Yugoslav Republic of Macedonia (FYROM)—is, of course, matched by the determination of the larger member states to preserve the veto.

If the Union is enlarged and the number of small states thus increases, the CFSP will face a major problem. One possible solution, recently suggested by France and Germany and cautiously endorsed by the UK foreign secretary, Malcolm Rifkind,[5] is that of "constructive abstention," whereby countries objecting to a particular aspect of CFSP would simply stand aside and not prevent others from pursuing it. Even bolder is the suggestion that a "variable veto"[6] be introduced. In this scheme, similar to that operating in the UN Security Council, the five large states—Germany, France, the UK, Italy, and Spain—would retain the unilateral right of veto in all CFSP decisions (other than with regard to those joint action implementation decisions for which the TEU already provides for majority voting). The remaining member states would lose their right of veto, and CFSP decisionmaking would be by qualified majority voting (QMV), but with a Big Five veto. In this way, in a further enlarged Union, only a very broad (and extremely unlikely!) coalition of small states could block a position on which the Big Five were in agreement. In a similar vein, it has been suggested that the CFSP might adopt an arrangement of "consensus minus one, two, or three" for small states who dissented. Provided the smaller states are exempted from participation in policies they do not agree with, the proposals mentioned above, which have been stimulated by the need to adjust to CFSP enlargement, might allow the larger and smaller member states to preserve the successful balance of interests they achieved in the past. These arrangements, along with other potential developments, would also increase the likelihood of a fragmented or multispeed Union developing.

Past Enlargements

Within the EU, decisions about enlargement have always been "high political" decisions. By and large, foreign policy considerations, expressed and developed in the EPC/CFSP framework, have dominated the enlargement agenda, while questions relating to the impact on the internal development of the EC/EU have been seen as secondary. In other words, enlargement is, and always has been, a diplomatic/security matter, dominated by the collective views of the member states and often involving either the rejection or the marginalization of the views of the Commission and the EP, despite the fact that they both now have a formal role in the enlargement process. The decision to reject Britain's initial application was linked to de Gaulle's foreign policy ambitions for the EC, as was his pursuit of linked and countervailing arrangements with Germany. The decision to eventually admit Britain, despite the fact that Britain was unenthusiastic about many of the internal integration objectives, was clearly linked with the Six's desire to make the EC more outward-looking and coincided with the establishment of EPC.

The enthusiastic endorsements of the Greek, Spanish, and Portuguese applications were foreign policy decisions imposed by the EC's foreign ministers on a reluctant Commission. The argument was that EC membership would support the foreign policy interests of the West by underpinning liberal democracy and market economics in three states that had only recently emerged from right-wing authoritarianism and that might otherwise be vulnerable to the attentions of the Soviet Union. While the EC member states were capable of agreeing about the primacy of foreign policy considerations, they subsequently did not prove so politically adept at implementing the enlargement decisions. Thus, Greece was allowed to join before Spain and Portugal and was therefore able to exploit its position both to delay their accession and to extract financial concessions from the rest of the EC.

There may well be a lesson here for the CEEC applicants, whose foreign policy stances toward each other and toward the outside world may be sufficiently different to cause difficulties if some find themselves inside the CFSP and influencing policy toward those who remain outside. The EU has, for example, experienced the most enormous difficulty in developing its stance (both economic and political) toward Turkey because of the determination of the Greek government to have its say. It would not be hard to imagine a situation in which Poland, Hungary, and the Czech Republic combined within the CFSP to frustrate the aspirations of those applicants next in line.

The admission in 1990 of the five East German Länder, as part of a reunified Germany, was also clearly the product of foreign policy considerations. Quite simply, the international situation demanded that economic and social criteria be overlooked. The neutral states of EFTA had been in a position to participate in the EC pillar for some time, but the international situation meant that, for them, the EPC arrangements presented an impossible hurdle. The EFTA neutrals could not consider accepting the obligations of full membership, and the member states could not have accepted their nonparticipation in EPC/CFSP. Once the international situation allowed a more relaxed view of neutrality and European foreign policy commitments, the way was clear for the applications that followed.

Future Enlargements

If the EFTA enlargement eventually presented few problems for either the EC or the CFSP (mainly because of the failure to develop the CFSP and, in particular, to build on the defense provisions of the TEU), the prospective eastern enlargement revives our interest in the conflict between long-term political objectives as developed in the CFSP and the shorter-term economic interests that dominate the EC process. The European Council and the EU foreign ministers have clearly decided, or have been so persuaded by political pressure from the applicants, that in time an extensive enlargement to the east is both desirable and unavoidable. However, so weak are the foreign policy arrangements that the EU has effectively lost control of this agenda and has been forced to respond hastily to accusations of duplicity by the potential applicants for promising cooperation in principle but failing to deliver in practice. Thus, the EU was forced by the CEECs at Copenhagen in 1993[7] to accept that Europe Agreements were designed to lead to full membership, and at Essen in 1994[8] to further accelerate the enlargement arrangements; this was done in such a way that the 1996–1997 IGC became greatly confused by the looming presence of enlargement considerations. This is not to say, however, that the IGC outcome was well designed to prepare the EU for enlargement.

Many people would go further and argue that the whole process of enlargement for all the surviving European organizations (the Warsaw Pact and the Committee for Mutual Economic Assistance [CMEA] have been wound up) represents some sort of failure of collective decisionmaking by the existing members. While it is reasonably easy to understand how all the former Soviet states, including the five central Asian republics,[9] became members of the CSCE/OSCE, it is difficult to understand how they became members of the North Atlantic Cooperation Council. Similarly, it could be argued that discussions about enlargement, within both the EU and NATO, have resulted in a potentially dangerous new division of Europe, the implications of which have never been properly thought out because of the weakness of the current foreign policy consultation apparatus. It is also clear, and the subject of some concern, that despite a considerable overlap of membership, little attempt has been made to coordinate enlargement considerations within and between the various institutions. Thus, NATO continues to refine its enlargement plans,[10] seeking to finesse the question of Russian exclusion, and probable CEEC inclusion, via the Partnership for Peace program, in apparent isolation from the EU's own plans[11] and indeed from the recent decision to admit Russia to the Council of Europe. The EU member states would appear to have decided that some states (those that have been given or have been promised Europe Agreements) will eventually join the Union while others will not. This most certainly meets the aspirations of the would-be members, which are all keen to have access to EU markets but are primarily motivated by a desire to seek security within a body that excludes Russia, the Ukraine, and Belarus. The EU, on the other hand, seems reluctant to face up to the foreign policy implications of its decisions or the actual aspirations of the applicants. Instead, having created an effective divide, the EU seeks to blur it by offering, in the near future, to go beyond the Partnership and Cooperation Agreements recently signed with Russia and the Ukraine and discuss the possibility of a free trade area with these states.[12]

The EU would appear to have a problem with its enlargement policy, which is itself a reflection of the weakness of the CFSP procedures, regardless of any enlargement. The EU clearly accepts the long-term inevitability of enlargement but is not collectively strong or confident enough to be clear about the nature of the obligation it is prepared to accept, or the wider international implications of its enlargement strategy. This is because it does not feel in a position to either agree on or deliver the sort of commitment that the CEECs want; this is partly because it is concerned about further alienating Russia or undermining President Yeltsin's delicate internal position.

Whether it likes it or not, and despite the fact that it is unable to accept the associated responsibilities, the EU is already regarded by a number of its member states as effectively being a security community. The CEECs and Baltic applicants believe that the EU is the answer to their security dilemmas, and I contend that so do Austria, Sweden, and, in particular, Finland. Regardless of whether they or the CEECs eventually join NATO, with its ambiguous security guarantee, or the WEU, with its more specific promise of support, these states feel that membership in the EU alone gives them security. After all, what sort of a union would it be if member states failed to give assistance to one of their number in the face or threat of an attack, from outside or within? This view was endorsed by Geoffrey Howe:

> It is difficult to believe that Russia might act against the Baltic states, for example, if they are regular participants, perhaps even equals, at a meeting of EU foreign ministers. It is still more difficult to believe that in the face of intimidation or aggression, EU leaders would be as inert as they were for so long over former Yugoslavia.[13]

Institutional Issues

Until recently, the impact of the successive enlargements on the institutions and procedures of EPC/CFSP had been slight; indeed, the major changes would seem to have been in the foreign offices of the acceding states. Ireland, Spain, and Portugal certainly had to restructure their foreign offices to comply with EPC arrangements, although Austria, Sweden, and Finland clearly profited from a close association with the CFSP mechanisms prior to entry. However, while all the previous new members could draw on a certain experience of cooperative participation in other Western organizations, the next round of applicants will be drawing on a quite different historical experience. Partly for this reason, and partly because the EU is anxious to respond to CEEC pressure for a closer involvement with the EU even before accession, complex arrangements have been set in motion, particularly since the Essen European Council, to establish a "structured relationship" that covers both EC and CFSP matters.

Structural Dialogue

There is already a high degree of structured contact between Malta, Cyprus, the CEEC states, and the CFSP, and this will presumably be extended to include the Baltic states and Slovenia as their Europe Agreements develop. During the German presidency, for example, the EU/CEEC heads of state and government met on the margins of the Essen European Council: the foreign ministers all met twice with the CEECs, and the foreign ministers' troika met with representatives of the Baltic states. More significantly, at official levels the EU/CEEC political directors met once and the European correspondents twice,[14] and to prepare for these deliberations there were no less than eleven meetings of experts (covering disarmament, nuclear nonproliferation, human rights, security, the CSCE, the CIS, planning, conventional arms export, the former Yugoslavia, terrorism, and the UN) mainly at the troika level.[15]

If this degree of contact is maintained throughout the 1990s, the socialization effect of the CFSP should have begun to have some impact long before the formal accession of these states. However, as with so many aspects of the EU's external activities, the elaborate procedures may well be more impressive than the substance they yield. It has been argued recently[16] that the structural dialogue is fundamentally flawed and that it has degenerated into a means whereby each side bores itself in a structural "monologue" in which each eastern European state vies for EU attention and approval. Things are not improved by EU pressure on the CEEC applicants to present common foreign policy positions. One EU observer is quoted as saying that "after four decades of being treated as a bloc, these countries are fed up with being lumped together."[17] Some might think that this does not bode well for these states' eventual participation in a CFSP procedure that seeks to develop a European foreign policy from a consensus of national foreign policies. It also suggests that an enlargement that is phased over a significant time period is bound to produce foreign policy tensions between those who have and those who have not yet entered the EU.

Enlargement and the EU Presidency

The greatest institutional challenge for a new EU member, and possibly for the EPC/CFSP system, has centered on the institution of the presidency. Because EPC and the CFSP were, and remain, "underinstitutionalized," the burden and responsibility of the presidency is so enormous that some would argue that it is too much for the smaller member states. However, with the single exception of Greece, it is difficult to find examples of new members who have been embarrassed or who proved embarrassing when their turn first came to take over the presidency. The fact that Greece assumed the presidency very soon after accession, combined with a certain apprehension about the policies it might wish to pursue, can be said to have had a major impact on the rapid development of the troika system. This enables the preceding and succeeding presidency states to ensure that ongoing business is not neglected and that the EU representational and negotiating role is not abused. Indeed, during the last Greek presidency, the German representatives were able to use their involvement in the troika to ensure that consultations relating to both Turkey and the FYROM were maintained.

Enlargement has had one major impact on the presidency in that the rotation, following the accession of the EFTA states, has been adjusted so that a sensible mix of large and small states is preserved. As a consequence of this change, the initiation of Austria has been put off until 1998, Finland until 1999, and Sweden until 2001, by which time all three states should be well versed in the mysteries of the CFSP.

The 1996–1997 IGC had plenty of presidency reform schemes to consider, all of which were made all the more urgent by the prospect of enlargement. The presidency problem is particularly acute in the second pillar because of the relative lack of supporting institutions (within the EC pillar, the Council Secretariat and the Commission are both able to assist those member states that are prepared to accept such assistance). It can be argued that as well as organizing capacity, in which the larger states would claim a superior competence, the representational role of the presidency within the CFSP is particularly important and is best entrusted to those states that have extensive representations of their own and that can claim to command greater authority in their dealings with the EU's interlocutors.

This sort of thinking has led some to suggest that with further enlargement it would make sense either to develop team presidencies (in which one large state would be joined by three or four smaller states in a year-long presidency) or, more drastically, to consider separating out the presidency of the EC pillar from the presidency of the CFSP (and the JHA pillar). Thus, while the presidency of the CFSP might be restricted to the Big Five states, the smaller ones might be compensated with the exclusive chairmanship of the JHA and a continued involvement in the rotating management (albeit as part of a team) of EC business. The problem with all these solutions designed to reconcile, including into the CFSP, a number of additional small states is that it has always proved difficult to sensibly separate out either the management or implementation of EPC/CFSP and EC business. While there are forces at work that might lead the Union to distinguish between the management of EC and CFSP business, there are clearly other forces that would mitigate against this, in particular the need to ensure consistency.

The Balance Between Large and Small States

Nevertheless, the periodic enlargements that the EU has experienced, along with the prospects for future enlargement, raise the question of the balance between the large and small states in a system that retains an insistence on consensus. Even if one accepts the arguments of participants that in practice the "club atmosphere" (can this be preserved as the numbers grow?) ensures that consensus forms around the median rather than the lowest common denominator, there remains a danger that the larger states will become frustrated by the ability of the smaller states to prevent reaching consensus. Many would argue that it was frustration with Greece over the Macedonian recognition issue, combined with other problems in recent years, that led to Britain, France, and Germany participating in the contact group (with the United States and Russia) on the conflict in the former Yugoslavia. Even though the agreements reached in Dayton, Ohio, were essentially achieved by the skill, will, and power of the United States alone, the contact group served, more effectively than the EU, to provide a basis for European (and Russian) involvement and legitimization of the peace process.

It could be argued that if the EU member states do not find satisfactory solutions to the presidency and voting problems, further enlargement and the problems of reaching consensus will force the major players increasingly to seek ad hoc solutions to international problems. The danger would be that, in an enlarged Union, the major players would be forced away from the CFSP process because it will be increasingly seen as restrictive rather than permissive. However, it should also be noted that even the larger states perceive great benefit both in the solidarity and cover functions that the CFSP, with its broad membership base, provides.

It may well be the case that all the member states are driven by the numerical complexities of enlargement to consider other ways of organizing themselves in the foreign policy sphere. While it seems unlikely that a consensus will develop around the idea of creating a central foreign policy institution within the European Commission, the member states might be attracted by the notion of giving more authority and tasks to the recently expanded CFSP secretariat, which is now a part of the Council Secretariat, and which has responsibility for supporting both EC external relations and CFSP.[18] Although the quantitative impact of enlargement on CFSP is often given too much attention, while the qualitative aspects are neglected (that is, many of the recent new members are themselves anxious to participate constructively in the CFSP and are therefore more prepared than some long-established members to make the necessary adjustments to achieve consensus), the lack of CFSP central institutions (such as a planning staff or a European foreign office or diplomatic service) is a problem that is considerably exacerbated by an increase in participants. Similarly, enthusiasm for the proposal to appoint a new EU foreign policy representative—a Mr. or Ms. CFSP—which some see as a short-term answer to the lack of central institutions, must be tempered by the realization that it will be more difficult if the person selected is to gain the support of more than twenty states.

The External Face of the EU

Similarly, the more member states there are under the current presidency arrangements, and the more commissioners there are with external responsibilities (there are four[19] in the present Commission, plus the president, who has assumed overall coordination responsibilities for the CFSP), the more confusing the Union appears to its external partners. If a large group of states with varying diplomatic competencies wish to make a collective and coherent impact on the outside world, they may well be forced to reconsider their fundamental opposition to the creation of effective central institutions. This point is made all the more powerful when one considers the enormous extra burden the Union's collection of "political dialogues"[20] imposes on all the member states, but on the presidency country in particular. At last count, either the presidency alone or the troika is required to have CFSP-related dialogues with the following: Albania, Australia, Canada, China, Cyprus, South Korea, the Baltic states, the United States, India, Japan, Malta, Morocco, New Zealand, Pakistan, Russia, Switzerland, Turkey, Ukraine, the CEECs, the Council of Europe, the Gulf Cooperation Council, the San José group, the Central American group, the Andean pact, the Rio group, the Non-Aligned Movement, ASEAN, and the ACP states. This represents a considerable burden for Britain, France, and Germany and, some would say, a near impossible task for Malta, Cyprus, and Slovenia, not to mention the Baltic states. Enlargement will reduce the number of dialogues by bringing some of them into the Union, but it will increase the number of those who have to try to agree on the substance and management of these dialogues, which are a central part of the current CFSP.

The institutions of the CFSP make the practice of collective diplomacy, based on common positions, a realistic ambition, but they are not sufficient to provide the basis for a common foreign and security policy for the Union. Further enlargement will make even the task of collective diplomacy that much more difficult and the successful pursuit of meaningful joint actions that much more unlikely. However, the fundamental problems of the CFSP have little to do with the need to adjust to an increased membership. The CFSP represents an attempt to continue and expand the successful EPC procedures. The problem is that EPC developed in a European system structured by the Cold War, in which, it could be argued, there was a degree of convergence imposed on the foreign policies of the member states by their common predicament. We are only just beginning to appreciate that, like all the other post-1945 institutions, the arrangements that underpin the EU and its CFSP may no longer be appropriate for the changed international situation the member states find themselves in. In other words, the CFSP has one set of problems that are enlargement related, but it also has a more fundamental set of problems that would exist even if further enlargement were not in the cards.

Policy Issues

All the enlargements of the EU have at one time or another been regarded as creating new "bridges" between the EU and the outside world. In 1973, Britain was regarded as a bridge to the wider international system in general and to its Commonwealth in particular—although the subsequent treatment of Commonwealth countries by the EC did not bode well for a profitable relationship. Denmark was seen as a bridge to the rest of Scandinavia and has indeed proved just that. It was always assumed within EPC that Denmark would keep the Scandinavian nonmembers informed (usually within the Nordic Council) about developments that might affect them or for which their support might be sought. Currently it is clear that Norway's self-imposed isolation from the developing CFSP has been eased to a certain extent by the information that is passed on by Denmark and Finland within the Nordic context.

Similarly, when Spain and Portugal joined in 1986, much was made of the bridge that would then be established between the EC and Latin America, and it was indeed the case that aid to that area increased as a result of Iberian efforts. More recently, the arrival of the two additional

Scandinavian states has given rise to the notion of a bridge to the Baltic states (but not Russia!), while Austria would appear to be performing the same service for Hungary that Denmark provides for Norway.

The Mediterranean

One consequence of all this bridge building by the new members is that it becomes that much harder to identify the priority of the EU's foreign policy interests, especially now that the potential EU external agenda is so much freer in the changed international environment. While the prospect of further enlargement has made relations with both the CEECs and Russia a recent foreign policy priority (with the new members particularly keen to push the case of the Baltic states), the Mediterranean states within the EU have recently begun to question this eastern focus for the Union. Obviously member states like Greece, Spain, Portugal, and Ireland have good cause to fear the financial costs to them of enlargement to the east. It is generally accepted that neither the CAP nor the structural funds can be offered to the eastern applicants on the same terms the present members currently enjoy, and therefore eastern enlargement is associated in their minds with a probable change in the current arrangements that will leave them worse off than at present. These states thus have a considerable incentive to push the case for a renewed foreign policy focus on the Mediterranean area (which will receive further support once Malta and Cyprus are admitted), linked with a slowing down of the timetable for eastern enlargement. Such an approach also found favor with France, Spain, and Italy at a time when their EU presidencies followed one another (January 1995–June 1996).

Future enlargement and pressure for a new foreign policy focus on the Mediterranean are therefore inextricably interlinked. Proposals by Britain for a stability pact for the Mediterranean similar to the one that is now the subject of a joint action toward the CEECs (the Balladur Pact) are designed to try to ensure that the southern focus is developed within the political remit of the CFSP rather than the potentially expensive area of EU external relations. The case for the EU balancing its eastern concerns with policies for the south has been made all the more convincing by recent events in Algeria, but the EU's problem in this area is that, while it has a clear interest in political stability and economic prosperity in the region—as it does in eastern Europe—it cannot use the prospect of membership as an incentive. In all other cases where the EC/EU has sought a relationship with its immediate neighbors, the prospect of enlargement has been the major foreign policy tool. Because this is not an option for the northern African states, despite Morocco's constant requests, the EU is going to have to devise a policy within the CFSP that does not rely on the prospect of EU membership.

In December 1995, the EU hosted in Barcelona a two-day conference that brought together twenty-seven Mediterranean countries with the aim of creating a "common area of peace and stability." The Euro-Mediterranean conference could herald the beginning of a process that would in many ways cut across the exclusiveness that is implied by further enlargement. Here, a major foreign policy issue is being addressed collectively by EU members, prospective members, and nonmembers.

Neutrality and Defense

It was argued earlier that EPC and the CFSP to date can be seen as essentially concerned with the narrow field of diplomacy rather than foreign policy proper. To the extent that much of European foreign policy cooperation is based on the production of common statements that together form the *acquis politique,* applicant states seem to have had little trouble accepting this *acquis* on accession. While this may well say something about the minimalist nature of many EU declarations, it also suggests that new members have so far shared a foreign policy outlook very similar to that of the original members. There was some concern at the start of the EFTA negotiations that Sweden, Finland, and Austria might have problems squaring their neutrality and their distinctive views on development policy with the EU *acquis politique,* but this did not prove to be the case, although a number of unanswered questions remain in the defense sphere. Only Austria felt the need (perhaps because it applied earlier than the rest) to specifically mention its neutrality—which is in any case based on legal provisions, unlike that of Finland and Sweden. However, not only is the definition of neutrality changing in line with changes in the European system of international politics, but the EU at present does not seem either willing or able to undertake the sort of foreign policy activity (the unilateral and independent use or threat of force) that might cause the neutral states difficulty.

If some of the present members of the EU seek to make significant progress in the defense area—perhaps within the IGC—the recent enlargement might give Denmark and Ireland some allies that would share their reluctance. But as long as the EU dares to use force only under the provisions of UN Security Council resolutions, the neutral states will have no problem. Sweden participated in the UN Protective Force (UNPROFOR) in both Macedonia and Bosnia; and Austria had little problem agreeing to allow Allied forces to overfly Austrian airspace and use Austrian roads on their way to the Gulf.

The EFTA enlargement has, of course, transformed the geopolitics of the EU, which now has a 2,000-kilometer frontier with Russia and has one state (Austria) close to the disputed Balkans. However, the three new members also added to the foreign and security policy resources of the Union; in particular, all three possess significant military resources and an advanced defense industrial base. If the EU is able to further develop its relationship with the WEU and resolve its place in the overall European security order, all three may, in time, be seen as net contributors to the CFSP.

The three small states of Cyprus, Malta, and Slovenia may pose some problems for the CFSP, especially if Cyprus somehow manages to join the EU before any settlement has been found regarding its division and partial occupation by Turkey. In the past, this problem was seen as an absolute barrier to Cypriot membership, but as things stand, Cyprus has a promise (like Malta) that negotiations will begin six months after the conclusion of the IGC. Malta itself is constitutionally committed to nonalignment, but as with the Scandinavian states, much of the rationale for this has disappeared with the Cold War. Like many of the eastern states, Malta would now seem to seek its security inside the EU. Slovenia, now that it has settled its territorial dispute with Italy, would not seem to be bringing any fundamental foreign policy problems into the EU, although, if successful, it would serve to highlight the aspirations (currently on hold) of the other former Yugoslav republics.

Security and the CEECs

Most of the CEEC applicants would be delighted if the EU sought to successfully turn itself into a formal security community. They would have no problem signing up to an effective WEU, and they would be keen advocates of any developments in the wider security area. The problem here is not with possible enlargement but with the reluctance, divisions, and uncertainties of the present members as well as the obvious hostility of those, like Russia, who cannot aspire to membership.

The CEEC states, all relatively poor, will not bring many foreign policy assets, other than their geostrategic position, into the Union. Although all the CEECs once had impressive military resources, these have been rapidly demobilized as part of economic reform. Although these states may be able to contribute in small ways to eventual EU peacekeeping forces, they are likely to be net recipients of security if the WEU eventually decides to extend its security guarantee to all EU members. The EU would do well to consult with NATO on this question because that organization is already thinking about the basic military capabilities it would require applicant states to possess and maintain. Thus, in the security area, enlargement to include the CEECs could be a problem for CFSP, because the prospective members probably want to go further down the integrative road than the present members do. Most of the problems relating to the defense and security aspects of CFSP are raised, with even greater force, by the potential membership of the three Baltic states. Although they have strong

Scandinavian supporters within the present EU, they must be seen as a foreign policy liability, contributing very little while being the potential source of considerable problems for the CFSP.

Conclusion

One of the difficulties in writing this chapter has been the realization that many of the fundamental problems CFSP faces have little to do with either the past, recent, or future enlargements (although enlargement has impacted the EPC/CFSP in the ways discussed above), but a great deal to do with the changed situation after the Cold War and the reluctance of most member states to contemplate any fundamental change in the mechanisms that appeared to serve their interests in the 1970s and 1980s. The EPC/CFSP procedures and policies are so limited that they have had little difficulty absorbing a succession of new members; only Greece, and then only intermittently, has proved to be a difficult partner. It may well be that the CEECs, the Baltic states, and the former Yugoslav states will bring with them fundamentally different foreign policy traditions and practices that present the CFSP with more severe problems of adaptation; but it seems likely that these will not prove insurmountable as long as the CFSP remains fundamentally unambitious.

The original six member states experienced no real difficulty in developing EPC and extending it to twelve member states. Although the EFTA enlargement has gone well to date, it has not been faced with any significant leap forward by the CFSP, nor does it now seem likely that any real progress, other than institutional tinkering, will be made in the IGC. It seems probable, for instance, that the future role of the WEU will be considered only in 1998 (its fifty-year anniversary), when the Treaty comes up for reconsideration. Nevertheless, for many of the prospective members, participation in CFSP is enormously attractive and potentially less painful in the short term than full exposure to the EC pillar. It remains to be seen whether CFSP can rise to the challenge of further enlargement. Failure to do so might well endanger not only the overall European order, but also the safety of the EU order itself.

Notes

1. For a discussion of the Fouchet plan, see Dinan, D., *Ever Closer Union: An Introduction to the European Community* (Boulder: Lynne Rienner, 1994), pp. 49–50. On intergovernmentalism see Holland, M., *European Integration: From Community to Union* (London: Pinter, 1994), pp. 117–129.

2. For the definitive history of the origins and development of EPC, see Nuttall, S., *European Political Cooperation* (Oxford: Clarendon, 1992).

3. *Treaty on European Union,* Title 1, Common Provisions, Article C.

4. Howe, G., "Bearing More of the Burden: In Search of a European Foreign and Security Policy," *The World Today* 52, no. 1 (January 1996), pp. 23–27.

5. Speech to the French International Relations Institute reported in the *Financial Times,* 6 March 1996.

6. Howe, "Bearing More of the Burden," p. 24.

7. For the buildup to the Copenhagen meeting, see Kramer, H., "The European Community's Response to the New Eastern Europe," *Journal of Common Market Studies* 31, no. 2 (June 1993), pp. 213–244.

8. See Cameron, F., "The European Union and the Fourth Enlargement," *Journal of Common Market Studies* 33, Annual Review (August 1995), pp. 31–33.

9. Kazakhstan, Kirgizstan, Tajikstan, Uzbekistan, and Turkmenistan.

10. Von Moltke, G., "NATO Moves Towards Enlargement," *NATO Review* 44, no. 1 (January 1996).

11. Ruhle, M., and Williams, N., "NATO Enlargement and the European Union," *The World Today* 51, no. 4, pp. 84–88.

12. Allen, D., "EPC/CFSP, The Soviet Union and the States of the Former Soviet Union: Does the EU Have a Coherent Policy?" in Regelsburger, E., de Schoutheete, P., and Wessels, W., eds., *The European Union in the World: The Common Foreign and Security Policy (CFSP) in the Maastricht Treaty* (Boulder: Lynne Rienner, 1996).

13. Howe, "Bearing More of the Burden," p. 25.

14. For an account of CFSP procedures, see Edwards, G., and Nuttall, S., "Common Foreign and Security Policy," in Duff, A., Pinder, P., and Pryce, R., eds., *Maastricht and Beyond: Building the European Union* (London and New York: Routledge, 1994), pp. 84–103.

15. CFSP Forum, Institüt für Europäische Politik, Bonn, *IEP No. 4,* 1994, p. 6.

16. Klau, T., "Tackling the Structural Monologue," *European Voice* 2 (22–28 February 1996).

17. Ibid.

18. Smith, M. E., "Achieving the Common Foreign and Security Policy: Collusion and Confusion in EU Institution," paper presented at the Tenth International Conference of Europeanists, Chicago, 14–16 March 1996.

19. Manual Marin (Spain) is responsible for Latin America, the Mediterranean, the Middle East, and Asia; Sir Leon Brittan (UK) is responsible for the developed world, including the United States and Japan; Hans van der Broek (Netherlands) is responsible for central and eastern Europe and for CFSP; and Joao de deus Pinherio (Portugal) is responsible for relations with the developing states of Africa, the Caribbean, and the Pacific.

20. For details of the political dialogue with the Visegrad states, see Klunkert, S., "The Dialogue with the Visegrad Group: Dynamics at Work," CFSP Forum, Bonn, *IEP No. 2,* 1994.

7

The Impact of Enlargement on EU Trade and Industrial Policy

Heather Grabbe & Kirsty Hughes

This chapter analyzes the implications that previous enlargements and the prospective eastward and southern expansion have had and will have for the trade and industrial policies of the European Union (EU). These policies have evolved over time in response to a number of internal and external influences, including in particular, on the trade side, the influence of multilateral trade negotiations under the auspices of the General Agreement on Tariffs and Trade (GATT) and then the World Trade Organization (WTO). In each enlargement, there are potential influences both from the accession countries on the EU, and from the EU on the accession countries. Furthermore, while some of the influences are direct, others are more indirect and possibly more difficult to disentangle from other factors.

Overall, the successive enlargements of the EU since 1973 have had a number of effects on the development of EU trade and industrial policy. With some exceptions, the main influences on trade policy have, in the long run, been indirect: enlargement has increased the size and weight of the EU and has influenced attitudes toward trade liberalization. There have been short-run direct effects on trade policy both through the development of specific trade agreements prior to accession and through transitional arrangements after accession. In the case of industrial policy, there have been more direct long-run effects, notably the impact of successive enlargements on the development of EU regional policy and its structural funds. More indirect has been the impact on how different countries view the role and scope of different aspects of industrial policy. This pattern looks likely to be repeated in the case of the eastward and southern enlargement of the EU: that is, there will probably be short- to medium-run trade effects owing to preaccession arrangements and postaccession transitional periods; longer-run indirect effects via size; and direct industrial policy effects through reform of the structural funds.

EU Trade and Industrial Policies

EU trade and industrial policies have changed and developed over time. Furthermore, it is not always a straightforward task to distinguish the scope and role of trade policy, industrial policy, and competition policy. For example, state aids are policies directly aimed at influencing industrial structure and performance, but control of state aids is seen as an aspect of competition policy—EU Articles 92 and 93 aim to limit distortion of competition through state aids. State aids can also form part of trade policy negotiations by influencing bargaining over tariff reductions. Industrial policy has itself changed over time, from being seen primarily as specifically directed toward the industrial sector to being a term applied to a range of microeconomic measures aimed at influencing competitiveness across the economy. Trade policy has also been concerned with questions of sectoral restructuring, particularly establishing special arrangements for sensitive sectors such as steel and textiles.

There have always been debates and tensions around the development of industrial policy. The essential divisions have been between those emphasizing the operation of free markets, using competition policy as the main tool, and those calling for a variety of more active and interventionist approaches. These tensions exist within and between EU member states and within the European Commission itself. The Commission's analysis of the benefits of the single market at times stressed the benefits of increased competition and at others stressed the potential of the single market for building large European firms that may benefit from the development of specifically EU technical standards.[1]

Another tension lies in the question of the appropriate division of responsibility between the EU and member states. With the exception of coal and steel, EU powers originally focused on competition policy (Articles 85 and 86) and on the regulation of state aids (Articles 92 and 93). The scope of policy has been extended over time, notably with the development of a range of EU technology policies in the 1980s, with the evolution of a wide-ranging regional policy, and with the coordination of restructuring policies for a number of sectors facing decline. The founding of the single European market expanded the scope of EU powers significantly, particularly in establishing a major new framework for trade and economic activity aimed at increasing economic integration and stimulating competitiveness. As such, the single market represents a substantial development of trade and industrial policies and also goes beyond the normal scope of such policies in promoting integration.

The development of EU industrial policy since the 1970s indicates, therefore, a mixture of underlying influences and rhetoric. On the one hand, by the late 1980s, substantially more emphasis had been placed on markets and competition through the single market program; on the other hand, the EU has developed its policy responsibilities in a number of areas, including technology and regional policy. The single market program itself appeared to encourage a major merger wave in the late 1980s, leading to a substantial restructuring and concentration of European industry.[2] This mixture of influences is also apparent in the Commission White Paper on competitiveness, growth, and employment, with its emphasis on promoting competitiveness and employment through initiatives such as the trans-European networks, together with an emphasis on more flexible labor markets.[3]

Different approaches across member states can also be observed by looking at the level and distribution of state aids. In the early 1990s, state aids as a percentage of GDP varied from 0.6 percent in the UK to 2.8 percent in Italy and 3.9 percent in Luxembourg.[4] The proportion of aid devoted to sectoral aids also varied from zero in Luxembourg to 34 percent in the case of Spain. Moreover, the poorer member states benefited particularly from the growing budget allocations to the structural—and then the cohesion—funds. Overall, the current policy consensus on industrial policy is that certain sorts of horizontal policy interventions are broadly acceptable, especially in a regional context—assistance to small and medium-sized enterprises, infrastructure, research and development, skills, and training—while sectoral assistance should be directed primarily at restructuring declining sectors rather than trying to promote the development of specific new ones. The influence of successive new members both on the development of specific policies and on overall attitudes toward industrial policy is explored below.

The evolution of trade policy has in many ways been more straightforward than industrial policy and much more influenced by external factors, the most notable being multilateral negotiations. The common external tariff has been lowered in stages over the past quarter of a century, and nontariff barriers have been gradually removed as a result of international obligations taken on by the EU. Successive enlargements had a role to play in this process by increasing the overall weight of the EU as a trader globally, and hence as a negotiating partner, and through the free trade inclinations of some of the acceding states, which tended to push the EU away from an inward-looking trade policy.

The EU's trade policy toward developing countries evolved under pressure from those countries and the multilateral framework, but the expansions of EU membership also affected policy. Each enlargement brought in a set of countries that already had trade ties with the new member; the result was often an expansion of preferential trading arrangements and a general upgrading of relations between those developing countries and the whole EU. In the longer run, the changes in membership affected the political balance that determines overall development policy and the preferences awarded to different groups of developing countries. The ways in which these influences on policy worked are discussed in this chapter.

The 1973 Enlargement: Denmark, Ireland, and the United Kingdom

Economic Positions on Accession

Because the UK is one of the largest European economies and a major international trader, its accession had a significant long-term impact on the direction of Community policies. Upon joining in 1973, the UK's GDP was over U.S. $180 billion (at current prices and current exchange rates), making it the third largest economy in the enlarged EU, whose total GDP was $1.1 trillion. Denmark had a much smaller GDP of $29 billion, and Ireland was tiny at just under $7 billion.[5]

Conditions of Accession and Policy Impact

The effects of the 1973 enlargement were more significant in trade policy than industrial policy, at least in the short to medium run. This was largely because of the openness of the UK economy to trade, the high proportion of GDP accounted for by exports, and the UK's extensive trade ties through the Commonwealth. The UK's and Denmark's previous membership in the European Free Trade Agreement (EFTA) was also significant in developing trade relations with the rest of Europe. However, the dominance of agriculture in the Irish economy played an important role in the long-term development of Community regional policy.

Trade policy. The largest and most immediate adjustments needed for enlargement had to be made by the acceding countries. Joining required the UK, Ireland, and Denmark to accede to the common customs tariff and common commercial policy toward third countries. The principle of a common commercial policy had been established in Article 3(b) of the Treaty of Rome, and common policies were developed in stages by the six member states.

Internal trade arrangements. With regard to intra-EU trade, the completion of the European Customs Union in 1968 provided a clear set of tariff reduction obligations for the new members. All three countries were given a transitional period of five years after accession, involving five stages of tariff cuts, to eliminate customs duties on industrial goods. Agricultural products were subject to a more elaborate set of arrangements designed to bring the new members into the Common Agricultural Policy (CAP). A five-year transitional period was established here too, including a system of "compensatory amounts" between the common price level and the prices to be applied by the new members during transition.

External trade conditions. Arrangements for acceding to Community policy on trade with third countries were more complex. The GATT Kennedy Round, which ended in 1967, had reduced the Common External Tariff (CET) by some 35–40 percent.[6] For all three new members, tariffs had to be approximated to the CET within five years of accession. The UK negotiated special arrangements for certain products because of its existing Commonwealth obligations, but these were transitional and offered no permanent guarantees to third countries.

Negotiations with the UK were the most difficult because of its extensive trade ties. Its Commonwealth Preference system was incompatible with EU policy toward developing countries, and preferential access to UK markets could not continue after accession. This issue was resolved by making Commonwealth countries in Africa, the Caribbean, the Indian Ocean, and the Pacific eligible to join the EU's Yaoundé convention with developing countries. The Generalized System of Preferences, which operated under UN auspices from 1971, provided some compensation for the other Commonwealth countries. Special arrangements were made concerning Indian sugar exports, tea tariffs, and EU trade with Malta, Cyprus, and Gibraltar.

The most problematic areas in the UK negotiations were New Zealand dairy exports, Commonwealth sugar, fisheries, and the UK budgetary contribution. Transitional arrangements were made for the first two issues, but reconsideration of fisheries policy had to be left until after accession. The British budget question dragged on until the Fontainebleau Agreement in 1984.

Negotiations were much less complex for Ireland and Denmark. Overall, terms for these two countries were similar to those obtained by the UK.[7] For Ireland, a transitional period was allowed for phasing out the existing Anglo-Irish Free Trade Area, and special arrangements were made for motor vehicles and some other products. Denmark negotiated solutions to issues concerning Greenland and the Faeroe Islands, especially over fisheries, and there were transitional measures for a small number of other areas.

Effects on Community policy. Apart from the changes undertaken by the acceding states, several EU external trade policies were changed as a direct result of negotiations. The most important were relations with EFTA and development policy.

As former members of EFTA, the UK and Denmark had opposed the reserection of trade barriers with their former partners, while the Six refused to agree to special links between the new members and EFTA.[8] Free trade with EFTA was therefore extended to the whole EU through separate bilateral free trade agreements between the EU and each EFTA member. The continuation of strong ties between Denmark and the other Scandinavian countries also encouraged the development of long-run trade and economic links with the Union, which culminated in applications to join.

With regard to trade with developing countries, EU policy began to change following the first set of negotiations with the UK.[9] On the UK's accession, the EU system of trade preferences was extended to the new member's former possessions, which encouraged a proliferation of association agreements and forced a change in the overall policy framework. At the time of accession at least, the EU took the view that adding the Commonwealth countries could help secure the supply of raw materials. Links with the African Commonwealth countries were seen as particularly important following the 1973 oil crisis.

The result of these considerations was the Lomé convention, signed in 1975, which replaced the Yaoundé and Arusha conventions of 1963 and 1969. It brought together and governed all trade and aid arrangements with African, Caribbean, and Pacific developing countries. Although Lomé was initially seen as a simple geographical extension of Yaoundé terms, it came to involve a change in the content of development assistance and terms, the most important of which was a commodity revenue stabilization system (STABEX) to be financed by the EU.[10]

In addition to this overall framework, relations with the southern Mediterranean rim were enhanced as a result of pressure from the countries of the Maghreb, which feared the loss of the UK market for their exports. The result was "overall cooperation agreements" offering preferential trade and other arrangements to the Maghreb and Mashreq countries. Overall, the enlargement led to a major expansion of EU relations with developing countries, extended the number of countries given preferential trading arrangements, and brought about the innovation of revenue stabilization for the large number of countries covered by Lomé.

After enlargement, EU trade policy retained protectionist elements through regional trade preferences, the CAP, and national measures. However, the UK had an important long-run influence in opposing an inward-looking trade policy on the part of the Community.[11] The insistence of the Six on negotiating a permanent solution to the Commonwealth issue in the framework of international agreements[12] was also important in maintaining the consistency of EU external trade policies and in continuing a tendency to resolve internal disputes through international agreements, especially the GATT rounds.[13]

Industrial policy. The impact of the 1973 enlargement in the area of industrial policy was primarily indirect. The negotiations resulted in few specific measures concerning industrial policy at EU level or in the member states.

In the area of state aids to declining industries, Articles 92 and 93 of the Treaty of Rome restricted types of aid that could be given, but it was up to the European Commission to determine which practices of national governments were to be permitted. At the time of accession, the Commission was relatively inactive in this area and did not react strongly to the increase in direct subsidies to national industries that resulted from the recession of the early 1970s. Its main focus in maintaining discipline on member states was on preventing subsidies that increased capacity or supported failing firms.[14]

In terms of an active policy to promote new areas of industrial development, an EU policy was beginning to evolve when the enlargement negotiations took place. The 1960s had seen greater interest in improving the industrial base and in technology policy. In 1973 and 1974, the Council of Ministers adopted two Commission memoranda on these subjects (CEC 1973a and b, based on the Colonna Report of 1970 and the Spinelli Memorandum of 1973), which advocated a much more active approach to industrial policy and proposed the creation of a single market. However, it was not until the 1980s that major programs were developed to pursue these aims.

The main impact of the 1973 accession on EU industrial policy seems to have occurred through the UK's emphasis during accession negotiations on having a European technology policy. The UK's interest in this area stemmed from its view of its own technological expertise[15] and high research and development spending, and contributed to the upsurge of interest in this area in the early 1970s.

In the long run, the provisions for economic and regional development Ireland negotiated for accession were significant in the development of EU regional policy. The Irish negotiators emphasized a need for EU-level measures to correct the "serious economic and social imbalances of a regional and structural nature" facing the country.[16] The Act of Accession accordingly allowed this issue to be taken into account when applying EU rules on state aids. The act also specifically mentioned Ireland's need to use EU resources available for promoting economic development and improving living standards. At that point, the main funds were the European Social Fund (ESF) and the European Agricultural Guidance and Guarantee Fund (EAGGF).

This aim of narrowing the gap between Ireland's state of economic development and the rest of the Union, combined with the UK's support for regional transfers from the EU budget, stimulated the founding of a formal EU regional policy. Before the 1973 enlargement, the EU had focused on support for national regional policy. A change in focus was provoked by the new members, who brought in more areas suffering from structural unemployment, at the same time this problem was receiving more attention from the Commission for the EU as a whole. Structural unemployment was especially severe in agricultural areas and in member states with declining industries. The positions of Ireland and Greenland,[17] along with the Italian Mezzogiorno, were given special mention in the Commission report on regional problems following enlargement,[18] and both Ireland and the UK were expected to be major beneficiaries of regional funds.[19] Establishment of the European Regional Development Fund (ERDF) in 1975 also helped to defuse UK concerns about having to give up control of aid to regions and provided some political relief in the budget dispute because of potential UK receipts from the fund.[20]

Overall, the 1973 enlargement established the basis for an EU regional policy that was expanded when the Mediterranean countries joined. In addition to this general stimulus to regional policy as an area of EU activity, the enlargement affected its focus on reducing disparities in economic development, particularly industrialization and social development.

Indirect Effects of Enlargement

Many of the changes in trade and industrial policy made because of the 1973 enlargement have proved to have much longer-term effects than anticipated. Policy toward developing countries and regional policy, in particular, took paths that were largely unforeseen at the time of the accession negotiations.

There were also indirect effects on policy. One was the size of the UK economy and the importance of the UK as a trading nation, which increased the EU's weight in multilateral trade negotiations. The UK's emphasis on free trade also encouraged the EU to move away from an inward-looking trade policy.

The enlargement had a significant impact on the EU budget as well. The effects on policy were amplified by the change in the political balance of the EU, with the UK becoming the second largest net contributor and Ireland by far the largest net beneficiary per capita of EU funding. Additional revenue because of the UK's accession gave EU policies greater scope. It gave a particular boost to the ERDF because of strong support from the UK for the establishment of a regional fund.[21] At the same time, Ireland's interests as a net recipient of regional and other funds added to the support for them and provided the basis for a political constituency of poor countries that was later extended with the Greek and Iberian enlargements.

However, the political acrimony caused by the British budget problem continued for over a decade. In combination with the Thatcher and Major governments' commitment to constraints on public expenditure, it consolidated UK opposition to any major expansion of the budget, including in the direction of industrial policy. In this regard, budgetary concerns were reinforced by UK free market policies in the 1980s, which increased the UK's resistance in the face of any pressures for the development of a strongly interventionist EU industrial policy.

The particular interests the UK, Ireland, and Denmark brought into the EU affected the political balance relating to a number of areas of trade and industrial policy. In terms of sensitive sectors, the UK had interests in coal, steel, fisheries, and shipbuilding. The agricultural basis of the Irish economy and the importance of fisheries to Denmark also had long-term influences. In addition, Denmark's high standard of environmental protection on accession added a voice to calls for a more comprehensive EU environmental policy.

The 1981 and 1986 Enlargements:
Greece, Portugal, and Spain

Economic Positions on Accession

The enlargements of 1981 and 1986 involved much greater industrial policy changes than were necessary to admit the UK, Ireland, and Denmark. The economic disparities between the EU and Greece, Spain, and Portugal were recognized early on to be great enough to warrant a major program of aid to the new members.

In 1975, Spain's per capita GDP was only U.S. $2,902 against an EC-9 average of $5,388, while Greece's was $2,306 and Portugal's was only $1,682.[22] Their industrial profiles were also very different, with a much higher proportion of the labor force employed in agriculture than in the EC-9. Declining industries had significant shares in their GDPs, especially textiles in Portugal.[23]

With regard to trade, all three had a considerably lower proportion of GDP accounted for by exports than the EC-9's average of 26 percent: in 1975, Greece had 13.8 percent, Spain 13.4 percent, and Portugal 17.5 percent.[24] The Spanish economy was also the most heavily protected, estimated at 11 percent in nominal terms and 13 percent in effective terms.[25]

On the other side, the EU had developed significantly as a political and economic entity since 1973. The negotiations with the UK, Ireland, and Denmark took place against the background of an only recently completed customs union and more limited international obligations to liberalize trade and capital flows. By the time of the Iberian negotiations, the Single European Act (SEA) was in view and momentum was already building toward the creation of a single market.

Conditions of Accession and Policy Impact

Because of the evolution of EU policies on internal and external trade, state aids, and technology policy since 1973, the Mediterranean enlargements involved considerable adjustments by the new members to conform with the EU's rules. However, the EU in return developed a regional policy that provided aid to help them adjust and to reduce overall economic disparities. In the long run, the structural funds became an important component of Community industrial policy and accounted for a very significant share of the EU budget.

Trade policy. Trade relations had developed between the EU and the new members for a number of years, and some progress on policy alignment had already been made before the start of formal negotiations. Greece had a Treaty of Association with the EU from 1962 (it was frozen during the 1967–1974 dictatorship) that provided for an eventual customs union. Tariff reductions for industrial trade between Spain and the EU were nego- tiated in the early 1970s, and limited concessions were made for imports of Spanish agricultural products.

Portugal was a member of EFTA from 1960; its free trade agreement with the EU (signed in 1972) provided for the elimination of all tariff barri- ers on Portuguese exports, although quantitative restrictions remained on some sensitive products until 1983. EU exports of industrial products to Portugal were to be liberalized in three stages, ending in 1985, and there were concessions for some Portuguese agricultural exports.[26]

Internal trade. The lengthy membership negotiations dealt with obstacles in the agricultural, industrial, and fishing sectors. For Greece, quantitative restrictions were removed on accession except for fourteen products. A five-year transitional period from accession in 1981 was set for the elimina- tion of customs duties on trade with the EU and alignment with the CET. Longer periods were allowed for certain agricultural and industrial prod- ucts.[27] However, effective protection declined little during the 1980s because of Greece's use of taxes and subsidies.[28]

For Spain and Portugal, a seven-year timetable was set from the start of full membership in 1986 for reciprocal dismantling in stages of tariffs for intra-Community trade and for aligning with the CET. The CAP was accepted by Spain and Portugal from 1986. Many quantitative restrictions were removed in 1986, and all had to be eliminated by 1990. Long transitional periods of between seven and ten years were set for freeing trade in agriculture, fisheries, and sensitive industrial sectors.[29]

Following accession, the new members also had to take on the removal of trade barriers, particularly the nontariff barriers, that accompanied the single market program launched in 1985. The new members received derogations from some aspects of the program based on their stage of economic development, often being allowed longer periods in which to implement directives than the Nine. The impact of the single market rules was also affected by the number of unsanctioned delays in incorporating directives into national legislation. In Greece, for example, domestic policy instruments were used actively to achieve selective protection of industrial activity throughout the 1980s.[30]

External trade. The 1981 and 1986 enlargements necessitated a change in the EU's trade relations with the rest of the Mediterranean. Financial and technical assistance to the southern Mediterranean countries was increased. The trade provisions of the existing agreements with Maghreb and Mashreq countries were modified eventually to compensate them for the enlargement, but adjustment was left largely to them.[31] However, in the long term, the trade and security concerns of the EU's southern members led to the "Euro-Mediterranean partnership" initiative of 1994 and a new phase in EU-Mediterranean relations.

Industrial policy. Enlargement posed further challenges for evolving Community industrial policy at both the sunset and sunrise ends of industrial development. Greece, Spain, and Portugal faced economic and social dislocation as a result of industrial decline, and all three countries maintained significant degrees of direct or indirect protection for certain industries before accession. At the same time, their technological bases lagged behind those of Community members.

Declining industries. Discussion had begun before the 1981 and 1986 enlargements about EU-level responses to supplement measures taken by national governments to deal with the economic and social consequences of crises in declining industries. The steel crises of 1974 and 1980 saw effective use of the European Commission's powers to intervene in the industry under the Treaty of Paris.[32] Other major industries experiencing excess capacity in the mid-1970s included textiles, shipbuilding, chemicals, and motor works.

The new members of the EU had to conform with measures aimed at preventing distortions in competition caused by national intervention in declining industries. In terms of financial intervention, EU discipline on state aids became stricter from the mid-1980s as a corollary of the single market program.[33] The main mechanism for this change was a tightening of European Commission policy in determining whether aids conformed with Article 92 of the Treaty of Rome.

However, the three new member countries have maintained a considerably greater proportion of their aids to the manufacturing sector in the form of sector-specific subsidies than have other member states.[34] Spain continued a particularly high proportion of sectoral aids to the steel and shipbuilding industries until 1989, when EU rules became fully applicable. Portugal was given until 1991 to conform with EU directives. Of all the member states, Greece alone increased its state aid to manufacturing between 1981 and 1988—by 37 percent.

All three new members were granted derogations in favor of state aid aimed at promoting development in regions with an abnormally low standard of living or serious unemployment. The whole of Greece, Portugal, and Ireland and 56 percent of Spain's population were eligible for derogations under Article 92(3)(a) of the Treaty of Rome under EU state aid policy.[35]

Technology policy. EU policy on strengthening the scientific and technological base of European industry began to develop rapidly in the early 1980s. The ESPRIT program covering information technology began operation in 1984, following a long collaboration between the European Commission and European industrialists. ESPRIT served as a model for other programs to promote new technologies introduced by the SEA, including the multiannual Framework programs and subprograms that began in 1987.[36]

Accession to the EU was an important stimulus for the development of national research and development policies as well as technology policy in the newcomer countries. All three became more active in these areas, and EC policies were prominent in helping shape national frameworks.[37]

Indirect Effects

In most of the areas of trade and industrial policy discussed above, the new member states had to accept the *acquis communautaire* and to implement EU policies they had had much less opportunity than the incumbent member states to shape. Although they may have been granted more leeway in implementation or longer transitional periods than other member states, the general direction of most major EU policies was not changed. The great exception to this picture is regional policy, which took a significant leap forward as a result of the enlargements and became an important component of EU industrial policy. The size of the structural funds in comparison with those made available for other instruments, such as the technology programs, resulted in the primacy of regional policy over other aspects of industrial policy.[38]

The Mediterranean newcomers brought regions into the EU that were significantly poorer and less industrialized than the other Nine, with the exception of Ireland. As a result, the enlargement stimulated a new set of policies—ultimately involving a third of the EU budget—to facilitate the structural adjustment of their economies and to promote greater economic and social cohesion in the enlarged EU.

Regional policy.   Before Portugal's accession, the EU helped that country adjust its agricultural and fisheries sectors. The EU also provided financial aid to Spain in the form of loans from the European Investment Bank for projects involving small business, regional infrastructure, and energy.[39] On accession, the ESF, ERDF, and the "guidance" section of the EAGGF became available to new members. The Commission's preaccession documents on Greece, Spain, and Portugal made clear the need for considerable financial flows from the EU through the structural funds to enable them to adjust to EU legislation.[40]

Following accession, the Greek government issued a memorandum demanding additional funds from the EU to aid the country's economic development.[41] At the European Council in Dublin in 1990, additional resources were allocated to compensate Greece, Italy, and France for the Iberian enlargement, resulting in the Integrated Mediterranean Programs (IMPs), which were to run until 1992.

Subsequently, the EU progressively took on greater responsibility for dealing with regional disparities. One of the primary aims of regional policy was to convert declining industrial regions.[42] In theory, the structural funds were not intended to supplement current incomes but to invest in the supply side of the assisted regions to improve their competitiveness and to facilitate integration,[43] although this was intended to lead to a greater convergence of incomes in the longer run.

In 1989, the structural funds were reformed to concentrate on five priority objectives; and they were doubled in real terms between 1987 and 1993, rising from ECU 7 to 14 billion.[44] The rationale behind the reform was that the Iberian enlargement increased the need for adjustment and greater cohesion. It was also an acknowledgment of the likely effects of the single market in increasing regional disparities.

Following the 1989 reform, EU regional policy differentiated between lagging poorer regions, regions in industrial decline, and rural regions in structural decline and provided additional funds to deal with structural unemployment. Greece, Spain, and Portugal benefited under all these criteria. From 1989, particular programs, which drew on the structural funds, were developed to deal with regions seriously affected by industrial decline: RECHAR for coal, RESIDER for steel, RETEX for textiles, and RENAVAL for shipbuilding. KONVER was set up in 1993 to cover regions in industrial decline following the end of the Cold War.

A new cohesion fund established in 1993 under the Edinburgh Growth Initiative was designed to promote environmental projects and trans-European networks in the field of transport infrastructure. Eligibility was restricted to member states with a per capita GDP of less than 90 percent of the EU average, which covered Greece, Spain, Portugal, and Ireland.

The development of the structural funds owes much to the lobbying power of the Mediterranean countries. In terms of overall EU GDP, it can be argued that the structural funds have so far been too small to have a significant redistributive impact,[45] although their size relative to the recipient countries' GDP had significant effects on the Greek, Spanish, and Portuguese economies. There is also considerable debate as to the effectiveness of the funds in achieving their aims. The transfers may have slowed structural adjustment in the case of Greece, according to Alogoskoufis,[46] and other authors have doubts about their impact in achieving economic convergence, particularly in employment rates.[47]

In terms of overall policy impact, regional policy has been of great political importance in ensuring the support of the Mediterranean countries for other initiatives in the context of multilateral bargaining in the EU.[48] To that extent, the Mediterranean enlargements have had a much wider impact on the political balance in the EU, which has itself indirectly affected the development of trade and industrial policies.

The 1995 Enlargement: Austria, Finland, and Sweden

Economic Positions on Accession

By the time of the 1995 enlargement, Austria, Finland, and Sweden already had a high degree of integration with the EU, particularly through the European Economic Area (EEA). They were relatively rich countries, with per capita GDPs above the EU average,[49] and they became net contributors to the EU budget. In terms of industrial structure and trading position, there were no striking differences with existing EU members that would require major policy changes on the part of either the acceding countries or the EU.

Conditions of Accession and Immediate Effects

Trade policy. The long development of EU-EFTA relations ensured that by the time of the negotiations for membership, there were few serious outstanding issues to resolve. Negotiations in 1986 had extended the use of the Single Administrative Document for intra-EU trade to the EFTA states, and the free trade agreements were extended into scientific and technological cooperation.

The European Economic Area. The single market program represented a threat to the EFTA states because of the likely discrimination against them due to closer integration among the full members of the EU.[50] Their response was coordinated through the negotiations to create the EEA, which began in 1990.

The EEA Treaty gave EFTA states many of the obligations and benefits of the single market and includes most of the *acquis communautaire* concerning the free movement of goods, services, persons, and capital, although there are still some exceptions. However, EFTA members remained outside the CAP and the CET.

When Austria, Sweden, and Finland submitted applications for full membership in the EU between 1989 and 1992 (along with Norway and Switzerland, which later withdrew their applications after national referendums), the major area of trade policy that remained outside the EEA was relations with third countries, including both trade and development policy. The average tariffs of the acceding countries had to be reduced and their trade preferences for groups of developing countries changed, but neither issue proved particularly problematic in negotiations.

In its opinions on enlargement, the European Commission had made clear the incompatibility of the single market with transitional arrangements involving frontiers between old and new members.[51] However, in the end, the most sensitive trade issue—the transit of heavy trucks through Austria—was dealt with by establishing a three-stage transitional period ending in 2003 and an accompanying policy review.[52]

Industrial policy. The EEA Treaty enables EFTA states to participate in EU research programs, and it enhances cooperation on environmental policy and consumer protection. Financial aid for social and economic cohesion in the EEA is administered by the European Investment Bank. Similarly, EU rules on competition, including state aids, are used as a model for rules throughout the EEA.

As a result, only a few issues were left for enlargement negotiations. The political importance of maintaining higher environmental, health, and safety standards in the applicant countries meant that transitional periods of four years were agreed, although border controls were abolished from accession. In regional policy, a new Objective Six was introduced into the structural funds for the Arctic Circle regions in Finland and Sweden, and additional funds for it were granted.[53]

Long-Run Impact of Enlargement

Because of the progressive integration of EFTA economies with the EU, and the alignment of their national policies with many aspects of the *acquis communautaire*, the 1995 enlargement had no dramatic effect on EU industrial and trade policy. However, pressure from the EFTA states for access to EU markets over the preceding thirty-five years helped to shape EU trade policy.

In the future, the enlargement seems likely to help strengthen the free-trading coalition in the EU and a more liberal stance in the EU's external trade policy.[54] It will also increase the EU's weight as a trading bloc in international trade negotiations. Likewise, the greater priority new members give to environmental, health, and safety issues seems likely to result in greater pressure at EU level for higher standards.

In terms of enlarging the EU to the east, Austria's trade and investment links with its eastern European neighbors, and Sweden and Finland's links with the Baltic states, are increasing the speed of economic integration between the EU and the latest set of applicants for membership.

Prospects for Southern and Eastern Enlargement of the EU

The enlargement of the EU to southern and eastern Europe has potentially major implications for EU industrial and trade policies, in particular for the former. The implications for trade policy mainly concern interim trade policies prior to enlargement, while eastward enlargement is likely to lead to substantial reform of EU industrial policy, particularly the structural and cohesion funds. Cyprus and Malta are the smallest of the twelve countries and also have had functioning market economies and stable democracies for a number of years; consequently, their accession has minor implications relative to the impact of accession by the Central and Eastern European countries (CEECs), especially the larger ones.

The accession to the EU of Cyprus, Malta, and the ten CEECs with Europe Agreements will result in a much larger EU (though not in economic terms in the short run); in a more diverse EU (in economic performance and structure); and in an EU with a greater number of poorer countries. While these twelve countries would increase the EU's population by over 100 million, they represent less than 4 percent of EU GNP. Given their population size, there is scope in the long run for these countries to be of major economic importance within the EU, but in the short to medium run, their economic weight is small, so many of the trade implications are limited. In contrast, the large population combined with low income is precisely the reason there are likely to be important implications for EU structural policy.

The CEECs differ greatly in size, economic structure and performance, and speed and nature of transition toward market economies. Table 7.1 sets out the proportion of GDP produced by the private sector in the CEECs, rates of GDP growth, unemployment rates, and GDP per head at purchasing power parity rates. Considerable variety can be observed: Hungary has the highest private sector share and Slovenia and Romania the lowest; official unemployment rates vary from 2 to 16 percent; and growth rates also vary greatly. While there has been substantial progress in most countries on small-scale privatization, there is more variation on large-scale privatization—with most progress by the Czech Republic, Estonia, and Hungary.[55] Analysis by the European Bank for Reconstruction and Development (EBRD) also suggests that much progress remains to be made on enterprise restructuring. Average GDP per head of the ten CEECs is only 30 percent of the EU average, and even the highest CEECs have a level below that of Greece and Portugal.

Table 7.1   Macroeconomic Performance in Central and Eastern Europe

	Percent of GDP in Private Sector	Unemployment Rate	Real GDP Growth, 1994	GDP per Head at Purchasing Power Parity, as Percent of EU Average
Czech Republic	56	3.2	2.6	42.2
Hungary	60	10.4	2.9	35.8
Poland	56	16.0	6.0	31.5
Slovakia	58	14.8	4.8	33.6
Slovenia	33	14.6	5.5	50.5
Bulgaria	40	12.8	1.4	33.0
Romania	35	10.9	3.9	15.7
Estonia	49	2.0	6.0	38.4
Latvia	58	6.5	2.0	28.7
Lithuania	55	4.2	1.7	17.7

Sources: CEC (1995), EBRD (1995), EBRD (1996).

EU-CEEC trade has grown rapidly since 1989. Table 7.2 shows export and import levels and the net trade balance from 1989 to 1994. Germany is the dominant country, representing over 50 percent of EU exports in 1994; it is the largest trader with many countries in the region and the dominant exporter to and importer from the Czech Republic, Hungary, and Poland.[56] For the Visegrad Four, Bulgaria, and Romania, exports from and imports to the EU grew at an average annual rate of 23.6 percent and 15.9 percent respectively from 1989 to 1993.[57] Foreign direct investment (FDI) into the

Table 7.2   EU-CEEC Trade

	1989	1990	1991	1992	1993	1994
EU exports to CEECs	24,208	23,343	31,640	35,243	41,899	48,987
EU imports from CEECs	27,350	29,220	34,449	36,619	38,728	49,301
EU net trade balance with CEECs	–3,142	–5,877	–2,809	–1,376	3,171	–314

Source: External Trade Statistics, Eurostat, 1995, 8/9.
Note: All figures are in ECU billions.

region grew relatively slowly in the early years of the transition but by 1994 appeared to be gathering pace. By mid-1995, FDI was approaching U.S. $28 billion, of which Hungary had received almost $10 billion, Poland almost $4 billion, and the Czech Republic almost $3.5 billion (OECD estimates). Germany and the United States were the dominant investors in the region, substantially ahead of other EU countries.[58] FDI was driven by both market and cost considerations, with markets the dominant motive.

Baldwin argues that the bilateral nature of the EU's Europe Agreements with the CEECs means there is a hub-and-spoke pattern that biases investors to locate in western Europe.[59] However, this argument depends on the importance of scale economies relative to low labor costs and is also less persuasive where markets are the key motive; the growth in FDI and the importance, especially for German firms, of cost-related FDI in CEECs also suggest that EU-CEEC trade arrangements are not necessarily inhibiting FDI. Taken together, the trade and FDI data indicate the dominant importance of Germany in the EU's relations with CEECs; a new central European division of labor may be developing that in the medium run could substantially change the structure and dynamics of the European economy.[60]

The EU has developed a preaccession strategy with respect to the CEECs as set out in the conclusions of the Essen European Council in 1994. The main components of this strategy are the Europe Agreements, the structured relationship (multilateral dialogue), the internal market White Paper,[61] and technical aid and assistance through the Phare program. With respect to industrial and trade policy, the relevant parts of the preaccession strategy are the Europe Agreements, the internal market White Paper, and the Phare program. The internal market White Paper covers a wide range of areas beyond the scope of this chapter but also covers areas and issues relevant to industrial and trade policy.

One of the key questions with respect to industrial and trade policy and the accession of the CEECs is whether—owing to the magnitude of the transition process they are going through—there will be long-run derogations and transitional periods that may represent or contribute to the establishment of a multispeed or multitier EU. The remainder of this section first considers EU trade policy in the context of southern and eastern enlargement and then EU industrial policy.

Trade Policy

Trade relations between the EU and the ten CEECs, Cyprus, and Malta are regulated both by international agreements and by bilateral association agreements between the EU and each country, referred to as Europe Agreements in the CEEC case. By early 1996, these had been ratified with all countries except Slovenia; that agreement was delayed because of Italian concerns about aspects of Slovenia's property laws and other issues. There has been little analysis of the implications of these agreements for EU trade policy, partly because of their small overall economic size; but there has been substantial analysis in the CEEC case of trade flows between CEECs and the EU, estimates of likely growth of trade, analysis of the Europe Agreements, and analysis of the costs and benefits to the EU of that trade.[62]

In the future southern and eastern enlargements of the EU, trade relations between the applicant countries and third countries may be relatively unimportant in the accession negotiations and therefore have few implications in terms of either temporary derogations or permanent changes in EU trade policy. In the case of Cyprus and Malta, this is due mainly to their small size; in the CEEC case, it is a function of the transition from planned to market economies. Previous trade relations within the Soviet bloc were substantially disrupted at the start of the transition, and there has been a substantial reorientation of CEEC trade westward. The CEECs are thus unlikely to have long-established trading relations with third countries they hope will be given preferential treatment in the context of their own accession.

In the short run, the small economic size of the applicant countries means that they will not substantially change the size of the EU as a trade bloc and hence its influence and weight in international trade negotiations. However, in the longer run, the CEEC enlargement will contribute to a substantial increase in the EU's economic weight. While it has been argued that enlargement will not lead to major trade diversion, it has been suggested that the larger EU may be more inward-looking and may also face yet more complex intergovernmental negotiations within the Union, making it a difficult partner in multilateral trade negotiations.[63]

The association agreements between the EU and Cyprus and Malta came into operation in 1973 and 1971, respectively. These agreements were, in both cases, intended to lead in two stages to the establishment of a customs union. In the case of Malta, the agreement has stayed at the first stage (which has been periodically renewed) essentially for domestic political reasons.[64] Whereas the first stage of these agreements focuses essentially on tariff reduction, the second stage is concerned with a wider range of policies—and their harmonization—including competition policy and state aids and approximation of laws. In the Maltese case, the EU imports industrial products free of duties, while Malta—despite reductions—still retains a substantial degree of protection. The Cyprus agreement initially allowed for completing the first stage in 1977, but this was extended to 1987; the second phase was intended to run from 1988 to 1997.[65]

In the CEEC case, the Europe Agreements came into force for nine of the ten CEEC countries between 1994 and 1995, while Slovenia's was delayed slightly. Interim Europe Agreements, covering trade, came into force earlier, from 1992 onward, pending full ratification of the Europe Agreements. The Europe Agreements also have two stages of five years each, during which free trade would gradually be established. The Europe Agreements aim to promote the expansion of trade and economic relations and seek to provide a framework for political dialogue and for the EU's financial and technical assistance to the CEECs. Furthermore, they are intended to facilitate the gradual integration of each country into the EU.

The Europe Agreements have been criticized for a number of reasons. They contain a number of exemptions for particular products and sectors deemed to be "sensitive"—different time periods are laid out in these cases for tariff reductions (according to three different categories of products), and some products and sectors are subject to quotas and/or ceilings. The Europe Agreements do not deal with the liberalization of agricultural trade. They allow for "contingent protection" where sectors face serious problems owing to rapid increases in imports, and include antidumping provisions and some allowance for infant industry protection and support for restructuring (this is discussed further in the industrial policy section). Sensitive sectors include textiles, coal, iron and steel, chemicals, furniture, and footwear.

These limitations of the Europe Agreements have led a number of authors to argue that the agreements are not liberalizing trade and opening EU markets to the extent that they should.[66] Nonetheless, the Copenhagen summit did speed up the process of liberalization, and there should be substantial trade liberalization in industrial products in the late 1990s, with removal of tariffs and quotas by 2001. Furthermore, in a number of areas, it appears that the CEECs have not come close to using their quota allowances. The quotas are therefore not as restrictive as they might be,[67] although this does not take account of quotas acting as a deterrent to economic agents ever trying to export or expand their export business.

Other criticisms of the Europe Agreements include Baldwin's argument that their hub-and-spoke—bilateral—nature is damaging, diverting investment to the west and inhibiting multilateral trade liberalization.[68] Other authors have expressed concern that after initial liberalization, the CEECs have been introducing more restrictions and that protectionist lobbies may be growing,[69] although the OECD (1994) assesses the CEEC trade regimes as rather liberal even by international standards.[70] The speed of enlargement may be important here; if accession to the EU looks to be lengthy, this could have negative effects. However, it may also be questioned how important the Europe Agreements have been in liberalizing trade. Faini and Portes[71] argue that Inotai[72] may have been right to contend that Generalized System of Preferences (GSP) treatment was the key breakthrough in market access. They also argue that trade could open up faster than envisaged in the Europe Agreements without detrimental effects to the EU.

A number of studies have investigated whether the CEEC economies may have competitive advantages that will be damaging to particular EU countries, regions, or sectors. Faini and Portes, summarizing the results of a number of studies, argue that there is no evidence suggesting EU adjustment costs would be large for either countries or sectors, even sensitive sectors such as textiles and steel.[73] Potential effects depend on the CEECs' current and likely future sources of comparative advantage or competitiveness, and on the nature of trade. Intraindustry trade has been growing between the EU and CEECs—especially between southern Europe and CEECs—and this may imply less structural adjustment than from interindustry trade.[74] Neven argues that southern Europe and CEECs have similar factor endowments and that CEECs may have an advantage in labor- and capital-intensive sectors, which could have regional impacts within the EU. Halpern suggests that CEECs could exploit their skilled labor more but that this requires rebuilding capital stocks.[75]

Different estimates have been made of how fast trade may grow between the EU and CEECs, but the general consensus is that there is scope for a substantial expansion of trade—doubling or much more in the medium term—with some countries in a position to expand more than others.[76] Germany dominates this trade, which implies that its future rates of growth may be less than those countries with low trade levels. But in absolute terms, it may continue to be the dominant trader as trade expands; this is also related to the extent of its FDI, which will tend to be positively related to trade.

Overall, in the medium to long run, eastward enlargement of the EU may have substantial economic effects in terms of both trade and FDI, but it is unlikely to have major implications for EU trade policy, though indirect effects through increasing EU size and weight in trade negotiations could become important. In the short to medium term, the aim of enlargement is affecting EU-CEEC trade relations, in particular through the application and development of the Europe Agreements.

Industrial Policy

The combined size—in population terms—and low relative income of the CEECs, Cyprus, and Malta raise a number of issues for EU industrial policies. As with trade policy, the small size of Cyprus and Malta means that their potential impact is very slight; the same may be said of the smaller CEECs. The most significant direct effects are expected to be on EU regional policy through the impact on the structural and cohesion funds. There may, however, be more indirect effects in both the shorter and longer term. As will be discussed further, the CEECs' experience, of central planning on the one hand and transition on the other, may affect their attitudes toward industrial policy in a variety of ways.

Both the Europe Agreements and the internal market White Paper have implications for the development of industrial policies within the CEECs, through their emphasis on EU competition policy, including harmonizing state aids, and on industrial standards, mutual recognition, and so on. The internal market White Paper sets out the main areas of legislation in twenty-three broad areas that the CEECs will need to adopt to comply with the single market. It stresses that implementing and monitoring legislation is as important as enacting the legislation. Furthermore, the single market does not represent the full *acquis communautaire*. This raises a much broader issue (going beyond industrial policy) as to whether and when the CEECs will be able to comply with the full *acquis*. Some derogations and transitional periods after accession may be expected, but if these are sufficiently long-term in nature they may represent the establishment of a multitier EU.

It is widely recognized that the main budgetary impact of EU enlargement will be through the potential costs of extending the CAP and the structural funds. Cost estimates of extending the structural funds on their current basis to the CEEC-10 and Cyprus and Malta suggest this could involve a doubling of the existing level of the structural funds. A common methodology for estimating the costs of extending the structural funds is to apply the amount per head Greece and Portugal receive—using either current figures or projected figures for 1999, by which time the structural funds will have to be reassessed anyway.[77] The CEEC-10 all have GDP per head below that of Greece and Portugal, which have the lowest in the current EU; Malta and Cyprus have levels that place them within the level of the four cohesion countries. Table 7.3 sets out estimates of the costs of extending the structural funds to the CEEC-10 on the assumption that they receive assistance at the rate of ECU 400 per head—the estimated amount for Greece and Portugal in 1999.[78] This gives a total of ECU 42.2 billion for the CEEC-10 compared with a total of ECU 3.3 billion for the EU-15 in 1999.

Table 7.3   Extending the Structural Funds to Central and Eastern Europe

	Population 1994 (millions)	GDP 1994 (ECU billions)	Structural Fund Estimates at ECU 400 per Capita (ECU billions)	Structural Fund Estimates as Percent of GDP	Structural Fund Estimates with 4% GDP Limit (ECU billions)
Czech Republic	10.3	30.8	4.12	13.4	1.23
Hungary	10.3	35.2	4.12	11.7	1.41
Poland	38.6	81.8	15.44	18.9	3.27
Slovakia	5.3	10.6	2.12	20.0	0.42
Slovenia	2.0	11.3	0.80	7.1	0.45
Bulgaria	8.4	8.6	3.36	39.1	0.34
Romania	22.7	27.1	9.08	33.5	1.08
Estonia	1.5	1.9	0.60	31.6	0.08
Latvia	2.7	2.9	1.08	37.2	0.12
Lithunia	3.7	2.9	1.48	51.0	0.12
Total	105.5	213.0	42.20		8.52

Sources: CEC (1995), EBRD (1995), and author's calculations.

Estimates of this or a similar scale have led many people to argue that the structural funds will have to be reformed before enlargement: the budgetary implications are otherwise seen as politically unacceptable. The European Commission also argues that because the structural funds are due for renegotiation by 1999, estimates of the cost of extending them on their current basis are irrelevant; this view in itself may indicate the political sensitivity of the issue.[79] It has also been recognized that extending the structural funds without reform would lead to the CEECs receiving such high levels of assistance that, first, they would find it difficult to provide matching funding; and second, they would have serious absorption problems. As shown in the fourth column of Table 7.3, the structural funds would represent amounts ranging from 7 percent of Slovenia's GDP to 51 percent of Lithuania's. Furthermore, the accession of these countries would also lower average EU GDP per head so that the cohesion countries—and regions of other EU member states—would no longer qualify for aid, particularly under Objective One of the structural funds (which requires GDP per head to be below 75 percent of the EU average).

Various proposals have been floated for the reform of the structural funds both to make them more efficient in their current operation and to reduce the amount the accession countries would otherwise receive. In essence, the structural funds will have to be reformed in a way that is acceptable politically to the northern member states (which will face increased budget contributions), the cohesion countries (which will be concerned about their receipts from the structural funds), and the eastern accession countries (which will not wish to be given second-class status). The commissioner responsible for regional policy has observed that "enlargement towards the East with no political guarantee of the continuation of the cohesion policy in the poorest of the Fifteen member states would be neither socially justifiable nor politically conceivable."[80]

Proposals for reform of the structural funds are likely to focus on concentrating the funds more (they currently cover over half the EU population), increasing their efficiency, possibly increasing the proportion of loan finance, and—in the case of enlargement—introducing a limit on the maximum amount of structural funds receivable in the form of a percentage GNP limit. The commissioner responsible for the budget has floated the idea of a 4 percent GNP limit.[81] The final column of Table 7.3 shows the effect on the costs of enlargement of imposing such a limit on the structural funds. It reduces the overall costs to just over ECU 8 billion for all ten CEECs—about one-fifth of the cost of extension without any reform. This would clearly be much more politically manageable. It does, however, have the rather perverse effect of providing more assistance to the higher-income CEECs. In addition, it would be necessary to negotiate some transitional agreement with the cohesion countries so that they would not lose all their funding. The CEECs would also not all join at the same time, and there are likely to be transitional periods before they obtain full access to the structural funds.

One problem with these various possible solutions is that they tend to undermine the overall justification for the structural funds of promoting convergence and giving assistance to the poorest member states, as well as the principle of equal treatment. There is also an argument that current assistance to the accession countries should be increased to speed their transition and so their convergence.[82] Without an acceptable and relatively swift solution to the budgetary costs of enlargement, there is a danger that budgetary concerns will lead to a deliberate slowing of the enlargement process and to unnecessary transitional conditions and create, at least in the medium term, a multitier EU. This would then have major implications for the nature and path of future EU development.

EU Assistance and the Development
of Industrial Policy in CEECs

The EU—and individual member states—have been providing technical aid and assistance to contribute to the transition and restructuring process. The EU's aid is concentrated in the Phare program, which has been seen since the Essen summit as promoting integration of the CEECs into the EU. It may also be seen as giving the CEECs experience with assistance similar to that of the structural funds. More generally, the Phare program may be considered a microcosm of EU views on "acceptable" industrial policy with its emphasis on infrastructure, FDI, education and training, small and medium-sized enterprises (SMEs), and technological know-how. The European Commission has also suggested[83] that an industrial policy dialogue should be established with the CEECs, based in part on the approach to industrial policy set out in the White Paper on competitiveness, growth, and employment.[84]

Total Phare assistance from 1990 to 1994 was ECU 4.2 billion, substantially less than these countries may get even from reformed structural funds. However, overall in that period, the CEECs received ECU 74.7 billion in assistance, of which over half was from the EU and its member states in bilateral assistance.[85] A number of EU programs are also being opened to the CEECs, but without additional funding.

Many of the CEECs are already developing industrial policies. In some cases, such as the Czech Republic, this involves a range of measures (SME assistance, skills, infrastructure, etc.) not actually brought together into an overall industrial policy framework. In other cases, such as Poland and Hungary, there is a similar range of policies set out within comprehensive industrial frameworks (in various White Papers).[86] The development of these policies is severely limited by funding constraints. Furthermore, while these policies are comparable to western industrial policies, especially in their emphasis on horizontal policies, many countries also have sectoral policies seen as short-run "crisis" policies. In the context of the Europe Agreements and during accession negotiations, the extent and nature of state aids will be an important topic. The CEECs will be expected to conform to EU rules in this area, although it is noteworthy that the cohesion countries in the current EU focus a higher proportion of their state aids on sectoral policies than other member states. There is also an ongoing tension in the development of EU industrial policies between an emphasis on competition and free markets and acceptable forms of intervention. The CEECs may, because of their experience with central planning, emphasize the free market; or, given their restructuring needs, they be more open to some range of interventionist policies. Just as with the current EU, different emphases may be expected across this diverse range of country policies, and so the indirect and long-run effects of CEEC accession on the development of EU industrial policy is difficult to predict.

Conclusion

EU trade and industrial policies have developed in a number of ways since the early 1970s. Successive enlargements of the EU since 1973 have played a role—both direct and indirect—in the development of those policies. The prospective enlargement of the EU to central and eastern Europe and to Cyprus and Malta is already having an impact on EU trade policy, notably through the Europe and association agreements; in the longer run, it will also have a substantial effect on the size of the EU as a trading bloc. Eastward enlargement is also expected to lead to substantial reform of the EU structural funds and may have further indirect effects on EU industrial policy. There are potentially far-reaching implications of reforming the structural funds, not only for industrial policy itself but also for the wider commitments and aims of the EU, in particular its support for solidarity, equality of treatment, and convergence among member states.

Notes

1. Hughes, K., "Competition and the Single European Market," *Policy Studies* 3 (1992).

2. Kay, N., "Mergers, Acquisitions and the Completion of the Internal Market," in Hughes, K., ed., *European Competitiveness* (Cambridge, Cambridge University Press, 1993), pp. 161–180.

3. Commission, "Growth, Competitiveness, Employment: Challenges and Ways Forward into the 21st Century," *Bulletin of the European Communities* 6/93 (1993), pp. 1–151.

4. Commission, *Fourth Survey on State Aids in the European Community in the Manufacturing and Certain Other Sectors* (Luxembourg: Office of Official Publications [OOP], 1995).

5. OECD, *National Accounts 1960–1994,* Vol. 1 (Paris: OECD, 1995).

6. Swann, D., *Competition and Industrial Policy in the European Community* (London and New York: Methuen, 1983).

7. Commission, "The Enlarged Community: Outcome of the Negotiations with the Applicant States," *Bulletin of the European Communities* Supplement 1/72 (1972), pp. 1–69.

8. Hine, R., *The Political Economy of European Trade* (Brighton, Eng.: Wheatsheaf, 1985).

9. Grilli, E. R., *The European Community and the Developing Countries* (Cambridge: Cambridge University Press, 1993).

10. Ibid.

11. Hine, *The Political Economy of European Trade.*

12. Swann, D., *The Economics of the Common Market* (London: Penguin, 1992).

13. Hine, *The Political Economy of European Trade.*

14. Curzon Price, V., "Competition and Industrial Policies with Emphasis on Industrial Policy," in El-Agraa, A., ed., *Economics of the European Community* (Hemel Hempstead, Eng.: Philip Allan, 1990), pp. 168–170.

15. Shearman, C., "Technology Policy," in Bulmer, S., George, S., and Scott, A., eds., *The United Kingdom and EC Membership Evaluated* (London: Pinter, 1992), pp. 78–82.

16. Commission, "The Enlarged Community."

17. Greenland joined as part of Denmark in 1973 but left the EU in 1986, although it remains an overseas territory and is therefore eligible for structural funds.

18. Commission, "Scientific and Technological Policy Program," *Bulletin of the European Communities* 14/73 (1973), pp. 1–47.

19. Harrington, R., "Regional Policy," in Bulmer, George, and Scott, *The United Kingdom and EC Membership Evaluated,* pp. 57–65.

20. Swann, *The Economics of the Common Market.*

21. Harrington, "Regional Policy."

22. Commission, "Enlargement of the Community: General Considerations," *Bulletin of the European Communities* Supplement 1/78 (1978), pp. 1–17.

23. Commission, "Enlargement of the Community: Economic and Sectoral Aspects," *Bulletin of the European Communities* Supplement 3/78 (1978), pp. 1–55.

24. Ibid.

25. Viñals, J., "Spain and the 'EC cum 1992' Shock," in Bliss, C., and Braga de Macedo, J., eds., *Unity with Diversity in the European Economy: The Community's Southern Frontier* (Cambridge: Cambridge University Press, 1990), pp. 145–234.

26. Swann, *Competition and Industrial Policy.*

27. Commission, *Thirteenth General Report on the Activities of the European Communities* (Brussels/Luxembourg: OOP, 1979).

28. Katseli, L. T., "Economic Integration in the Enlarged European Community: Structural Adjustment of the Greek Economy," in Bliss and Braga de Macedo, *Unity with Diversity.*

29. Commission, *Nineteenth General Report on the Activities of the European Communities* (Brussels/Luxembourg: OOP, 1985).

30. Kateseli, "Economic Integration."

31. Grilli, *The European Community and the Developing Countries.*

32. Geroski, P. A., "European Industrial Policy and Industrial Policy in Europe," *Oxford Review of Economic Policy* 5, no. 2 (1989), pp. 20–36.

33. Commission, "Fair Competition in the Internal Market: Community State Aid Policy," *European Economy* 48 (1991), pp. 7–114.

34. Commission, *Third Survey on State Aids in the European Community in the Manufacturing and Certain Other Sectors* (Luxembourg: OOP, 1992); and Commission, *Fourth Survey on State Aids.*

35. Commission, "Fair Competition in the Internal Market."

36. Sharp, M., "The Community and New Technologies," in Lodge, J., ed., *The European Community and the Challenge of the Future,* 2d ed. (London: Pinter, 1993), pp. 200–223.

37. Vernadakis, N., "Research and Development Policy," in Kazakos, P., and

Ioakimidis, P. C., eds., *Greece and EC Membership Evaluated* (London: Pinter, 1994), pp. 128–136; Alvarez, A. C., "Technology Policy," in Amparo, A. B., ed., *Spain and EC Membership Evaluated* (London: Pinter, 1993), pp. 30–37; Gonçalves, F., and Caraça, J. M. G., "Costs and Benefits of EC Membership for Portugese Research and Technological Development," in da Silva Lopes, J., ed., *Portugal and EC Membership Evaluated* (London: Pinter, 1993), pp. 123–132.

38. Molle, W., "Industry and Services," in Molle, W., and Cappellin, R., eds., *Regional Impact of Community Policies in Europe* (Aldershot, Eng.: Avebury, 1988), pp. 45–64.

39. Commission, *Nineteenth General Report.*

40. Commission, "Enlargement of the Community: General Considerations"; and Commission, "Enlargement of the Community: Economic and Sectoral Aspects."

41. Commission, *Commission Communication to the Council of the Greek Government Memorandum of 19 March 1982,* COM(82)348 Final (Luxembourg: OOP, 1982).

42. Commission, *The Regions of Europe,* Second Periodic Report COM(84)40 Final 2 (Brussels: OOP, 1984).

43. Begg, I., Gudgin, G., and Morris, D., "The Assessment: Regional Policy in the European Union," *Oxford Review of Economic Policy* 11, no. 2 (1995), pp. 1–17.

44. Commission, *Guide to the Reform of the Community's Structural Funds* (Luxembourg: OOP, 1989).

45. Fuente, A., and Vives, X., "Infrastructure and Education as Instruments of Regional Policy: Evidence from Spain," *Economic Policy* (April 1995), pp. 11–51.

46. Alogoskoufis, G., "The Two Faces of Janus: Institutions, Policy Regimes and Macroeconomic Performance in Greece," *Economic Policy* (April 1995), pp. 147–192.

47. Begg, Gudgin, and Morris, "The Assessment."

48. Wallace, W., *Regional Integration: The West European Experience* (Washington, D.C.: Brookings Institution, 1994).

49. OECD, *National Accounts 1960–1994,* Vol. 1 (Paris: OECD).

50. Baldwin, R. E., and Flam, H., *Enlargement of the European Union: The Economic Consequences for the Scandinavian Countries* (London: Center for Economic Policy Research, 1994).

51. Commission, "Europe and the Challenge of Enlargement," *Bulletin of the European Communities* Supplement 3/92 (1992), pp. 1–24.

52. Commission, *General Report on the Activities of the European Communities* (Brussels/Luxembourg: OOP, 1995).

53. Ibid.

54. Pederson, T., *European Union and the EFTA Countries: Enlargement and Integration* (London: Pinter, 1994).

55. European Bank for Reconstruction and Development, *Transition Report* (London: EBRD, 1995).

56. Estrin, S., Hughes, K., and Todd, S., *The Nature and Scope of Foreign Direct Investment in Central and Eastern Europe,* mimeo, 1996.

57. Faini, R., and Portes, R., eds., *European Union Trade with Eastern Europe: Adjustment and Opportunities* (London: Centre for Economic Policy Research, 1995).

58. Estrin, Hughes, and Todd, *Nature and Scope.*

59. Baldwin, R. E., *Towards an Integrated Europe* (London: Center for Economic Policy Research, 1994).

60. Hughes, "Competition and the Single European Market."

61. Commission, *Preparation of the Associated Countries of Central and Eastern Europe for Integration into the Internal Market of the Union* (Luxembourg: OOP, 1995).

62. For example, Baldwin, *Towards an Integrated Europe;* Faini and Portes, *European Union Trade;* Winters, L. A., ed., *Foundations of an Open Economy: Trade Laws and Institutions for Eastern Europe* (London: Center for Economic Policy Research, 1995).

63. Rollo, J., "EU Enlargement and the World Trade System," *European Economic Review* 39 (1995), pp. 467–473.

64. Commission, "The Challenge of Enlargement: Commission Opinion on Malta's Application for Membership," *Bulletin of the European Communities* Supplement 4/93 (1993), pp. 1–49.

65. Commission, "The Challenge of Enlargement: Commission Opinion on the Application by the Republic of Cyprus for Membership," *Bulletin of the European Communities* Supplement 5/93 (1993), pp. 1–49.

66. See Faini and Portes, *European Union Trade;* Winters, *Foundations of an Open Economy;* and Inotai, A., "From Association Agreements to Full Membership? The Dynamics of Relations Between the Central and Eastern European Countries and the European Union," *Institute for World Economics Working Paper,* No. 52, Budapest, 1995.

67. Commission, "The Economic Interpenetration Between the European Union and Eastern Europe," *European Economy,* Reports and Studies 6 (1994).

68. Baldwin, *Towards an Integrated Europe.*

69. Winters, *Foundations of an Open Economy,* especially chapter by Sapir, A., "The Europe Agreements: Implications for Trade Laws and Institutions."

70. OECD, *Integrating Emerging Market Economies into the International Trading System* (Paris: OECD, 1994).

71. Faini and Portes, *European Union Trade.*

72. Inotai, A., "Some Remarks on Developments in Foreign Trade in Central and Eastern European Economies," *Institute for World Economics Working Paper,* No. 36, Budapest, 1994.

73. Faini and Portes, *European Union Trade.*

74. Neven, D., "Trade Liberalization with Eastern Nations: How Sensitive?" in Faini and Portes, *European Union Trade,* pp. 19–60.

75. Halpern, L., "Comparative Advantage and Likely Trade Pattern of the CEECs," in Faini and Portes, *European Union Trade.*

76. Baldwin, *Towards an Integrated Europe;* and Baldwin, "The Eastern Enlargement of the European Union," *European Economic Review* 39 (1995), pp. 474–481. Also see Cadot, O., and de Melo, J., "France and the CEECs: Adjusting to Another Enlargement," in Faini and Portes, *European Union Trade,* pp. 86–122; and Commission, "The Economic Interpenetration."

77. For example, Brenton, P., and Gros, D., "The Budgetary Implications of EC Enlargement," *Centre for European Policy Studies Working Document No. 78,* Brussels, 1993; and Commission, "Stable Money—Sound Finances: Community Public Finance in the Perspective of EMU," *European Economy* 53 (1993).

78. Commission, "Stable Money—Sound Finances."

79. Commission, *Interim Report from the Commission to the European*

Council on the Effects on the Policies of the European Union of Enlargement to the Associated Countries of Central and Eastern Europe, CSE(95) 605 (Brussels: OOP, 1995).

80. Wulf-Mathies, M., "The Future of European Regional Policy," speech given at the Center for European Policy Studies, 19 October 1995, Brussels.

81. Liikanen, E., quoted in *Agence Europe,* 13 January 1996.

82. Brenton and Gros, "The Budgetary Implications of EC Enlargement"; and Inotai, A., "The System of Criteria for Hungary's Accession to the European Union," *Institute for World Economics Trends in World Economy,* No. 76, Budapest, 1994.

83. Commission, *Industrial Cooperation with the Countries of Central/Eastern Europe,* Communication from the Commission to the Council and the European Parliament COM (95)71 Final (Brussels: OOP, 1995).

84. Commission, "Growth, Competitiveness, Employment: Challenges and Ways Forward into the 21st Century," *Bulletin of the European Communities* 6/93 (1993), pp. 1–51.

85. Commission, *Technical Assistance for Central and Eastern European Countries and the Newly Independent States Phare and Tacis Programmes,* Background Report (London: European Commission, 1996).

86. Hughes, K., "The Development of Industrial Policy in Transition Economies: A Comparative Analysis," mimeo.

Part 3

Looking Forward

8

The CEECs: From
the Association Agreements
to Full Membership?

András Inotai

It is more than surprising how much the professional political and economic literature dealing with the relations between the European Union (EU) and the Central and Eastern European Countries (CEECs) is dominated by an evident imbalance. On the one hand, there are a rapidly growing number of publications on specific but not necessarily strategically important issues—from the impact of trade policy measures through special areas of cooperation to an overall assessment of the association agreements (AAs). On the other hand, there are rather few studies that examine different strategic approaches to the future of the European pattern of security, political, economic, and social cooperation. This imbalance is all the more striking because the history of EU-CEEC relations in recent years has provided an unprecedented dynamism of bilateral relations that clearly has not been brought to an end by the signing of AAs.

It was less than seven years ago that, after a decade of deadlock, the joint declaration between the EU and the late Common Market Economic Area (CMEA) was signed. This document opened the way for trade and cooperation agreements, but with only very modest potential for real improvement. Dramatic transformations within the CEECs made these agreements obsolete almost overnight. The granting of Generalized System of Preferences (GSP) treatment, the start-up of the Phare program, and the signing of AAs all followed within the next two years. As a result, all CEECs have substantially upgraded their position on the pyramid of trade preferences granted by Brussels to third countries.[1] Once the AA was ratified in February 1994, Hungary and Poland almost immediately applied for full membership, in April 1994; most other transforming countries that might reasonably aspire to EU accession soon followed.

Meanwhile, substantial changes have equally characterized the attitude of the EU. Still, the AAs do not contain any EU commitment to future full membership for any of the associated countries. Rather, the EU, very much

157

against the interests of the CEECs, has clearly stated that there is no linkage between present association and future membership. The subsequent EU summits at Edinburgh and Copenhagen acknowledged the efforts of the CEECs to become full members once the basic political and economic criteria, set by Brussels, were fulfilled.[2] The German presidency, in the second half of 1994, qualified future membership for the CEECs as a main priority. Therefore, outlining clear criteria for joining, further opening EU markets, and intensifying political dialogue were considered the most important policy steps to be taken. Only three years after the refusal of potential future membership, the December 1994 Essen summit took full account of the EU's eastern enlargement. The question was no longer *if* the CEECs would gain membership, but when and how. A comprehensive network of "structured dialogue" has begun in several integration-related areas (foreign and security policy, domestic and legal issues, education, environment, research, telecommunications, etc.).

This dynamism has to some extent been incorporated into the EU's schedule for the coming years. Negotiations on membership may commence in the second half of 1997 or early 1998, after the conclusion of the Intergovernmental Conference (IGC). At the December 1995 summit in Madrid, all associated CEECs with formal applications were offered the start of negotiations within six months after the close of the IGC. They have thus been given the same status as Malta and Cyprus.

But there is likely to be an even greater stimulus for decisionmaking and institutional reform of the EU beyond this in-built dynamism. In the next few years, substantial impetus can also be expected both from the CEECs themselves and from internal developments within the EU. Clearly, the dramatic changes that began to sweep across Europe in 1989 are not over. But now western Europe is where we can expect to see pronounced changes, for both domestic and external reasons. Evidently, we do not know the precise nature of these changes, which are expected to shape the future of Europe. It is, however, obvious that the western European political, security, economic, and social status quo, as established in the late 1950s and early 1960s and based on a firmly divided Europe, cannot continue.

The rest of this analysis is divided into six parts, the first of which examines the adjustment criteria preceding CEEC membership in the EU. This is followed by a section on sensitive issues in EU-CEEC relations and one on the question of financial transfers. The next section looks at intermediate or alternative proposals to full membership, and the penultimate section considers the impact of eastern enlargement or nonenlargement on the general balance of power in Europe. The final section offers some conclusions.

The Development of Adjustment Criteria

The Copenhagen Criteria

The Copenhagen criteria were prompted, at least partly, by the (then) associated central European countries (Czech Republic, Hungary, Poland, and Slovakia). At its Copenhagen summit in the summer of 1993, the EU formulated some conditions to be fulfilled by the would-be members. The list of conditions covers a wide but rather "soft" range of political, legal, and economic conditions, including the stabilization of law and democracy, readiness to adopt the *acquis communautaire*, the establishment of an effective market economy, and the adoption and fulfillment of the convergence aims of the Maastricht Treaty.

For several reasons, this set of criteria represents an unprecedented step by the EU in comparison with earlier enlargements. For the first time, specific conditions have been imposed on acceding countries. The Treaty of Rome laid down only one condition: the entrant nation must be European. So the Copenhagen decision, in fact, discriminates against the transitional countries.[3] Of course, there were prerequisites in the previous enlargements too, but these affected only the conditions of accession, not the starting of negotiations and the very chances of joining. In this context, the question can be formulated as to whether the system of criteria can be considered as an instrument to facilitate membership, or rather as a substantial barrier to future accession. In other words, does this concept help sustain the dynamics of European evolution set free after the collapse of the Berlin Wall and the Soviet Union, or does it slow down and even stop them altogether?

The Copenhagen set of criteria indicates the EU's interest in shifting the emphasis of future enlargements from political to economic merits. Both Mediterranean enlargements were characterized mainly by political motives. Paradoxically, after the collapse of the Yalta-based European security system, Brussels has not expressed any short-term political interest in favor of eastern enlargement. On the contrary, in the absence of such pressure, it tends to concentrate on the economic performance of potential newcomers.

In addition, and for at least two reasons, the associated CEECs are in a worse initial position than previous applicants. First, they have to adjust to a flexible and unpredictable EU. Accession criteria may be amended according to changing circumstances and the interests of Brussels and the member countries. Second, the level of EU integration is much higher today than it was a decade ago when the Mediterranean enlargement occurred.

Finally, there are serious questions about how readiness for membership ("integration maturity") might be assessed and measured. Should this maturity level be measured on the basis of current economic performance (static assessment) or—arguably more important—on the basis of the speed and quality of the adjustment process (dynamic assessment)? And even if the first, static criterion applies, should macroeconomic adjustment or microeconomic developments be considered more important? And is it appropriate to compare the performance of nonmember countries with that of member states, when the latter enjoy a very special status—from free market access to substantial financial transfers—and the former are largely deprived of these opportunities until they become full members?

The Enlargement Capability of the EU

It should be stressed that the viability of European integration depends on more than an eastern enlargement. The original architecture of the EU was created for six to ten countries, more or less on the same level of economic development and with similar political cultures. Major restructuring is overdue even without the prospect of an eastern enlargement. Therefore, the new integration framework is not only a precondition for further enlargement, but also a pressing requirement for the survival of the existing Union.

First, the EU has to respond to serious international challenges, such as regionalization, globalization, the changing patterns of competitiveness, and technological developments.

Second, Brussels has to update its philosophy about the dynamics of European processes. This does not require simply a shift in emphasis or another mix of policy instruments, but a fundamental rethinking of the whole concept of integration and Europe. The decades-long status quo mentality based on the protection of Western values against an imperialistic Soviet empire should give way to an active, offensive, and future-oriented attitude.[4]

Third, most of the member countries are plagued by the "European disease," which is characteristic of the former socialist transforming economies as well. Two-digit unemployment, exploding budget deficits and state debts, obsolete agricultural and industrial structures, serious limits to financing the current level of social welfare, and a rapidly aging population can be mentioned as some of the principal negative factors.

Fourth, and most unfortunate, these external and internal challenges affect the EU at a time when, mainly as a result of internal developments, the integration process is itself facing new problems. The integration patterns that emerged out of the priorities of the 1950s and 1960s (for example, iron and steel community, customs union, and agricultural self-sufficiency) cannot efficiently answer the challenges of the late 1990s. In addition, as recent referendums have shown, popular support for a large

Union, as conceived by Brussels and some politicians from member countries, is far from enthusiastic.

Finally, for the first time in its history, the EU is facing an increasing balance-of-power crisis due to German reunification, its European Free Trade Association (EFTA) enlargement, CEEC AAs, and the highly unpredictable situation inside Russia—all part and parcel of the emerging dynamics of European politics and economics.

The capacity of the EU to expand yet further has to be assessed within this framework. Key importance will be attached to the handling of new "fault lines" that may arise because of different definitions of the ultimate objective of European integration, the management of the North-South conflict, or the control of the internal balance of the Union.[5] The IGC was expected to deal with some of these issues. It is, however, unlikely that it will be able to develop a completely new pattern of European integration; there is no fixed linkage between its success and eastern enlargement. The only link was that negotiations on further enlargement would not be initiated until after the IGC.

The White Book

During the 1995 German presidency, Brussels produced a White Book containing more detailed conditions of membership for new applicants, based mainly on the *acquis communautaire* and the rules of the internal market. The criteria in the White Book are not binding, but they do contain important elements for assessing the integration capability of the applicant countries. Unfortunately, the White Book follows EU tradition by making future accession exclusively dependent on the ability of the associated countries and not on mutual adjustments.[6] There was no indication as to how applicants should evolve from their present status toward full membership, or how the EU would support this process. Moreover, for political reasons, a clear timetable was not offered.[7] Although the EU has already acknowledged the fundamental differences among CEECs, no "geographic sequencing" of an eastern enlargement is envisaged.

New Obstacles to Membership?

None of the transforming economies is ready for full membership at present. However, most of them have made substantial progress in recent years, and their adjustment capability and transformation dynamics have proved to be much higher than those of western Europe. In some areas they are at least on the same level as some EU members.[8] In other—mainly economic—areas, their adjustment performance has been overshadowed by the transformation crisis. However, as the old problems fade away, a more competitive economic structure is emerging, at least in the central European countries. Industrial restructuring is under way, agriculture's share of the economy is decreasing, and the service sector is rapidly expanding. Intraindustry trade is growing dynamically, and its share of CEEC exports is already higher than that of some EU members. In addition, the CEECs can call upon a sizable human resource.

Looking at these trends, it may be increasingly difficult to argue against the membership of these countries for major political or economic reasons. Such an attitude becomes even less acceptable when it is recognized that some of the CEECs seem to be more comfortable and willing to fall in line with many EU principles than are some of the existing member states. Thus, if eastern enlargement should be postponed, new ideas will have to be found to explain why the CEECs would still not be able to join the EU.

Various ideas are already taking shape. According to the most recent French position, new entrants should immediately have to cope with the prescriptions of the Social Charter and with the environmental rules. Other ideas include examining the exchange rate in the CEECs, eliminating any major (even temporary) gap between productivity and wage growth, and linking foreign direct investments and employment in the capital-exporting countries.

It is not difficult to identify the common roots of all of these measures—which is a growing fear of competitiveness throughout western Europe, and particularly among the EU's economically weaker members. As a result, the view expressed by CEEC experts that the adjustment criteria have been formulated not for them to be fulfilled but to keep the doors of the Union closed to the transforming economies as long as possible is gaining support.

Sensitive Issues on the Way to Full Membership

Free Trade

Except for agriculture, the complete elimination of trade barriers is foreseen by the AA. Tariff and nontariff barriers have to be asymmetrically abolished on both sides over a ten-year period. It is generally considered that free trade in industrial products belongs in the hard-core category of criteria for membership. At the same time, little attention has been paid to how sensitive this issue may become as a consequence of possible economic and social developments.

The associated countries may be challenged by two major adverse developments. First, the process of asymmetric elimination of trade barriers approaches its second stage, in which the CEECs will have to dismantle the remaining restrictions. In other words, after 1997, a "reversed asymmetry" will come into force in which the transforming economies will have to accelerate their processes of trade liberalization, including most of the sensitive areas. For various reasons, this is a more difficult task for the transforming economies than for the EU. Average tariffs are generally higher in the former. Therefore, the impact of tariff dismantling is expected to be more substantial for domestic production than for the EU.

In addition, and parallel to the global tariff reduction process, the EU developed a highly efficient "secondary wall of protection," which consists of a jungle of technical norms, such as environmental, veterinary, and sanitary prescriptions. Such nontariff protection hardly exists in any of the CEECs. Therefore, without swiftly introducing similar policy measures, the elimination of tariffs would result in a much more vulnerable situation for central and eastern European producers than for their EU counterparts. This vulnerability is exacerbated by the fact that, as of 2001, free trade (not including agricultural products) would cover 96 percent of EU exports to the CEECs, but only about 70 to 80 percent of the CEEC exports to the EU.

One has to be increasingly aware of the political and sociopsychological repercussions that emerged recently. After the first years of overhasty trade liberalization in extremely adverse economic conditions (the collapse of the eastern markets and the dramatic shrinking of domestic demand), the transforming economies are now experiencing growing pressure from protectionist lobbies, which consist of both domestic producers and foreign-owned firms located in the region.[9]

Second, temporary asymmetry in bilateral trade relations was not able to produce a sustainable trade surplus for the CEECs. After an initial export boom caused by a number of domestic and external factors, imports from the EU started to grow much more dynamically than exports to the EU. Most important, the higher level of economic development, a much stronger bargaining position, financial solidity, better marketing methods, and general competitive strength of EU companies have more than compensated for the initial impact of asymmetric trade liberalization. In other words, the "development asymmetry" proved stronger than temporary and rather selective "trade asymmetry." The western European recession of 1993 then gave specific impetus to this adverse development by boosting EU exports and slowing down imports.

The inevitable consequence for all the associated CEECs was a rapidly growing trade deficit with the EU. While between 1989 and 1994 the EU had accumulated a trade deficit of more than ECU 201 billion in its trade with non-EU countries, there were only two bilateral trade relations in which the EU could register a trade surplus. Besides the Mediterranean region, characterized by traditional EU surplus, it was the trade with the

Visegrad countries that helped improve the EU's trade balance by ECU 11 billion between 1992 and 1994.[10] As a result, the sustainability of trade liberalization crucially depends on the capacity of the transforming economies to finance growing trade deficits with the EU. Temporary or lasting balance-of-payments problems, at least partially caused by the growing imbalance of trade with the EU, could slow down or even stop the process of trade liberalization stipulated in the AAs. In certain circumstances, this could be interpreted by Brussels as a lack of "EU maturity" for some CEECs.

Simultaneously, sensitive areas of trade relations can also be identified on the EU side. The still very restrictive market access for CEEC agricultural products is just one example. It cannot be completely ruled out that the rapidly growing competitiveness of the CEECs in selected areas would increase protectionist pressures within the EU. Acute tensions in the labor markets of several EU countries, or real or alleged implications of adverse economic developments on essential political processes, could further reduce the EU's readiness to maintain free trade with the transforming countries.

Another factor that may lessen the EU's interest in eastern enlargement could be the temporary shrinking of the CEEC import market as their balance-of-payments situation deteriorates. The sensitivity of future trade relations could be substantially reduced if the EU recognized the need to finance the natural "modernization deficit"—at least in the more progressive CEECs. Over the coming years, huge investments will be needed to create a modern production and export structure in all the CEECs. A significant proportion of the investment goods will be purchased abroad, and there is little doubt that the EU (and foreign companies located in the EU) will be the principal supplier. According to international experience, a rapidly widening trade gap can hardly be avoided during the first years of economic modernization. Restrictions on the exports of available (agricultural) commodities make this problem even more serious. Assuming a high efficiency of investments and an export-oriented economic policy in the CEECs, this gap can be narrowed or even closed in the medium term. It is, however, far from clear how the emerging "modernization deficit" will be financed during the most critical years of transformation.

Adjustment to the Acquis Communautaire

The second key element of future membership is the acceptance of a constantly increasing package of EU rules and regulations. Some of the CEECs have already started this adjustment process and have been integrating the EU rules into their national legislation. Nevertheless, legal adjustment cannot be completed before membership, for several reasons.

First, none of the present member countries was able to prepare itself fully for membership before accession. In each case, there were, and still are, important derogations that enabled both the new member and the EU to adjust gradually. Taking into account the development gap between the EU and the CEECs, and the sensitivity threshold of the latter, burdened with the unique tasks of transformation, the difficulties of the adjustment process become manifest. Therefore, a clear medium-term strategy, elaborated jointly by the applicants and Brussels, would be needed.

Second, part of the *acquis communautaire* can be implemented only after a country has become a member of the EU. The whole package of the Common Agricultural Policy (CAP), for example, belongs in this area.

Third, the EU is itself undergoing constant change, the outcome of which is unpredictable. It would be a serious mistake to make a perhaps economically and socially costly adjustment to something that will be changed before the CEECs become members of the Union.

Agriculture

While most experts do not devote special attention to the sensitivity of trade relations and legal adjustment, there is a widespread consensus that agriculture is a very sensitive area that could hinder or substantially delay the EU's eastern enlargement. Of course, there are substantial differences among the individual CEECs. At the moment, only Poland and Hungary are significant exporters of agricultural goods, while agriculture is not a major negotiation issue for the Czech Republic.

For the first time since Ireland joined the Union in 1973, the accession of most of the CEECs challenges the producers of continental commodities. These countries, which happen to be the most influential members of the EU, have not only greatly benefited from the CAP but also consider it crucial for their domestic political balance to maintain this system.

It is generally acknowledged that the present system of agricultural support cannot be sustained, and that both the budgetary problems of the Union and the international obligations deriving from the GATT Uruguay Round make reform of the CAP unavoidable. However, even the most radical transformation plans, vehemently opposed by influential lobbies within the EU, fall considerably short of the transformation that would be needed to absorb the expected impact of an eastern enlargement.

A further problem rests in the fact that the EU, according to some experts in the CEECs, regards the CEECs as an additional market for highly subsidized EU agricultural goods and not as a low-cost supplier for EU markets. In fact, the most dramatic developments reflecting the most extensive "reversed asymmetry" have taken place in the agricultural trade between the EU and the CEECs in the last six years. At present, all CEECs except Hungary are net agricultural importers in their bilateral trade relations with the EU. In addition, Hungary's traditionally substantial trade surplus has started to shrink rapidly. Moreover, subsidized EU exports and food aid packages to the successor states of the Soviet Union have largely devastated the traditional agricultural markets of the associated CEECs. As a result, the EU registered a cumulative surplus of more than ECU 10 billion between 1992 and 1994 in its agricultural trade with CEECs, which is more than ten times higher than the surplus of the EU in its total trade with the CEECs.[11] This not only implies that the EU-CEEC nonagricultural trade balance would have been negative for the EU but, more important, it is also in sharp contrast both with the EU's agricultural trade deficit of ECU 18 billion with non-CEEC extra-EU partners and, even more, with the natural pattern of division of labor between "developed" and "medium developed" countries.

Looking at the present situation in the agriculture of the transforming economies, the EU's fear of "eastern competition" can hardly be justified. For several reasons, agriculture has become the sickest sector in all CEECs. Its contribution to GDP fell dramatically, from about 15–20 percent to less than 10—no higher than in the less developed EU countries. Similar tendencies can be observed in the pattern of the labor force. Of course, some CEECs, notably Poland and Hungary, still have a substantial production and export potential, but some of the basic preconditions, such as efficient production structure, money, technology, and marketing organizations, are missing. Therefore, the real problem of an eastern enlargement is not so much how to integrate a highly competitive eastern agricultural sector into the CAP, as how to finance those regions that, as a consequence of declining or indeed terminated agricultural production, are becoming ever poorer.

Most experts are convinced that a sound and competitive central and eastern European agricultural sector would cost less to the EU than would a devastated one. Calculations have to consider not only agriculture itself, but also the impact of agricultural production on several other areas (notably, financing of imports from the EU, employment, regional development, and political stability). Starting from such an assessment, a coordinated plan should be designed to combine the restructuring of agriculture in the EU with restructuring in selected CEECs. In this way, the costs of adjustment could be substantially reduced and some fundamental barriers to future membership removed. In addition, the impact of an eastern enlargement on the EU's agricultural budget would be only moderate.

Labor

The highly sensitive issue of the free flow of labor has not been regulated by the AAs; this is still the responsibility of the member states. Hence, the flow of labor has to be settled in bilateral negotiations with the individual EU countries. At the moment, only Germany and the newcomer Austria have signed such a document, and even in the case of the former, the yearly quota of central and eastern European labor to be employed in Germany is being reduced.

It is likely that the issue of free movement of labor will be one of the fundamental areas in which the EU will apply a long period of derogation, as was the case with the second Mediterranean enlargement. This restriction will, however, be felt differently in the individual CEECs. The problem is much more important for Poland and Romania than for the Czech Republic or Hungary.

Two special aspects of this issue concern all CEECs. On the one hand, the first stage of eastern enlargement may occur at a time of two-digit western (and eastern) European unemployment. On the other hand, labor problems are not confined to unskilled or low-skilled labor, as was the case with the guest workers from southern Europe in the 1960s and 1970s. More important, the real competitive pressure is expected to come from highly skilled labor with clear competitive advantages in terms of both wage levels and, in several cases, "skill flexibility."

It is not unlikely that EU restrictions on the free flow of labor will further strengthen the flow of capital to the CEECs in both traditional and new skill-intensive sectors as the wage and productivity differences become more manifest. This could contribute to accelerated economic development and a quicker adjustment to the EU more than the reinvention of a new "guest worker system." What is not yet clear is the future answer of EU governments and trade unions to the increasing flow of capital and, with it, the (alleged) "export of employment" to the CEECs. High social and environmental standards, as mentioned in Chapter 1, are an early indication of the potential behavior of some pressure groups that could cause some difficulties for the eastward enlargement of the EU.

Financial Transfers

According to the most recent literature on the possibilities of, and the limits to, an eastern enlargement, all the difficulties listed above are dwarfed by the financial needs of such a decision. Without doubt, in their present situation, all CEECs would be net beneficiaries of the current EU transfer mechanism. Most of them would be entitled to money for their agriculture, and all of them would be net receivers of the structural, cohesion, and regional funds.

It is understandable that the present member countries that are net beneficiaries of the system strongly protest against any kind of enlargement that would attack their present position and harm any of their vested interests. They would oppose any enlargement that would lead to any kind of redistribution of the existing funds. There is nothing new in this; the same happened with earlier enlargements.

The really new development is that the mechanisms that were previously able to remedy the above problems do not seem very likely to work in the late 1990s. First, the net contributors to the EU budget are not ready to commit themselves to "recapitalize" the existing funds and create extra resources for the CEECs without hurting the vested interests of other net beneficiaries of the system. Just the opposite is happening; most of the contributors would like to reduce their contribution as they struggle with serious internal imbalances. Neither their increasingly high budgetary deficit and exploding state debt, nor the strong adjustment criteria they must fulfill to become a member of "Maastricht-Europe," allow meaningful scope for financial activities. The most important country with a strong interest in eastern enlargement, Germany, has been struggling for years with the astronomical costs of its own reunification. Second, earlier enlargements were regularly accompanied by the creation of a new fund tailored to the applicant(s), to avoid conflicts that could have been caused by a major redistribution of previously committed resources. At present, no such initiative seems to be financially feasible, even if it were not difficult to find a number of justified labels for it ("modernization fund," "preaccession fund," "physical and human infrastructure fund," "stability fund," and "regional development fund," for example).

The situation is complicated by three additional factors, which may increase the total costs of eastern enlargement. First, there is a widespread fear within the EU of the unexpectedly strong competitiveness of the CEECs in a wide range of commodity markets. At a time of high-level unemployment and substantial social and political resistance to structural changes in the EU, influential interest groups will do their best to get some kind of compensation as a consequence of eastern enlargement. Second, those member states that are currently net beneficiaries of the EU budget will also present their bill, as they did shortly after the signing of the AAs and the coming into force of the Phare program. In fact, they were given several times more additional money than what was envisaged for the financing of the transformation in the CEECs.

Finally, the Essen summit provided a first indication of an emerging political struggle between advocates of an eastern enlargement and those preferring contacts with the (southern) Mediterranean. The growing fear of Islamic fundamentalism and, more directly, the interest in maintaining the increasingly delicate balance between France and Germany may require substantial "political compensation," expressed in financial terms, for northern Africa in exchange for any eastern enlargement. Summing up, the total costs of an eastern enlargement may turn out to be much higher than the resources to be directed toward the applicant countries.

But there is also an extremely large gap in the calculation of the direct costs themselves. Figures fluctuate from ECU 18 billion to over ECU 100 billion annually. It is not difficult to discover political considerations behind the calculations. The higher the amounts are, the more the experts try to point out why an eastern enlargement is impossible or is at least unwanted. Most of the unreasonably high figures turn out to be the result of serious miscalculations and may even be withdrawn. However, once published they take on their own momentum and will have a lasting impact on the mentality of policymakers. For both economic and political reasons, and in the interest of both the EU and the CEECs, it would be highly desirable to rule out politically motivated "scientific approaches."

Any realistic assessment of the potential costs of an eastern enlargement has to take into consideration the following elements. First, all calculations based on the present transfer mechanism of the EU are exaggerated because none of the CEECs believes in the financial capability of the EU to extend this system without major reform in the new entrants.

Second, an assessment of the economic performance of the CEECs cannot be realistically based on old figures, as often happens with their agricultural potential (based on the late 1980s). Neither can the present figures be considered realistic, because such an approach ignores the expected development prior to full membership. In this context, per capita GDP, as a key indicator of entitlement for transfers from the regional and the cohesion funds, is relevant. At present all CEECs are entitled to such transfers, but some of them may get out of this framework more quickly than expected, because GDP per capita, as expressed in ECU terms, depends not only on GDP growth rates but also, sometimes to a larger extent, on the appreciation of the national currency, a general consequence of economic recovery and structural upgrading.

Third, there is no plan that would envisage a "bloc accession" of all CEECs to the EU. Therefore, all reliable calculations have to make it clear that the individual CEECs will be entitled to substantially different amounts of net resource transfer from the EU budget. Therefore, any overall estimate or the frequently used "basket principle" is detrimental to the interests of the individual countries, especially those expected to become full members in the first wave.

Fourth, no comparison can be made between the financial requirements of German reunification and the resources an eastern enlargement would require. The CEECs did not become part of another country, they did not give up their national currency, and, most important, they know very well that they cannot anytime soon attain West German living standards. For economic, political, and psychological reasons, the financing of their modernization is much less expensive. Neither can the financial requirements of the CEECs be compared with the those of Russia or Ukraine.

According to realistic calculations, Poland would need an annual net transfer of about ECU 5–7 billion, the Czech Republic and Slovakia ECU 1.5–2 billion each, and Hungary ECU 2–3 billion. Thus, the Visegrad countries would require EU financing of ECU 10–16 billion annually. This would increase the annual budget of the EU (about ECU 70 billion) by 15 to 23 percent, provided that the Visegrad countries could join the EU at the same time. Between 1993 and 1997, the four less developed EU member countries, with the same level of population as the Visegrad Four (about 64 million), receive an annual transfer of ECU 18 billion from the structural and cohesion fund only.[12] The calculated *total* transfer to the four central European countries would be 60–90 percent of this sum. Finally, a 1 percent growth of the EU means a GDP increase of about ECU 67 billion. In the coming years, a rapid and sustainable growth of about 3 percent can be forecast. The establishment of a special fund devoted to the financing of central Europe's economic modernization would need less than a quarter of 1 percent economic growth within the EU.

The timing of the financial transfers is extremely important. The CEECs would need this money before becoming members of the EU. The financing of the preaccession period is crucial for several reasons. Such a mechanism could partially finance the emerging modernization costs and maintain the momentum of economic and social transformation and its political support. At the same time, it would be a clear sign that the EU is really committed to an eastern enlargement. Most important, however, is that such a fund could contribute to the financing of those industrial and infrastructural investments that would substantially enhance the development level of the CEECs, a precondition for efficient membership on both sides. In addition, the financing of a successful preparation would decrease the transfer amounts that would be necessary following accession.

To implement such a policy, some basic strategic decisions have to be taken. The EU has to decide which would cost more: financing modernization or financing constant instabilities. The first option has a better chance of creating sustainable security and development and increasing European global competitiveness; and it would certainly strengthen pressure for adjustments in western Europe. In turn, a "strategy" based on repeated damage limitation not only requires much more money but also fails to eliminate the roots of instability; and, more important, it fails to create the "grassroot cells" of modernization. The dynamics of European development will not allow the EU to delay much in making this decision: specifically, will it finance (painful) modernization or finance a minimum level of social welfare promising short-term stability? The EU's answer to this challenge will influence not only the future of eastern enlargement but also, and at least to the same extent, the future of the EU.

Transitory Concepts
Between Association and Membership

Considering the difficulties, it is not surprising that a wide range of suggestions have emerged for bridging the time gap between the present situation and future objectives. All these recommendations are based on the common assumption that European dynamics will not produce any dramatic and sudden shift in the current balance of power and, more important, that Russian political developments will remain sufficiently predictable and under control. In other words, there will be no reason for emergency access of the CEECs to the EU.

Practically all such suggestions have been formulated in the EU. In turn, the associated countries believe that association and full membership are directly linked and treat the association agreements as a stepping-stone toward future membership. Consequently, they are rather suspicious of plans to break this linkage.

One of the main western European arguments is that the transforming economies have to reach the average level of the EU before accession. But this has never been the case in any integration scheme, and particularly not in the EU. The argument has to be reversed. All applicants would like to become full members of a more developed and prosperous integrated Union because they consider membership a conduit to higher levels of development. In the same vein is the concept of regional integration preceding membership in the EU. Baldwin's idea of an "Association of Association Agreements" can be refuted on the same grounds.[13]

The second set of transitory measures tries to separate economic and security issues. This is particularly manifest in French approaches, including the Balladur Stability Pact. From a shortsighted western European point of view, this concept is understandable, for the EU would like to achieve the highest level of security without having to cofinance the economic modernization process in the CEECs. This goal is based on the fatally erroneous assumption that stability in Europe can be sustained without fundamental economic modernization, at least in central Europe. As long as the latter fails to be realized, no lasting stability on the continent will emerge.[14]

The third approach offers new members full membership in some areas (mainly those that are of key importance for the EU, such as security and political cooperation), but excludes them from other areas that would be vitally important for them. Membership without participation in the CAP and membership without financial transfer are the two most significant suggestions, neither of which the CEECs would accept.

There are also plans that recognize the importance of economic issues for the CEECs but try to manage them in non-EU frameworks, such as the OECD, a new EFTA, or the European Economic Area. Although how the CEECs establish a satisfactory role for themselves within some of these frameworks, mainly the OECD, are important policy issues, and may even be a precondition for EU membership, they are not substitutes for the EU in two basic areas: agricultural trade and financial transfer.

Finally, the CEECs do not share the idea that emphasizes the importance of European cultural identity and a common value system but does not support economic modernization in the transforming economies.

At first glance at least, there is a more common view that the transition from association status to full membership will be drawn out. It is, however, extremely important to determine which transition adjustments the EU will implement before the accession of new members, and which ones the transforming economies will implement after accession. All new entrants, including the highly developed ones, have long derogation periods; and the EU needs some time for adjustment to integrate the new members fully. Moreover, some adjustment tasks, such as the CAP, cannot be implemented until a country is in the EU.

Widely argued is the relative importance of deepening and widening. Those who give priority to deepening argue that only a strong and united EU can provide the necessary support for the transforming countries and absorb the problems that are likely to arise as a result of eastern enlargement. In addition, a premature eastern enlargement could easily dilute the EU and even threaten existing integration. This argument is based on the assumption that the dynamics of deepening are much stronger than the dynamics of European restructuring. Experience during the past few years does not prove this hypothesis. If the EU does not consider the new European dynamics adequately in its strategic plans, it is likely to face tremendous challenges from both outside and inside the EU—mainly in the form of growing German dissatisfaction with integration. The danger of at least temporarily diluting integration is a real one, but so is the danger of disrupting the Union.

From the point of view of the CEECs, those accession plans jointly designed by the individual CEECs and the EU seem to be the most convenient. A clear-cut preaccession strategy can substantially decrease the costs of enlargement, for both the applicants and existing members of the Union. This plan should be gradual in three respects: time, geography, and content. In other words, it has to offer a clear timetable, integrate the individual CEECs step by step, and contain a list of derogations.

A feasible modernization plan financed by the EU could substantially reduce the present pressure on the EU for quick eastern enlargement. The CEECs look at the EU as their economic modernization anchor. However, if they could get most of the resources needed for a medium-term modernization strategy (mainly free access to the EU's agricultural market and substantial modernization transfers), perhaps the question of membership could be postponed for some years.

Eastern Enlargement and the Future of European Balance

Germany's "binding into Europe" is in the common interest of western, central, and eastern Europe and Germany itself. This is the decisive issue that should lead the EU and its member countries in shaping integration strategies. In fact, the EU's agricultural and financial transfer problems and its generally weak arguments for postponing the eastern enlargement are likely to be dwarfed by this key element in the sustainability of European order.

Two points should be made regarding this proposal. First, adversaries of eastern enlargement may argue that it would virtually consolidate already dominant German positions in the region. Second, any eastern enlargement would definitely put Germany into a geographically central position in Europe.

As regards the first point, German influence is likely to be relatively greater if the CEECs are not integrated into the EU; consider, for example, Austria's economic history from the 1960s to the early 1990s. Interestingly, in the mid-1960s, France vetoed Austrian membership in the EEC for exactly the same reasons. CEEC membership in the EU would provide those countries with better opportunities for strengthening cooperation with other EU countries, attract more foreign investors—including from outside Germany and the EU—and, most important, introduce a strong political, legal, and economic control imposed by the institutions of the Union.

The second argument is more difficult to refute. In fact, Germany will gain a central geographic position in Europe, which is consistent with changing realities on the continent and may hurt some western European (mainly French) interests. If, however, this shift is adequately bound into the integration framework, most impacts could be favorable for European stability and cooperation and could compensate for eventual negative impacts. As a result, a positive-sum game is easily attainable. In turn, Germany's prolonged "eastern" position in the EU would create much more of a problem, without the positive impacts of integration on European stability and cooperation.

In summary, two basic scenarios can be forecast. The first does not consider early eastern enlargement a realistic option. The consequences would be a growing instability, a deepening economic gap, and a heavy emphasis on German-CEEC cooperation. As the direct neighbor of some CEECs, Germany would be forced to pay more attention to its eastern neighbors and ultimately divert more resources to them. Concurrently, German firms will increasingly use the comparative advantage of being able to shift part of their production to low-cost transforming countries well endowed with skilled labor. The EU would be damaged in two ways. First, some German resources, a major component of the EU budget, will be diverted for damage limitation and stabilizing purposes. Second, Germany, as it makes more extensive use of competitive production capabilities in the CEECs, will emerge as a more competitive economy within the EU. Both elements are likely to generate developments that may substantially affect the intra-EU balance.

The second scenario is based on quick eastern enlargement and Germany's binding into a larger European framework. Most probably, instabilities on Germany's eastern border can be eliminated (even if they are partly shifted to the new eastern border of the EU), available resources could be dedicated to economic modernization of the transforming countries, and all EU members would benefit from the rapid development and high import demand of the CEECs.

These two options will not be available indefinitely. The later the decision in favor of the second option is made, the less possible it will be to build a stable and competitive Europe based on the EU.

Conclusion

The chain reaction of dramatic shifts in Europe ended with the collapse of the Warsaw Pact, the Soviet Union, and East Germany. The process of political democratization and economic transformation in the CEECs is but one of the major elements of these changes. The EU is the obvious modernization anchor of the continent. However, it can play this role only if it can provide the right answers at the right time to the new challenges. A return to the earlier status quo mentality is definitely the wrong answer, even if it is described in "modern terms" (deepening, cautious enlargement, a balance between the Mediterranean and eastern Europe, and an all-European stability contract). Also, the EU's pursuit of unilateral adjustment by the CEECs is untimely. A new European pattern that provides a sufficient level of security and a high level of economic integration requires substantial adjustment efforts on both sides. Economic and political adjustment should be accompanied by a more positive communication strategy. This should emphasize the positive results that can be expected from the eastern enlargement and not the high costs—which hinder the geographic extension of the EU—or the relevant threats that may force the EU to widen integration.

Without doubt, gradual eastern enlargement will cost additional money, but much less than the financing of any nonmembership alternative. The AAs do stipulate the creation of free trade in industrial products by the end of the century, and, thus, give the EU full access to the CEECs' markets. However, the market of the CEECs can expand and offer sustainable dynamic demand for EU goods only if these economies recover, start a high export- and investment-led growth, and are able to finance their exploding trade deficit in the crucial years of economic modernization ("modernization deficit"). While eastern enlargement is likely to enhance competition on western European markets and increase pressure on the EU's industrial structure and labor markets, it can substantially contribute to higher levels of European competitiveness on the global scale.

Both all-European restructuring and the integration of low-cost and highly skilled labor into the international division of labor are expected to work in this direction. Finally, western European stability and security cannot be sustained without eastern enlargement. The latter would not only provide a relevant support to a new security scheme, but would also strengthen European stability by creating a solid balance-of-power structure.

This essay has sought repeatedly to counter western European arguments that qualify the scenario of rapid eastern enlargement as an illusion. However, what is the real illusion: an attempt to develop a new concept of Europe in the face of rapidly changing European dynamics, or a stubborn insistence on trying to maintain the outdated pattern of the (pre-1989) western European status quo?

Notes

1. Inotai, A., "Looking Forward to Full Membership," *Hungarian Economic Review* (June-August 1994), pp. 64–69.
2. Ibid.
3. Inotai, A., "The System of Criteria for Hungary's Accession to the European Union," Institute for World Economics, Budapest (Trends in World Economy, No. 76).
4. Weidenfeld, W., "Ernstfall Europa," *Internationale Politik,* no. 1, pp. 11–19.
5. Dauderstädt, M., and Lippert, B., *Differenzieren beim Integrieren: Zur Strategie Einer Agbestuften Osterweiterung der EU* (Bonn: Friedrich Ebert Stiftung, 1995).
6. Inotai, A., "Die Deutsche Präsidentschaft und das Essener Gipfeltreffen im Kontext des Europäischen Integrationsprozesses," Budapest (manuscript).

7. Altmann, F. L., Andreff, W., and Fink, G., *Future Expansion of the European Union* (manuscript), January 1995.

8. Altmann, F. L., and Ochmann, C., "Mittel und Osteuropa auf dem Weg in die EU," *Europäische Rundschau,* no. 1, pp. 41–61.

9. Inotai, "Looking Forward to Full Membership."

10. Eurostat, *External Trade: Monthly Statistics,* nos. 8–9.

11. Own calculations based on Eurostat, *External Trade: Monthly Statistics,* 1995.

12. Nötzold, J., "Wann Werden die Staaten Ostmitteleuropas Mitglieder der EU?" *Europäische Rundschau,* no. 4, pp. 53–65.

13. Baldwin, R. E., *Towards an Integrated Europe* (London: Center for Economic Policy Research, 1994).

14. Inotai, A., "Die Beziehungen Zwischen der EU und den Assoziierten Staaten Mittel und Osteuropas," *Europäische Rundschau,* no. 3, pp. 19–36.

9

The Mediterranean Challenge

Birol A. Yesilada

The Mediterranean region is the third largest customer of the European Union (EU) and the fourth largest supplier of imports. During the last twenty-five years, the Global Mediterranean Policy (GMP), adopted at the 1972 Paris summit, defined the then European Community's (EC) relations with this region in areas of commerce and foreign assistance. The goals behind this initiative were to promote regional stability, improve trade between the EC and the Mediterranean Basin, and counter the Soviet Union's advances in the area.[1] However, because of the economic recession in Europe during the 1970s, the GMP did not attain its original goals and the EC lost substantial influence among the Mediterranean countries.

This chapter evaluates the EU's relations with nonmember Mediterranean Basin countries as they relate to future enlargement of the Union. The Mediterranean is a concern for the EU not only because Cyprus, Malta, and Turkey have applied for membership, but also because their application provides a major challenge for the member countries in their attempts to revive the EU's trade, financial, cultural, and political relations with the nonmember states of the region.

The importance of the Mediterranean Basin for the EU is unquestionable. During the Barcelona conference of 27–28 November 1995, fifteen EU countries and twelve Mediterranean countries met to discuss how relations between them could be improved. The goals of creating a Mediterranean free trade area, establishing closer economic ties between the Mediterranean countries and central and eastern European associate members of the EU through the Union, and establishing free trade agreements among the twelve Mediterranean countries represent a grand design. However, there are important lessons to be learned from the earlier GMP and the accession of Greece, Portugal, and Spain to EU membership. In my earlier study, I documented that two important developments—the global economic crisis of the 1970s and the membership of three Mediterranean

177

countries in the EC—had profoundly negative implications for the implementation of the GMP. Furthermore, the memberships of Greece, Portugal,
and Spain had a negative impact on exports of the nonmember
Mediterranean countries to the EU markets.[2] The new Mediterranean initiative is a response both to the failure of the GMP and to the important security concerns of the EU. Economic problems in northern Africa, rising
Islamic fundamentalism in that region and in the Mashreq (Egypt, Lebanon,
Jordan, and Syria) and Turkey provide a major impetus for policy reformu-
lation. According to a communication from the Commission to the Council
of Ministers and the European Parliament (EP):

> The establishment of a Euro-Mediterranean Economic Area should go
> hand in hand with the creation of an area of peace and stability. The
> Economic Area itself should involve not only free trade arrangements, but
> also a range of measures on the part of the Community to help countries
> of the region modernize their economies in the interests of sustainable
> development while still preserving their societies' equilibrium and identi-
> ty. There should also be greater cooperation in the new fields covered by
> the Maastricht Treaty (particularly Title VI).[3]

Title VI of the Maastricht Treaty pertains to the field of justice and
home affairs. The proposals of the Commission further appear in the
Council report on relations between the EU and twelve Mediterranean partners as a basis for the Barcelona conference. The report emphasizes political and security, economic and financial, and social and human issues.[4]
While these three issues will be discussed later, it is important to note that
the new initiative is being undertaken at the same time as three
Mediterranean countries (Cyprus, Malta, and Turkey) are applying for
membership in the Union. Thus, there is reason to be concerned about how
eventual membership of these countries and memberships of the Central
and Eastern European Countries (CEECs) will affect the new
Mediterranean initiative.

The Cases of Malta, Cyprus, and Turkey

Turkey applied for EU membership in 1987, when the government of
Turgut Özal felt confident about the completion of the country's economic
transformation and integration with global capitalism. Soon after the
Turkish application, Malta and Cyprus applied, in July 1990. Despite the
Turkish enthusiasm, however, the European Commission concluded on 18
May 1989 that the EU was not ready to enter into accession talks with
Turkey and rejected the application. The Commission's decision was based
on the fact that the Turkish economy was not as developed as the EC's, that

there were serious concerns about Turkey's human rights record, and that unemployment in Turkey posed a serious threat to the EU's markets.[5] Furthermore, the Greco-Turkish conflict over Cyprus, the Aegean airspace and territorial waters, the continental shelf, and the rights of the Greek and Turkish minorities in the respective countries meant that the Greeks would object to Turkey's membership in the EC/EU. The Cypriot and Maltese applications, on the other hand, did not receive a rejection but did not make it into the next wave of membership expansion, which included the European Free Trade Association (EFTA) countries. As I will explain later, the Cypriot case is closely tied to the rivalry between Greece and Turkey.

The Turkish Application

Does Turkey meet the membership requirements of the EU? The answer depends on whom one asks and when the question is raised. Often at times of serious security concerns, when Turkey can play a major role in protecting Western interests, the answer is an unconditional yes. However, when security interests are absent, the Europeans tend to view the Turks as part of the Middle East.

In geographical terms, Turkey is a member of all the European inter-governmental organizations—the Organization for Economic Cooperation and Development (OECD) (1948), the Council of Europe (1949), and NATO (1952); associate member of the EU (1963); and associate member of the Western European Union (WEU) (1992). So where does the problem lie? The objection is hidden within cultural and religious considerations. Although the Turkish state is secular, and indeed the U.S. and European officials refer to it as a model for the newly independent Muslim nations of the former Soviet Union in their state-building efforts, there exists in Europe a settled bias toward Muslims in general and Turks in particular. The Europeans point to the Islamic heritage of the Turks and fear that the recent rise in fundamentalist activities in Turkey would somehow "poison" the Christian-secular culture of the EU. But short of Turkey becoming an Islamic state, it would be difficult to maintain opposition to Turkey's membership solely on religious grounds—especially given that Turkish officials are helping their Turkic cousins in Azerbaijan and central Asia establish secular and market-oriented states. Furthermore, there is nothing in the Maastricht Treaty, or in any other EU legislation, that states that a prospective candidate for membership must be Christian. It can be argued that as long as Turkey remains a secular republic, Islam would not present a problem for the EU. After all, several EU member states have significant Muslim minorities.

With regard to the political conditions for membership, it is important to note that the postcoup civilian governments have made significant moves toward of democracy. In an earlier study, I argued that the new Turkish political system resembled a heterogeneous form of interest representation, which is a cross between state corporatist and pluralist forms of interest representation.[6] Under the 1982 constitution, the state controls the activities of citizens, interest groups, and political parties as much as any other exclusionary state corporatist system. Yet, despite these restrictions, politics has gradually moved in the direction of pluralism following the transition to civilian rule in November 1983. Today, all the pre-1980 political parties are reestablished, all restrictions on party officials have been lifted, and in June 1993, Turkey became one of the few Western democracies to have a female head of government. Furthermore, since the signing of the customs union agreement between Turkey and the EU on 6 March 1995, the Turks have been amending the 1982 constitution to rid it of the authoritarian articles that restrict individual civil and political rights. Closer relations with the EU would help the secular government(s) check the threat of Islamic fundamentalism in Turkey.

On economic grounds, EU officials can find reasons both to support and to reject Turkey's membership. In a recent analysis of economic conditions in Turkey, David Wood and I concluded that there were significant negative factors: "high inflation, high unemployment rate, low GNP per capita, and, most importantly, Turkey would qualify for 5.4 billion Ecus from the EU budget as regional aid. This last figure is based on the criteria used by the Union in paying out 7.4 billion Ecus of regional aid, also known as structural funds, to the member countries in 1991."[7] Turkey's high unemployment rate of about 20 percent is an added concern for EU officials. It was this problem, and fear of Turkish unemployed workers flooding the EU countries, that convinced the EU to back away from its commitment to allow for free movement of labor between the EU countries and Turkey, as stipulated in the Ankara agreement (association agreement) of 1963 and the Additional Protocol of 1970. According to these agreements, the transition period would have ended in 1986, allowing for free movement of individuals.[8] On a positive note, the Turkish economy is highly developed and the country provides an important link between the EU and newly emerging markets of the Middle East and central Asia.[9] In light of these complex issues, the EU decided to give Turkey a more favorable relationship with the EU, short of full membership, in the form of a customs union (CU). However, this was not an easy task. When the EU and Turkish officials met to discuss the CU, Greece vetoed the idea at the EU Council meeting on 19 December 1994. The Greek move did not surprise anyone, as Greece had already, on one occasion, voted to block another economic agreement with Turkey: in 1984, "Greece vetoed and effectively blocked EC economic assistance to Turkey in the amount of 400 million

Ecus."[10] The Greek government explained that it would oppose the CU as long as Turkey's alleged human rights abuses against the Kurds and military occupation of Cyprus continued. The supporters of the CU argued that Turkey was in the process of reforming its authoritarian constitution and that the Turkish military presence in northern Cyprus was the result of a complex problem that was caused in part by the Greek junta in 1974. However, it quickly became clear that Greece was not about to drop its objection to the CU until it obtained some concessions from the other EU countries.

The apparent deadlock ended as a result of intense negotiations between the EU and Greece, under the leadership of the then French foreign minister, Alain Juppé. In exchange for lifting its veto, the Greek government asked for specific concessions from the EU:

1. That the EU agrees to enter into negotiations with Cyprus for membership six months after the end of the 1996 Intergovernmental Conference (IGC) on the Maastricht Treaty
2. That Cyprus participates in dialogues with the EU on the same level as that between the EU and eastern European states
3. That the EU provides monetary compensation to the Greek textile industry, which stands to lose due to competition from Turkish textiles in the EU markets
4. That the proposed monetary assistance to Turkey over five years, ECUs 1 billion, be reduced[11]

The EU agreed to the first three items, which satisfied the Greek government. However, the signing of the CU agreement by the Council of Ministers did not mean that the problem was over. The agreement still required ratification by the EP, where Turkey faced some tough opposition. The Socialist bloc and the Greens opposed the CU because of Turkey's poor human rights record, especially in relation to the Kurdish problem, and the presence of authoritarian elements in the Turkish constitution.

The supporters of the CU argued that since transition to civilian rule in 1983, Turkey's political system has been gradually becoming more democratic in the Western pluralist fashion.[12] The Kurdish problem, on the other hand, was more than a domestic concern for the Turks, since the militant Kurdish Workers Party (PKK) operated out of Iraq and Syria. Nevertheless, the Turkish government of Tansu Çiller moved to reform the constitution of the country to secure the ratification of the CU.

In July 1995, the National Assembly passed amendments to fifteen articles of the constitution, easing the restrictions on individual civil and political rights. Important changes included

1. Granting trade unions the right to engage in political activity (Articles 33 and 52)
2. Granting civil servants the right to join trade unions (Article 53)
3. Lowering the voting age to eighteen (Articles 67 and 68)
4. Permitting professional organizations to engage in politics (Article 135)
5. Permitting university staff and students to engage in politics (Articles 67 and 68)

However, six other amendments were defeated, which drew criticism from the EP members and human rights groups and prodemocracy politicians in Turkey. These amendments would have made it more difficult for the government to ban strikes, would have allowed strikes by civil servants, and would have withdrawn the present immunity from prosecution of former members of the military government of 1980–1983.[13] More alarming was that the government failed to amend Article 8 of the Law for the Suppression of Terrorism. This article makes even a verbal support of Kurdish nationalism a crime against the state. It was this law that the state used as the basis for punishing the six ex-DeP (pro-Kurdish Democracy Party, which was closed down in 1994) members of the National Assembly. These parliamentarians received long prison sentences.

Against this background, the Turks and their European allies intensified their diplomatic efforts, aided by the United States, to secure the ratification of the CU agreement. They argued that, besides providing important economic benefits to European businesses, the CU held the promise of assisting Turkey with greater economic liberalization and structural reforms and, eventually, further democratization. Furthermore, the CU would give leverage to the coalition government of Çiller as it faced growing Islamic fundamentalist opposition from the Welfare (Refah) Party of Necmettin Erbakan. This Islamic party opposed the CU and favored withdrawal of Turkey from NATO. With the national elections scheduled for 24 December 1995, the pro-CU forces intensified their efforts and succeeded in obtaining the ratification of the agreement by the EP on 13 December 1995. Unfortunately, the CU victory did not translate into an electoral victory for Çiller. Her party, the True Path, won 19.2 percent of the vote, while the opposing, center-right Motherland Party obtained 19.7 percent, and Refah 21.3 percent.[14] As a result of these elections, the Turkish political scene entered a period of uncertainty. After an ill-fated and short-lived coalition between the two center-right parties, Motherland and True Path, Çiller eventually agreed to form a new coalition government with Refah in mid-1996.

The CU, which came into effect on 1 January 1996, gives the Turks closer economic relations with the EU than any other nonmember countries except Iceland and Norway. It opens Turkey's huge market of 60 million consumers to EU products and encourages investments in Turkey by third parties (for example, U.S. and Japanese companies that can manufacture goods in Turkey for sales in the EU). Moreover, the CU provides an access to central Asian markets for the European companies through Turkey's growing economic and political influence in this region. Turkey, in return, will receive large economic assistance from the EU, and Turkish companies will benefit from increased competition from their European counterparts. One Turkish industry that stands to gain from the CU immediately is textiles, as the EU will lift all quotas against Turkey's clothing and textiles exports.

While the CU agreement benefits Turkey, it could cause major concern for the other nonmember Mediterranean countries that met with the EU countries in Barcelona, as it gives a Mediterranean member an added advantage over the rest in trade relations with the EU—similar to the problem when Greece, Portugal, and Spain became members of the EU, though not as serious. This is a concern for nonmembers because the CU between the EU and Turkey calls for

> free movement of ECSC products and reciprocal concessions on agricultural products, macroeconomic dialogue in order to ensure the best economic environment possible for the functioning of the CU; broadening of cooperation on social matters, Trans-European networks, energy, transport, telecommunication, environment, agriculture, science, statistics, home affairs, consumer protection, and cultural cooperation; political dialogue; and cooperation in institutional matters through the organization of consultative relations between Turkey and the EU especially in areas of a Trans-European nature.[15]

Cyprus and Malta

Cyprus and Malta have small economies that are easily absorbable by the EU. Neither country presents a major economic burden for the EU. The mutual problem for both candidates is the smallness of their economies, which makes them vulnerable to assimilation by major European companies. Another concern pertains to the voting rights in the Council of Ministers and the disproportionate representation of small countries in EU institutions.[16] The Cypriot case, however, is a powder keg and requires special consideration.

Cyprus has always maintained close relations with the EU. When the United Kingdom showed interest in joining the European Economic Community (EEC) in 1961, Cyprus followed suit in 1962. The decision to apply for membership came about with the consent of the Greek Cypriot and Turkish Cypriot members of the House of Representatives. This is an important issue, because Article 50, Paragraph 1(a) of the Cyprus constitution states that

> the President and the Vice-President of the Republic, separately or conjointly, shall have the right of final veto on any law or decision of the House of Representatives or any part thereof concerning: foreign affairs, except the participation of the Republic in international organizations and pacts of alliance in which the Kingdom of Greece and the Republic of Turkey both participate.[17]

Thus, the consent of the president and the vice-president was necessary to go ahead with the application. Although this was obtained, the subsequent outbreak of civil war in December 1963 indefinitely postponed this idea.

Although full membership did not materialize, Cyprus did obtain an association agreement with the EC in 1972, which became effective in 1973, the year the UK became a member. At this time, the Turkish Cypriots were not party to the association negotiations because they were forced out of the central government and were living in small enclaves surrounded by Greek Cypriot armed forces.[18] Nonetheless, the EU indicated that "rules governing trade between the Contracting Parties may not give rise to any discrimination between the member states, or between nationals or companies of these states, nor nationals or companies of Cyprus."[19] The association agreement, therefore, prohibited discrimination against the Turkish Cypriots or the Greek Cypriots by their EU trading partners.

This agreement called for the elimination of all tariffs and quotas between Cyprus and the EC within five years. Following the end of the five-year period, the agreement was renewed annually until 1987, when the two sides signed a CU agreement. At the time of CU negotiations, the Turkish Cypriots cited Article 5 of the association agreement and asked to participate in the negotiations. They were successful only in obtaining informal meetings with the EC officials.

The CU between the EC and Cyprus, which came into effect on 1 January 1988, provided two phases for preparing the Cypriot economy for eventual membership in the EU: the first phase for ten years, and the second phase for four or five years.[20] According to Article 2 of the agreement, the movement of goods between Cyprus and the EU had to obey the principle of "rules of origin" during the first phase except for men's and boys' outer garments (heading no. 61.01).

In an attempt to assist the development of the Cypriot economy, the EU further agreed to give financial assistance to Cyprus under the financial protocols. The First Financial Protocol, signed on 15 July 1977, was aimed at financing projects that would be beneficial to both communities in Cyprus. The total amount of aid was ECU 30 million and was distributed during the next five years. The Greek Cypriot side received ECU 24 million, and the Turkish Cypriot side received 6 million. The Second Financial Protocol (1984–1988) provided ECU 44 million in aid, yet none of the proposals offered by the Turkish Cypriot side were reviewed favorably by EC officials; all the Turkish Cypriot projects failed the EU's "communality" requirement. This protocol was followed by the signing of the Third Financial Protocol in January 1989, providing another ECU 62 million in aid to the Cyprus republic, which for all practical purposes meant the Greek Cypriot side.[21]

As explained earlier, Cyprus applied for full EU membership in 1990. At that time, the decision was made solely by the Greek Cypriots and did not in any shape or form include the opinion of the Turkish Cypriots. An additional issue concerning the potential membership is the nature of the Cypriot constitution: membership of the Cyprus republic in international organizations of which Greece and/or Turkey are not members requires the joint consent of the two communities. In legal (constitutional) terms, the applications can be viewed as being unconstitutional and therefore could not be considered to be valid! However, this point seems to have been sidelined in recent diplomatic discussions and is now only a matter of preoccupation for the Turkish Cypriot side. Yet the problem did not become serious until 1995, when the EU decided to reach a compromise with the Greek government in exchange for Greece lifting its veto over the CU agreement with Turkey. In effect, a very complex game of chess was being played in Brussels that had serious implications for the Turkish Cypriots. The EU agreed to enter into accession talks with the Greek Cypriots, representing Cyprus, six months after the completion of the 1996–1997 IGC between the member states.[22]

In assessing Cyprus's application for membership, it is important to keep in mind that the island continues to be divided, with no apparent hope for reconciling differences between the Greek and Turkish Cypriots. Is the EU really interested in inheriting this problem, which has been one of the insoluble conflicts of the second half of the twentieth century?

For its part, the EU has been attempting to provide some assistance in resolving the Cyprus problem while preparing for future accession talks with the Greek Cypriots. Some of these efforts have centered on bringing together representatives of the two communities in some form of prenegotiation discussions. For example, in January 1995, the Commission sponsored an all–trade union forum in Cyprus, under the leadership of Director General Ivor Roberts, to promote better understanding between the Greek Cypriot and Turkish Cypriot labor leaders. If the joint declaration is any indication of the willingness of the Cypriots to work out a solution to this problem, the EU might be able to contribute to the prenegotiation confidence building. The joint declaration called for the following:

- A federal and democratic political system for Cyprus
- One type of system of employment and labor relations
- A unitary system of social insurance
- Unified standards of wages and salaries
- Complete safeguarding of the rights of freedom of movement and freedom of choice of employment in any part of Cyprus, coupled with entrenched right of freedom of organization
- No discrimination whatsoever in employment, or emoluments arising in connection with ethnic origin, religion, color, or sex
- A unitary economy[23]

While this is an example of a positive development, the European Court of Justice (ECJ) had earlier thrown up a major obstacle to the intercommunal negotiations that were being held under the auspices of the UN Secretary-General.

As Secretary-General Boutros Boutros-Ghali asked the leaders of the two communities to consider some confidence-building measures, which included concrete steps to promote the economic well-being of northern Cyprus, the Greek Cypriots filed a lawsuit in the UK to prevent the importation of citrus fruits and potatoes from the self-declared Turkish Republic of North Cyprus. Because the matter pertained to EU trade legislation, the case ended up in the ECJ. The Court ruled, on 5 July 1994, that these commodities should not receive preferential treatment under EU law because the "official" Cyprus government did not inspect the exports for approval. Specifically, the Court ruled as follows:

> The agreement of 19 December 1972 establishing an Association between the European Economic Community and the Republic of Cyprus, annexed to Council Regulation (EEC) No. 1246/73 of 14 May 1973, and Council Directive 77/93/EEC of 21 December 1976 on protective measures against the introduction into the member states of organisms harmful to plants or plant products must be interpreted as precluding acceptance by the national authorities of a member state when citrus fruit and potatoes are imported from the part of Cyprus to the north of the United Nations Buffer Zone, of movement and phytosanitary certificates issued by authorities other than the competent authorities of the Republic of Cyprus.[24]

That is, the ECJ ruled that health certificates issued by the authorities of the self-declared Turkish Republic of Northern Cyprus (TRNC) could not be accepted as substitutes for the documents issued by the Cyprus government. This meant that the TRNC citrus fruit and potatoes exports to UK markets would no longer receive preferential trade treatment as stated in the association agreement and the CU. To make matters worse, the British authorities, interpreting this decision to cover all exports from the TRNC, began to impose trade restrictions by eliminating preferential trade status of export commodities from northern Cyprus. The net result for the Turkish Cypriots was a monetary loss equal to 2.57 percent of TRNC's GNP and 26.6 percent of its export earnings in 1994.[25] Under these circumstances, it is hardly surprising that the Turkish Cypriots accused the Greek Cypriots of a double standard for going to the ECJ while simultaneously pursuing UN confidence-building measures; as a consequence, the Turkish side decided to take a hard-line position in the intercommunal negotiations.

Given this situation, it is rather difficult for the EU to commit itself to Cypriot membership. Unless the UN, the United States, and the EU work closely to promote confidence-building measures between Greek and Turkish Cypriots, Cyprus will continue to be a thorn in the side of the international community. Regardless of Greek desires, it would be highly irrational for the EU to inherit this messy state of affairs. Thus, Cyprus is a powder keg, and the most that Turkey can expect for the foreseeable future is a customs union. This leaves Malta, which the EU found in many ways to be the most attractive of the three Mediterranean applicants until the new Labour government, elected in October 1996, ruled out EU membership for the time being.

Relations with Other Mediterranean Countries

The Mediterranean Basin represents economic, political, and security concerns for the EU. The countries of the region are the EU's third largest customer and its fourth largest supplier of imports. The initial Mediterranean policy of the Union was in the form of an economic and technical assistance package, the GMP, after the Paris summit of 1972. According to Roy Ginsberg, the GMP was driven by political and economic motives: the strategy called for using economic influence to promote stability, while checking Soviet intentions in the Mediterranean.[26] However, as Wood and Yesilada explain, despite such ambitions, several problems stood in the way of the GMP:

> First, the economies of the EC and the NMBCs [nonmember Mediterranean Basin countries] were not sufficiently compatible to promote the desired level of trade. Second, while the industrial products of the NMBCs received easy access to EC markets, agricultural goods were not included in the GMP because of the CAP. Third, even in industrial products, key exports of the NMBCs faced quota restrictions (i.e., textiles and clothing, shipping, steel, synthetic fibers, paper and paper products, machine tools, and cars) because the EC labeled these industries as "sensitive industries" that required Community protection. And finally, there was the question of the migrant workers from the NMBCs. The EC viewed this issue as a potential problem if not controlled.[27]

The problems of the GMP worsened as Greece, Portugal, and Spain joined the EU. Alfred Tovias explains that these countries' membership resulted in making the EU more Mediterranean-like, resembling countries like Israel and Turkey, and with a very strong agricultural base.[28] Furthermore, as explained above, studies have shown that the membership of Greece, Portugal, and Spain hampered the NMBCs' trade relations with the EU.[29] Under such conditions, the GMP became highly ineffective and the EU was unable to provide assistance to the nonmember countries. As economic conditions worsened in the Arab Mashreq and Maghreb, social unrest increased and Islamic fundamentalism became a serious challenge to the governments of these countries. In addition, large-scale unemployment meant that more people from northern Africa would seek refuge in the EU. The European officials had no choice but to come up with a more realistic program for technical, economic, and political cooperation between the EU and nonmember Mediterranean countries.

On 25 April 1990, the vice-president of the Brussels Commission, Frans Andriessen, stated that there was a need to readdress the GMP because "increasingly closer geopolitical rather than political links will be forged between the Mediterranean countries in the coming decades [and] the European Community will be involved in this process."[30] After much debate and competition between the EU countries to author the future plan for partnership with the Mediterranean countries, the Commission prepared a draft plan for renovating the GMP: *Vers une Politique Méditerranéenne Renovée: Propositions pour la Période 1992–96*. This plan established the framework for high-level discussions on the subject.

The EU leaders provided some answers to the Mediterranean challenge at the June 1994 summit in Corfu, Greece. At this meeting, the EU leaders invited the Commission to draft a new southern strategy for the Mediterranean Basin.[31] The Commission's response came in the form of a proposal to create the largest free trade zone in the world, to include the EU and its North African and Middle Eastern neighbors.[32]

The recommendations of the Commission became the basis of the Council document that presented recommendations for the Barcelona conference. The proposals of the Council provided specific suggestions:

1. Political and security partnership covering two areas of concern: (a) human rights, democracy, and the rule of law; and (b) stability, security, and good-neighborly relations
2. Economic and financial partnership: (a) Euro Mediterranean free trade area; (b) cooperation priorities (investment, regional cooperation, business, environment, fisheries and energy; and (c) other areas of cooperation (agriculture, rural development, infrastructure

development, information technology and telecommunications, regional planning, research and development, and statistics)
3. Partnership in social and human affairs (educational training, social development, migration, drug trafficking, terrorism, international crime, judicial cooperation, racism and xenophobia, combating corruption, culture and media, health, and youth)[33]

To sell this plan at the Barcelona conference, the Commission also recommended that EU assistance to these countries be increased to U.S.$6 billion.[34] The countries that agreed to take part in this Mediterranean bloc are Algeria, Cyprus, Egypt, Israel, Jordan, Lebanon, Malta, Morocco, Syria, Tunisia, Turkey, and the Autonomous Palestinian Territories. Their trade and financial relations with the EU can be seen in figures provided in Table 9.1.

Table 9.1   Financial Relations Between the EU and Mediterranean States

Country	Development Aid From the EU (1992, as % of total multilateral aid)	Exports to EU (1994, as % of total exports)
Algeria	78.0	67.7
Cyprus	14.0	36.2
Egypt	40.4	55.8
Israel	12.6	29.4
Jordan	27.3	9.3
Lebanon	56.1	15.5
Malta	n.a.	68.9
Morocco	69.0	68.5
Syria	33.5	55.3
Tunisia	69.8	80.2
Turkey	n.a.	47.9

Source: "A New Crusade," *The Economist,* 2 December 1995, p. 49.

These figures clearly show the importance of the EU for the participating Mediterranean countries. However, collectively these countries' trade deficit with the EU has worsened since 1992, when it stood at around ECU 4 billion. In 1993, this figure reached ECU 13 billion and remained around 10 billion in 1994. The Barcelona Declaration pledges to create a Mediterranean Free Trade Area by 2010 and to provide economic and technical assistance to these countries to develop their domestic industrial base. The EU, which is about to negotiate bilateral trade agreements with most of the Barcelona participants, if it has not already done so, hopes to bring stability to the region as a means of countering Islamic fundamentalism and chronic unemployment. The EU already has association agreements with Israel, Morocco, and Tunisia and was aiming to conclude similar ones with Jordan and Egypt in 1996–1997. EU officials have opened talks with Lebanon, are in preliminary discussions with the Algerian officials, and have made it clear that they will also begin talks with the Syrian and the Palestinian authorities when the time is right.[35]

Despite the initial enthusiasm, one should be cautious about the goals of the Barcelona Declaration, as several developments could undermine the objectives of the participant states. First, the Mediterranean countries view one another with great suspicion; unless they work on confidence-building measures and promote trade among themselves, the existing suspicion between their peoples will not disappear. Second, the Mediterranean countries can expect to see certain protectionist measures in areas designated as sensitive industries by the EU. This is similar to the earlier problem these countries faced under the GMP. Farm products, textiles, and other low-technology products compete with the products of Greece, Portugal, and Spain. Finally, France, Greece, Italy, Portugal, and Spain all compete to define the Mediterranean policy of the EU. A further addition to these potential problems is the future impact of an EU-Turkey CU agreement on exports of the other Mediterranean countries. If previous cases are any indication, the impact would be a negative one.

Conclusion

The Mediterranean Basin provides an important challenge for the EU in economic, political, and social terms. As the EU moves ahead to deepen integration among the member states, it needs to address the question of how EU countries could provide assistance to the Mediterranean states in their quest for economic and political development. The problems of economic decline, high unemployment and inflation, and political instability in the Mediterranean countries spill over to the EU states in the form of illegal immigration, drug trafficking, and Islamic fundamentalism—which also threaten the moderate Arab states and Turkey.

The EU has chosen a two-tier approach to these challenges. First, it decided to increase its economic and political ties with Cyprus, Malta, and Turkey. It approved a CU agreement with Turkey to solidify its relations with the West, at a time when Turkey's secular democracy faced a serious challenge from the fundamentalist Welfare Party. The EU also agreed to consider membership of Cyprus and Malta, though the Cypriot case is likely to be delayed because of the never-ending Greek-Turkish conflict, and the Maltese case is now in suspension. Second, the EU also decided to revive the old GMP in the form of a grand design—the Mediterranean Free Trade Area. The success of this plan, however, depends on the willingness of the Mediterranean countries to work together, and also on the EU's efforts not to repeat the mistakes made under the GMP.

Under these circumstances, it is highly probable that the next wave of EU enlargement will include no Mediterranean countries, with Malta excluded through its own choice and Cyprus and Turkey postponed by the EU to some unspecified time. Even though the EU agreed to consider the Cypriot case six months after the completion of the 1996–1997 IGC, this is no guarantee that Cyprus will become a member prior to a settlement of the island's problems. In addition, Turkey would be likely to block Cyprus's membership if the accession included only the Greek Cypriot side. Finally, the CU with Turkey seems to be the compromise that satisfies European and Turkish interests for the foreseeable future. As the analysis in this chapter demonstrates, the EU cannot admit Turkey as a full member because of serious economic and political considerations. At the same time, the EU cannot afford to tell the Turks to go their own way. The CU is similar to a redefined Ankara agreement and provides significant economic and political payoffs for both sides.

Notes

1. Ginsberg, R., "The European Community and the Mediterranean," in Lodge, J., ed., *Institutions and Policies of the European Community* (New York: St. Martin's Press, 1983), pp. 161–162.
2. Yesilada, B. A., "The EC's Mediterranean Policy," in Hurwitz, L., and Lequesne, C., eds., *The State of the European Community: Policies, Institutions, and Debates in the Transition Years* (Boulder: Lynne Rienner, 1991), pp. 362–365.
3. Commission of the European Communities, *Strengthening the Mediterranean Policy of the European Union: Proposals for Implementing a Euro-Mediterranean Partnership,* COM(95) 72 Final, Brussels, 8 March 1995, para. 1.4.
4. "Council Report on Relations Between the European Union and the Mediterranean Countries, in Preparation for the Conference on 27–28 November in Barcelona," EUROPE Documents, Brussels, 27 April 1995, p.2.
5. Commission, *Commission Opinion on Turkey's Request for Accession to the Community,* Sec.(89) 2290 Final, Brussels, 18 December 1989.
6. Yesilada, B. A., "Problems of Political Development in the Third Turkish Republic," *Polity* 21, no. 2 (winter 1988), pp. 345–347.
7. "Survey: The European Community," *The Economist,* 11 July 1992, p. 17, as cited in Wood, D. M., and Yesilada, B. A., *The Emerging European Union* (White Plains, N.Y.: Longman, 1996), p. 208.
8. Pomfret, R., "The European Community's Relations with the Mediterranean Countries," in Redmond, J., ed., *The External Relations of the European Community* (London: Macmillan, 1992), p. 83.
9. For a detailed discussion of the Turkish economic development in the 1980s, see Yesilada, B. A., and Fisunoglu, M., "Assessing the January 24, 1980

Economic Stabilization Program in Turkey," in Barkey, H., ed., *The Politics of Economic Reform in the Middle East* (New York, St. Martin's Press, 1992), p. 207.

10. Wood and Yesilada, *The Emerging European Union,* pp. 208–209.

11. Athens News Agency Bulletin, 20 February 1995, as cited in Wood and Yesilada, *The Emerging European Union,* p. 209.

12. For a detailed discussion of the authoritarian-corporatist and pluralist contest in the Turkish political system during the 1980s, see Yesilada, "Problems of Political Development in the Third Turkish Republic," pp. 345–372; Heper, M., and Landau, J. A., eds., *Political Parties and Democracy in Turkey* (London: I. B. Tauris, 1991); and Eralp, A., Tünay, M., and Yesilada, B. A., eds., *The Political and Socioeconomic Transformation of Turkey* (Westport, Conn.: Praeger, 1993).

13. Economist Intelligence Unit, *Country Report, Turkey,* Third Quarter (London: EIU, 1995), pp. 10–11.

14. *Financial Times,* 27 December 1995, p. 2.

15. Commission, *Association Between the European Community and Turkey,* Association Council, 3 March 1995. CE-TR 106/95, as cited in Wood and Yesilada, *The Emerging European Union,* p. 209.

16. For a good analysis of these cases, see Redmond, J., *The Next Mediterranean Enlargement of the European Community: Turkey, Cyprus, and Malta?* (Aldershot, Eng.: Dartmouth, 1993).

17. *Constitution of the Republic of Cyprus,* Art. 50, para. 1(a).

18. For a detailed discussion of these issues, see Solsten, E., *Cyprus: A Country Study* (Washington: Federal Research Division of the Library of Congress, 1991); and Stearns, M., *Entangled Allies: US Policy Toward Greece, Turkey, and Cyprus* (New York: Council on Foreign Relations, 1992).

19. Commission, *Agreement Establishing an Association Between the Republic of Cyprus and the European Economic Community,* SEC (72) 4552, Brussels, 1972, p. 3.

20. EEC, *Protocol for the Implementation of the Second Stage of the Agreement Establishing an Association Between the European Economic Community and the Republic of Cyprus,* Brussels, 1987.

21. EC Council Decision, *Protocol on Financial and Technical Cooperation Between the EC and the Republic of Cyprus,* Art. 2, Brussels, 1989, p. 1.

22. Wood and Yesilada, *The Emerging European Union,* chap. 10.

23. Donated to the author by Ivor Roberts, director-general at the Brussels Commission.

24. ECJ, *Judgment of the Court,* Case C-432/92, 5 July 1994, p. 16.

25. Yesilada, B. A., and Biçak, H. A., "The European Court of Justice Decision on Trade with Northern Cyprus: Implications for the Cyprus Conflict," paper presented at the annual American Political Science Association conference, Chicago, 31 August–2 September 1995.

26. Ginsberg, "The European Community and the Mediterranean," pp. 161–162.

27. Yesilada, "The EC's Mediterranean Policy," p. 361.

28. Tovias, A., *Foreign Economic Relations of the European Community: The Impact of Spain and Portugal* (Boulder: Lynne Rienner, 1990), p. 2.

29. For a detailed discussion of the issues surrounding the second enlargement and trade with the NMBCs, see Donges, J., et al., *The Second Enlargement of the European Community* (Tübingen: J. C. B. Mohr, 1982; Pomfret, R., "The Impact of EEC Enlargement on Non-member Mediterranean Countries' Exports to the EC," *The Economic Journal* 91 (September 1981), pp. 726–729; Yannopoulos, G.,

"Prospects for the Manufacturing Exports of the Non-candidate Mediterranean Countries in a Community of Twelve," *World Development* 12, no. 11–12 (December, 1984), pp. 1087–1094; and Yesilada, B. A., "The Impact of the European Community's Second Enlargement and Project 1992 on Relations with the Mediterranean Basin," paper presented at the annual meeting of the Midwest Political Science Association, Chicago, 5–7 April 1990.

30. Andriessen, F. H. J. J., "Europe at the Crossroads," paper presented at the Tenth Annual Paul-Henri Spaak Lecture, Harvard University, 25 April 1990, pp. 11–12.

31. "Brussels Urges Wider Trade Zone," *Financial Times,* 20 October 1994, p. 2.

32. Commission, *Communication from the Commission,* COM(95) 72 Final.

33. "Council Report on Relations Between the European Union and the Mediterranean Countries."

34. Commission, *Communication from the Commission,* COM(95).

35. *Reuters,* 14 November 1995.

Part 4

Conclusion

10

The Impact of Enlargement on the Role of the European Union in the World

Roy H. Ginsberg

Enlargement—the European Union's most important foreign policy power under Article 237 of the Treaty of Rome—has broad implications for the EU's position in the world. Each enlargement changes the size, geography, composition, scope, and direction of this Union. The process of enlargement carries contradictions—in the risks of diluting the cement that holds the EU together and in the opportunities of strengthening the EU and its values of structural peace and reconciliation among formerly warring parties. Although the EU becomes more diverse and decisionmaking becomes more complicated with each expansion, enlargement has made the EU an economic and financial superpower, and many applicants become committed and energetic members.

The EU acts as a magnet for surrounding states, many of whom have determined that the benefits of membership outweigh the costs of nonmembership. Since the EU decides which applicant states join, and under what conditions, it has enormous influence over the fates of nations. The UK, Ireland, Denmark, and Norway in the 1960s and Morocco and Turkey in the 1980s wanted to join but were kept out for various reasons, forcing them to either reapply or seek another form of accommodation with the EU.

For those who have made it into the Union, enlargement has had enormous effects on their own interests as well as those of the EU. Britain's entry was a milestone: it not only represented a fundamental break with the centuries-old pattern of Anglo-European relations, but it was also one of the country's most important and painful postwar decisions. It was also a turning point for the EU: Britain rounded out the Common Market's membership to include all former colonial powers, overcame old divisions dating back to the split between the old European Economic Community (EEC) and the European Free Trade Association (EFTA), and catapulted the Common Market onto the world stage. No less significant for the EU and its southern neighbors was the entry of the former dictatorships of Greece, Spain, and Portugal during the 1980s. This not only consolidated democracy in those countries in ways perhaps not possible without the incentives of membership, but it also made the EU a Mediterranean power in its own right.

Each enlargement causes a metamorphosis in the EU's relationship with the outside world. New members adjust to, and mold, the EU's international relations; in turn, they must adjust their policies to those of the foreign policy *acquis communautaire* (the foreign agreements of the EU) and the *acquis politique* (the declarations made and positions taken in the context of political cooperation). Thus, Spain had to recognize Israel by virtue of the EU-Israeli cooperation accord; and Ireland, Finland, Sweden, and Austria have had to adjust their neutrality in light of the EU's partisan positions and actions taken in the context of the Common Foreign and Security Policy (CFSP).

Enlargement brings the EU closer to border regions—the Mediterranean, the Middle East, and eastern Europe—and to countries with whom the new members have close historical and trade ties, in Latin America, Asia, and Africa. Enlargement has brought the EU closer to the United States via British membership: the accession of the UK, Denmark, Greece, and the Iberian states has made all but the four EU neutral states members of the North Atlantic Treaty Organization (NATO). New members also bring their own foreign policy interests, specializations, connections, and expertise to the EU. The UK, for example, brought to the EU a global network of diplomatic, political, and economic interests that factored directly into the establishment of many new EU foreign policy actions. These range from the establishment of the Lomé convention and the Mediterranean Policy to the high-level consultations with the United States and the growth and development of the forum for foreign policy coordination among the EU member governments known as European Political Cooperation (EPC). Meanwhile, although small in size and clout, Ireland championed Third World development and national liberation causes within the EU, and the Danes served as a bridge to the Nordic Council after the two joined in 1973. Denmark showed how a small member can have an enormous effect on the goal of the European Security and Defense Identity (ESDI): in its first referendum on the Treaty on European Union (TEU), a slight majority of Danes rejected the TEU, partly due to opposition to participation in ESDI.

Greece's 1981 accession brought the EU closer to the Balkans and to Middle East affairs; the Greeks have not shied from influencing EU policies toward both regions. Spain and Portugal, which joined in 1986, spurred the development of deeper EU–Latin American ties in the 1980s, as well as the EU-Mercosur Pact and the Euro-Mediterranean Partnership in the 1990s. Swedish, Finnish, and Austrian accession in 1995 is also making a mark on EU foreign policy. The causes of democratization and market reforms in the Baltic republics, Baltic accession to the EU, and the environmental situation in the Baltic Sea are championed by Sweden and the other Nordics. Finland gives the EU a long border with Russia, with all the implications this has for ESDI. Austria deeply implicates the EU in the affairs of Central and Eastern European Countries (CEECs) and the affairs of the Organization for Security and Cooperation in Europe (OSCE). All three of these neutrals will complicate the quest for, or put the brakes on, the development of ESDI. Although they support EU participation in peacekeeping operations endorsed by the UN, they are not members of the Western European Union (WEU), the EU's defense arm, and do not want to commit themselves to collective self-defense.

Although the EU's expansions have diluted the original cement that held the original six members together, and a more diverse membership makes common positions much more difficult in some instances—for example, Greece's problematic relations with Macedonia and Turkey—enlargements have generally strengthened the EU's role as an international political actor. Successive enlargements have created the world's largest import and export market, and the EU is now one of the world's three economic superpowers; few states are untouched by the effects of its trade policies. The act of enlargement itself causes a flurry of foreign trade policy activity. After each enlargement, the EU renegotiates bilateral trade agreements to account for the enlarged membership and negotiates compensation agreements according to World Trade Organization (WTO) rules.

This chapter asks three questions that explore the impact of enlargement on the EU's world role:

1. What is the relationship between enlargement and foreign policy?
2. What are the effects of enlargement on EU foreign policy decision-making?
3. What are the effects of enlargement on the EU's position in Europe and the world?

Foreign policy in this chapter refers to the civilian (nonmilitary) policies and actions of the EU as a sui generis international actor. Neither a state nor a conventional international organization, the EU nonetheless has distinctive international legal, political, and economic arrangements with a large number of nation-states and international organizations. Foreign policy thus refers to the two related methods of EU foreign policy: the foreign economic, commercial, and diplomatic actions of the European Community (EC) pursuant to the 1958 Treaty of Rome, the 1987 Single European Act (SEA), and the 1993 TEU; and the political declarations, common positions, and joint actions of the CFSP, formerly EPC, pursuant to the TEU.

Enlargement and Foreign Policy

Enlargement is both a cause and an effect of EU foreign policy. The EU must first respond to the pressures from outsiders who want full or associate membership; and as it must respond and ultimately decide on the fates of others, enlargement is a cause of action. Once the decision to enlarge has been made and accession has occurred, the larger and more powerful EU has additional influence over other countries and regions both within and outside Europe. The outside world makes all sorts of new demands on the EU to act as a responsible and coherent unit in international politics, even when the EU members are not ready to fill that role. Although the outside world has higher expectations of the EU than the EU itself can deliver, the spur of outside expectations forces the EU to better organize itself to address foreign needs and to formulate and implement new policies in response to those needs.

The EU does not initiate enlargement; rather it responds to formal membership bids from eligible countries. The EU is a pole of attraction for surrounding states. Although the Norwegians and Swiss have their reasons for staying outside, contrary to the wishes of both governments, there are nonetheless powerful economic, political, and security reasons that drive the decision of other outsiders to join and the EU to welcome them.

For aspirants, the lure of membership is in the free access to, and the economies of scale of, the world's largest internal market (for example, Britain needed the shock therapy of competition from the continent to overcome political opposition to industrial modernization and economic transformation; Denmark gained substantially more from duty-free access to the common market than the reverse because of the small size of its market). For some, access to regional development aid and agricultural subsidies provide inducements (Ireland, Greece). For others, the fear of being left outside, while feeling the effects of EU decisionmaking, is a good enough reason to seek membership (Sweden, Finland). For smaller states dependent on the markets of larger states that have applied for membership, the decision to seek EU membership is dictated in part by the decision of others. Thus, the dependency of Ireland and Denmark on the British market and of Portugal on the Spanish market is an example of how smaller states have had to adjust to the actions of their larger neighbors. The loss of Finland's markets in the former Soviet Union was a major catalyst to seeking EU membership.

Regional integration theory reveals useful explanations behind the enlargement process and how it relates to foreign policy.[1] The EU's Common External Tariff (CET) requires it to negotiate with trading partners because the EU sets and negotiates tariffs. EU common commercial, agricultural, development, competition, standards, and other policies may have adverse effects on outsiders that in turn seek accommodation in the form of a bid for membership (Lithuania in 1995, for example), association (Greece in 1960), preferential status (Israel in 1970), or specific bilateral agreements governing trade terms (United States in 1995). The EU is pressed to deal with the demands of outsiders even though it may not wish to do so. Its response to the needs and pressures of outsiders drives the integration process as new responsive policies are developed.

Economics alone do not drive enlargement. A politics of scale is at work as aspirants seek membership to further their own influences in a wider body that carries more collective than individual weight in the world.[2] A politics of scale enables members to conduct joint foreign policy actions at lower costs and risks than when they act on their own. Members generally perceive that they carry more weight in certain areas when they act together as a bloc than when they act separately. As for the smaller members (such as the Dutch), the EU offers them an indispensable gateway to international politics. For the larger countries that no longer wield the power in the world they once did (Italy, Spain), the EU offers a collective platform to pursue national interests. Other large states (France, Britain) are torn between their residual prerogatives as former great powers—and thus naturally cling to foreign policy independence—and the imperative of Europe-wide cooperation, resulting in many conflicts within the CFSP.

Although the EU does not initiate enlargement, it does have its own agenda when extending the membership. Willy Brandt's Germany and post-Gaullist France wanted Britain in the EU to balance the other's ambitions; the Common Market needed Britain's network of global ties as it faced increasing demands from the outside world to act in international political terms; and all recognized that it was time to overcome the divisions in western Europe caused by the split between the two rival trade blocs of the late 1950s (EFTA and what is now the EU).

Enlargement has been seen as a means to secure the EU's external borders. The EU's concern with stabilizing its exposed southern flank during the Cold War was an important element in overcoming significant French agricultural opposition to Iberian accession in the 1980s. Enlargement in 1995 to include all but three of the remaining EFTA states enriched the EU coffers and cleared the path for the much more difficult challenge of enlargement to the former communist east. The EU's future eastern enlargement to include the central and eastern European aspirants (Hungary, Poland, Czech Republic, Slovakia, Romania, Bulgaria, Slovenia, and the Baltic republics) and southern enlargement to include Cyprus and

Malta also entail very significant security considerations for both the applicants and the EU.

The Effects of Enlargement on EU
Foreign Policy Decisionmaking Structure and Process

Deepening while widening has been the norm. Enlargement has been a catalyst for the creation of new, or the reform of existing, foreign policy making procedures, mechanisms, meetings, and institutions, as the EU is forced to adjust to the impact on its foreign relationships of its larger size and more diverse membership. The run-up to, and aftermath of, the EU's first enlargement, in 1973, was no exception. The heads of state and government met in The Hague in 1969 to clear the path for British (and Danish, Irish, and Norwegian) membership. Facing a larger union with increasing international political responsibilities and the integration into the EU of Britain's formidable foreign policy interests, the government leaders took an important step that extended the economic integration experiment to foreign policy: they charged the EU foreign ministers to make recommendations on how the members could best meet global challenges collectively. Their recommendations led to the establishment of EPC in 1970. An intergovernmental framework of consultations and meetings conducted outside the traditional Rome treaty framework, EPC was designed to facilitate foreign policy cooperation and coordination among the member governments. Hundreds of foreign policy declarations and common positions have sprung from EPC during its lifespan from 1970 to 1993, when it was replaced by CFSP. Foreign ministers began meeting biannually within EPC, and members committed themselves to consulting with one another on all important foreign policy matters. The foreign ministers' chief European advisers, the political directors, formed the Political Committee in 1970 to prepare for these foreign ministers' meetings.

At the 1972 Paris EU summit, the heads of state and government charged the foreign ministers to produce a second foreign policy report. In the 1973 Copenhagen Report, the leaders committed themselves to consulting on all important foreign policy matters *before* members took final positions, gave the Commission a role in EPC, increased the number of foreign ministers' meetings from two to four per year, set up the Correspondents Group of the political directors' chief assistants to prepare for PoCo meetings, called for consultations among members' foreign embassies and permanent representations to international organizations, and directed the Council president to implement conclusions adopted at the foreign ministers' and PoCo meetings. These major innovations in EU foreign policy structure were designed to facilitate common negotiating positions at the

OSCE and toward the Middle East, Mediterranean Basin, and Asia—areas of the world brought closer to EU concerns as a result of British accession.

At the 1974 Paris summit, the heads of state and government created the European Council, the twice-yearly summit meeting also attended by the Commission and the foreign ministers. The European Council, the pinnacle of the EU decisionmaking structure, is chaired by the EU Council presidency, which rotates among the members on a six-monthly basis. The Council president is charged by the TEU to be the EU's voice to the outside world and thus is the most critical position in the EU foreign policy edifice. In response to pressure from Washington, the European Council agreed in 1974 to brief the United States and other like-minded states on matters taken up in EPC that affect their interests.

At the time of Greek accession in 1981, the heads of state and government strengthened the Council presidency by establishing the troika—representatives from the past, present, and succeeding Council presidencies—designed to assist the current Council president in EPC. The leaders also agreed to do the following:

- Extend EPC to the political aspects of security
- Take into account one another's position and give due weight to the desire to achieve common positions
- Emphasize the need for consultation at international conferences in which one or more of the EU states participate and at which the agenda includes matters under discussion in EPC or in which the EU has a common position
- Emphasize the need to achieve not just a common attitude but joint action
- Accept a British-inspired crisis management plan whereby any three or more members may call an emergency meeting of the foreign ministers, who would convene within forty-eight hours of the call

Again, these significant changes to the way the EU conducted international business were in response to increasing external demands to react more resolutely and speedily to international crises. The enlarged membership catapulted the EU toward a higher political profile in international politics.

Negotiations for the SEA were concluded in 1986, the year Spain and Portugal joined the EU. It was no accident that the SEA beefed up the EU's foreign policy powers at the time of another enlargement. The SEA did the following:

- Linked the EU and EPC for the first time under the rubric of the European Council

- Codified the existence and spelled out the international functions of the European Council
- Codified the troika concept
- Committed members to coordinate positions more closely on the political and economic aspects of security and to maintain the technological and industrial conditions necessary for their security
- Gave EPC a small secretariat
- Gave the European Parliament (EP) powers of assent over the EU's international agreements

These small but significant steps to strengthen the EU's foreign policy cooperation framework reflected the growing demands on the EU to respond collectively to the pressures on the common market from the international political economy. The SEA's goal of completing the internal market by 31 December 1993 provoked new external demands on the EU to ensure market access by nonmember states. The SEA also had an effect on the decision of a number of countries to apply for membership: Cyprus, Malta, Austria, and Turkey feared being left outside the reinvigorated common market.

The TEU, ratified in November 1993, was in its first full year of operation when the EU's fourth enlargement (to include the Finns, Swedes, and Austrians) occurred in 1995. The foreign policy aspects of the TEU were designed to deepen EU political cooperation to complement the goal of monetary union and to prepare for the future challenge of eastern enlargement. The TEU took the following steps:

- Replaced EPC with CFSP
- Brought the EPC secretariat inside an EU institution, the Council Secretariat, and strengthened it with additional personnel and resources
- Replaced PoCo with the Committee of Permanent Representatives (COREPER), an EC institution served by the Council Secretariat, to prepare for all meetings of the foreign ministers
- Called for an ESDI and designated the WEU as the EU's defense arm
- Further extended the EP's decisionmaking authority over enlargement and international agreements
- Gave the Commission the right of nonexclusive initiative in CFSP
- Charged the European Council with the responsibility of speaking for the EU in world affairs

The TEU did not go far enough in binding the members to a CFSP and an ESDI. The next round of enlargement to possibly include Cyprus and the

CEECs (but, for the moment, seemingly not Malta) sometime within the next decade drove proposals for foreign policy decisionmaking and institutional reform at the 1996–1997 Intergovernmental Conference (IGC). Creating a central policy planning capability, bringing the WEU closer to the EU, introducing qualified majority voting into some CFSP decisionmaking, and creating more consistency between the political and economic dimensions of EU foreign policy are objectives of the next round of treaty revisions. Many in the EU, especially Germany, maintain that further enlargement is not tenable without institutional deepening; thus, the next enlargement is likely to be preceded by at least some foreign policy decisionmaking reforms consistent with past patterns.

The Effects of Enlargement on the EU's Place in Europe and the World

There have been many influences on EU foreign policy—the Cold War, the oil embargo and price hikes, the growing interdependence of the EU and the world, relations with the United States, Islamic fundamentalism, terrorism, war in the former Yugoslavia, and the domestic politics and national interests of the member states, to name but a few. This section, however, concentrates on enlargement as a catalyst for foreign policy actions and as an agent of change in the EU's European and global positions.

By 1995, all but Iceland, Norway, Switzerland, and Liechtenstein in western Europe had joined the EU, and by 1997 all CEECs had applied for membership. For all intents and purposes, the EU and Europe—including the Baltics but minus the rest of the Commonwealth of Independent States (CIS)—have become synonymous, testifying to the enormous growth of the EU since the original six members merged their coal and steel sectors in 1952. The EU is a model and magnet for nonmember European countries. Membership is based on various conditions: applicants must be European, democratic, have a competitive market economy, respect human rights, and accept the *acquis communautaire* and *acquis politique*. Thus, the EU is a force for political and economic change in Europe. Its stabilizing effect on Iberian and Greek democracy is a model for what the EU can do for the aspirants of the CEECs, although the enormous problems that lie ahead for the integration of eastern into western Europe appear far more daunting than the Iberian accession.

Enlargement has also created a civilian superpower in international economic, commercial, financial development, and diplomatic terms as the incorporation of new members transforms the EU in global terms. Enlargement has

- made the EU agriculturally self-sufficient, thus less dependent on traditional nonmember suppliers;
- increased the EU's share of world trade so that it has become the world's largest importer and exporter;
- increased the EU's coastline and thus control of some of the world's richest fishing zones;
- increased the EU's gross domestic product, which now exceeds that of the United States; and
- expanded the diplomatic reach of the EU to nearly all nation-states and a large number of multilateral organizations, including other regional trade blocs, which see the EU as a model of cooperation.

One way to measure the impact of the EU's first enlargement on foreign policy is to examine the scope and nature of EU policy actions before and after enlargement. During the preaccession years, 1958–1972, the EU was internally preoccupied, and its foreign policy actions were limited to setting up diplomatic relations and representations at international organizations and responding to demands from former colonies for preferential trade access. Examples of preaccession actions included enforcing the association accord with Greece in 1962, followed by trade sanctions against the Greek military government (1967–1974); implementing the Yaoundé convention in 1962 (forerunner of today's Lomé convention); rejecting British membership bids in 1963 and 1967; imposing UN-led economic sanctions against Rhodesia in 1965; and adopting the Generalized System of Preferences (GSP) in 1971.

It was not until British accession in 1973—and the impacts of the oil cartel's embargo and price hikes, the Middle East War, and the domestic political crisis in the United States—that the EU began to act in more global terms. As already emphasized, enlargement itself catalyzes foreign policy actions and institutional development. The four enlargements to date have generated substantial levels of foreign policy activity that would not otherwise have taken place. The following analysis shows that each enlargement triggers a flurry of foreign policy activity as the EU renegotiates with nonmembers who have trade contracts and negotiates new relationships with nonmembers who are tied to the acceding states.

The British have remained more ambivalent than many noncharter members over membership: they have had severe budget disputes with their fellow members and have resisted integration in some areas they feel cut too deeply into state sovereignty, particularly in foreign policy. However, it is also true that the British were quick to leave indelible marks on the EU's foreign relations both in Europe and abroad. In Europe, Britain was a motivating force behind the negotiation of industrial free trade arrangements between EFTA and the EU; behind renewed efforts to mediate the dispute on Cyprus; and behind further institutionalization of EPC and the establishment of the European Council. On the world stage, Britain was a motivating force behind the following:

- The negotiation of cooperation accords with the Maghreb and Mashreq countries that together took the form of the EU's Mediterranean Policy, a forerunner of the 1995 Euro-Mediterranean Partnership
- The forging of EU diplomatic relations with many more states, especially with the People's Republic of China
- Trade contracts with such countries as India, Pakistan, and Bangladesh
- The Euro-Arab dialogue
- High-level consultations with and briefings for like-minded states (the United States, Canada, New Zealand, and Australia)
- Interbloc relations with the Association of Southeast Asian Nations (ASEAN)
- The Venice Declaration in 1980, which called for, among other things, a Palestinian homeland

Since the second enlargement in 1981 involved just one small applicant, Greece, the impact on EU foreign policy was more limited than with the first enlargement—with some notable exceptions. The Greek case illustrates how enlargement can have adverse effects on EU foreign policy consensus building. For example, Greece did the following:

- Withdrew from an EPC declaration condemning the imposition of martial law in Poland in 1982
- Foiled an EPC declaration condemning the Soviets for the downing of the civilian Korean jetliner that accidentally strayed into Soviet airspace in 1983
- Broke ranks with the EU's public backing of the agreement between Israel and Lebanon and of the withdrawal of Israeli troops from Lebanon in 1983
- Rejected calls by the EP to align its position on Israel with the other member states and to establish full diplomatic relations with Israel (with whom Greece had only de facto relations)
- Maintained a pro-Serbian stance, which contributed to the difficulties the EU faced between 1993 and 1995 as it attempted to form a unified policy concerning the war in the former Yugoslavia
- Unilaterally embargoed all trade with the former Yugoslav Republic

of Macedonia in 1994, an action opposed by the entire EU, in order to force concessions from the newly declared state until extensive U.S. mediation helped resolve the problems between Greece and Macedonia in 1995

The experience with Greece offers insights into how a small state can affect EPC and how enlargement may dilute consensus. Greece's problematic relations with Macedonia and Turkey, its close ties with a number of radical Arab states, and its heavy dependence on oil from countries such as Libya put brakes on Greece's cooperation with its EU partners in foreign policy. Greece has also influenced EU policy in other ways: it has been a champion of the Greek Cypriot government and the reunification of Cyprus, and it has used its influence to extract concessions from Turkey over its position on Cyprus in exchange for lifting Greek objections to the EU-Turkish customs union.

The second enlargement was followed between 1981 and 1985 by a growing number of EU foreign policy actions: for example, an unprecedented cooperation accord with Romania in a peace plan for Afghanistan; the opening up of new and regular EU-U.S. ministerial meetings; the implementation of the EU-Andean Pact Cooperation Accord; EU endorsement of its members' participation in the multilateral peacekeeping force for Sinai; a ban on all imports of baby seal pelts; OSCE follow-up meetings; and EU trade and/or diplomatic sanctions against Argentina, Israel, Poland, the Soviet Union, Grenada, Iran, Iraq, the self-declared Turkish state on northern Cyprus, and South Africa.

The third enlargement opened up new areas of interest and concern for the EU as a result of Spanish, and to a lesser extent Portuguese, foreign policies. The EU brought the Iberians into some aspects of EPC before accession—for example, in the EU's participation in the 1984 San José ministerial conference of the EU, Iberian, Contadora, and Central American states to examine ways in which the EU could help defuse the conflict in Central America. The model of engaging applicant states in political cooperation has already been applied in advance of the fourth enlargement and for the CEECs. Spain has become more paternalistic toward the Latin American and Mediterranean states since joining. The EU, under Spain's very successful EU Council presidency in 1995, negotiated new bases for relations with the Mediterranean states (the Euro-Mediterranean Partnership) and the United States (the EU-U.S. action plan); submitted the Reflection Group's report on institutional and decisionmaking reform to the foreign ministers; committed the EU to open negotiations for the next IGC in March 1996; kept the EU members on track for the third phase of Economic and Monetary Union (EMU); and sent reassurances to the CEECs and Cyprus and Malta, who wish to open accession negotiations with the EU soon after the closing of the IGC. Spain has come of age as an important EU member. Conversely, Portugal, with a much smaller foreign ministry and fewer resources, has had much less impact on EU foreign policy, apart from championing the interests of its four former colonies in the Lomé convention.

EU foreign policy actions continued to increase in the five years following Iberian accession. The EU imposed diplomatic and/or economic sanctions against Libya, Syria, South Africa, China, Romania, Iran, and Iraq; lifted economic or diplomatic sanctions against Turkey, China, and Romania; rejected Morocco's bid for membership; opened diplomatic relations with the Council for Mutual Economic Assistance, the Soviet Union, Cuba, Mongolia, Hungary, Czechoslovakia, East Germany, Bulgaria, and Poland; negotiated cooperation accords with Yugoslavia, Hungary, Poland, Czechoslovakia, the Soviet Union, Bulgaria, East Germany, and Romania; banned chemical exports to belligerents; and negotiated the Transatlantic Declaration with the United States.

The EU's third enlargement was followed by a huge trade row between the EU and the United States over the amount of compensation the latter was due over loss of trade when Spain's much lower import levies on corn and grain were raised to meet the CET and the EU's set-aside of 15.5 percent of the Portuguese grain market to EU suppliers. The United States rejected the EU's offer of compensation and threatened retaliation by raising levies of U.S. imports of EU products covering about ECU 1 billion, at which point the EU threatened counterretaliation. When negotiations did not yield the results the United States desired, Washington imposed retaliatory duties of 200 percent on $400 million worth of European products, but before that action took effect a peace accord was reached. The EU eliminated the 15.5 percent share of the Portuguese grain market reserved to EU suppliers and committed Spain to importing certain amounts of corn and grains from non-EU suppliers over a four-year period. Enlargement can have adverse effects on outsiders that press the EU to respond to their demands for compensation, which in turn forces the EU to react as a unified bloc. The EU's threat of counterretaliation signaled that it would not be easily bullied, and in the end, both sides compromised.[3]

In the fourth enlargement, the EU entered into compensation negotiations with the United States, Canada, Australia, and other trading partners that claimed trade loss as a result of Finnish, Austrian, and Swedish accession in 1995. After months of negotiation, in December 1995, the EU offered compensation acceptable to the other parties. As was the case in the third enlargement, applicant states shadowed CFSP—for example, they were invited to participate in the September 1994 EU-ASEAN annual meeting in Karlsrühe, and they associated themselves with various CFSP policy statements on the Mediterranean and Maghreb. The CEECs have also begun associating themselves with the EU and aligning their foreign policy positions with those of the EU at multilateral organizations such as the UN and the OSCE. Ministers and heads of government of CEECs who have applied for membership were invited to attend the Madrid EU Council summit in December 1995. The model of engaging applicants during the preaccession period, established before the third enlargement, has proven to be a useful way for the EU to play a role in the democratization process, in the case of the CEECs, and to otherwise begin easing accession, in the case of Austria and the Nordics.

Although the accession of Austria, Finland, and Sweden will not block the development of ESDI, these neutrals are not likely to participate as full WEU members in the foreseeable future; the EU will therefore not be able to develop a security dimension that includes a collective self-defense commitment in which all members participate fully.[4] These countries are likely to pull the ESDI in the direction of UN-mandated peacekeeping missions. Although there are still many unanswered questions about how the fourth enlargement will affect ESDI, the neutrals did accept the EU's present and future commitments to developing ESDI. As for CFSP, the accession states are expected to be active proponents within the EU for policies that promulgate respect for human rights and the environment, support multilateral cooperation, and support the integration of the Baltic republics into the EU.[5]

The EU has committed itself to a southern and eastern enlargement after it completes the negotiations for the IGC that began in March 1996. The TEU mandated this IGC to review, and make improvements to, the functioning of the CFSP. Many EU members prefer to deepen the EU before further widening in order to reform institutions and facilitate decisionmaking.

Because the EU's previous enlargements were accompanied by foreign policy decisionmaking reforms, there is a preexisting culture of enlargement-driven reform. The EU's goal of further developing the CFSP and the ESDI may be jeopardized as a decisionmaking structure designed for the original six members buckles under the weight of twenty-seven members. The difference between the fifth and previous enlargements is in the number of applicants.

To what extent can the EU replicate its accommodation of the Mediterranean states in the 1980s for the democratizing states of the former Soviet bloc in the 2000s? For many aspirants, the EU is a symbol—however imperfect—of an epic process of interstate reconciliation and structural peace unparalleled in the history of international relations. Thus, the model of Franco-German, Dutch-German, and Anglo-Spanish reconciliation through economic integration is relevant to Poland, Hungary, and other CEECs that also wish to break out of the cycle of history that has locked them into political conflict and economic underdevelopment. The EU's favorable impact on the return to, and consolidation of, democracy in the Iberian states and Greece is a partial model for those CEECs that are also in the process of shaping new democratic institutions; but the case of CEECs is much more dramatic and urgent.

On the one hand, both sets of applicants were plagued by authoritarian regimes and saw EU membership as a means to consolidate democracy once authoritarian structures were replaced by democratic ones. The TEU stipulates that only democracies may join the EU. Although membership entails some costs, such as competition from the more advanced members and the surrender of certain degrees of sovereignty, it also entails benefits—for example, free access to a larger market, agricultural and regional subsidies, participation in decisionmaking, and membership in an exclusive democratic club. The EU offered the former authoritarian regimes legitimacy in ways reminiscent of the reinforcing effect of the European Coal and Steel Community on West Germany's democratic transition and consolidation in the 1950s.[6] Spain and the CEECs had regimes that represented ideological extremes to the far left and far right of the EU democratic center. Spain, a fascist dictatorship since the 1930s until Franco's death in 1975, was isolated vis-à-vis the EU for as long as the CEECs were ruled by the communists. Thus, there is a precedent for the EU to play a constructive role in helping shepherd democracy in the CEECs. Indeed, the case of EU support for democracy in CEECs through association and membership is even greater than it was for the Mediterranean states because of the scale of the fifth enlargement: there are more countries and people; there is only a narrow window of opportunity that may exist between the present and the possible failure of Russian democratization; and the risks of failure are great for the security of the EU and of the CEECs.

On the other hand, the Mediterranean states that joined in the 1980s had market economies (Spain's industrialized economy was the world's tenth largest), and the CEECs had centrally planned ones. The process of market reforms will take a very long time for some of the CEECs, thus making early accession for some of them highly problematic.

For the EU in both sets of enlargements, security considerations were of paramount importance. The EU's need to promulgate stability along the northern shores of the Mediterranean was so great that the members bought out French and Italian farmers' opposition to enlargement by substantial subsidies under the Integrated Mediterranean Programs (IMPs). In the forthcoming eastern enlargement, the EU is faced with even more pressing security concerns.

The EU offered the Mediterranean states cooperation or association accords as a halfway house to membership. The EU has done the same with so-called Europe Agreements with most of the CEECs. These accords offer industrial free trade with the EU and other preferential treatment, although the CEECs would prefer more generous treatment for their farm and textile products. To prepare for membership, the CEECs are beginning to adapt their production standards, competition laws, and other economic and financial measures to those of the EU.

Iberian accession involved a long transition period that provided both the EU and the acceding states with time to adjust. The model of a long transition period is appropriate again in the context of the fifth enlargement. The EU will be pressed to enlarge as a gesture of political support for democratization in the east but will need a long transition to prepare its farmers and other producers for the new competition. Likewise, a long transition offers time for the newcomers to adjust to the stiff competition and to adapt their laws and regulations to those of the internal market. It took twelve years for the British to move from their initial application to actual entry; it took six years in the Greek case and nine years in the Iberian case. It then took a minimum of ten, eight, and six years, respectively, to move from accession to full integration for each of these entrants.[7] Since enlargement is a very slow and internally combative process, the EU can make the political gesture of welcoming new members but still buy time to adjust.

Without reforms of the CFSP, the Common Agricultural Policy (CAP), and the EU scheme for regional development aid, the fifth enlargement will have deleterious effects on the EU. The CFSP needs to be reformed to facilitate decisionmaking. Without substantial reform of the CAP and regional development programs to cut down on costs, eastern enlargement will be prohibitively expensive. Although the members generally support the need to press on with the fifth enlargement, these highly charged domestic political concerns will have to be addressed. Ultimately, as in past enlargements, there will be a bargain struck between the political imperative of extending membership to stabilize the EU's frontiers and the costs of who pays what and over what length of time.

What impact will another enlargement have on EU foreign policy? The prospect of membership is expected to facilitate the reunification of Cyprus. Malta's membership would offer the EU an important strategic position in the Mediterranean as the EU grapples with the spread of Islamic fundamentalism, transborder terrorism, and drug interdiction. The two Mediterranean states would reaffirm, but are unlikely to change substantially, the EU's Mediterranean vocation.

The CEECs will transform the EU from a western European common market to a European one and complete the geographical process of European integration. The CEECs will compete with the Mediterranean for scant development resources. Because the CEECs are not former colonial powers, they will not bring to the EU the global connections that some other accession states have brought in the past. The CEECs have already begun to align their foreign policies with those of the EU at the OSCE, UN, and other multilateral forums. The EU has engaged the CEECs in preventive diplomacy by using the carrot (of membership) and the stick (of non-membership) to strongly encourage those with border and minority disputes to solve them peacefully (although the lack of progress in the proposed accord between Romania and Hungary is worrisome). Many of the CEECs that do join are likely to be as enthusiastic about their membership in the EU as the Spanish, Portuguese, and Irish have been.

What will be the impact of another enlargement on ESDI? Eastern enlargement will transform the EU from a western European to a European organization, from the eastern borders of western Europe to the eastern borders of eastern Europe. Since the WEU is the EU's defense arm, and membership in the EU opens the door to membership in the WEU, many of the CEECs will want to join the WEU and the benefits of collective self-defense provisions in Article 5 of the Brussels treaty. Thus, the EU, via the WEU, will in the future become a defense guarantor of some or many of the CEECs. To avoid an EU-NATO bloc pitted against Russia and the CIS states, the EU and NATO will want to do all they can to engage Russia and Ukraine in a pan-European security framework, either through the OSCE or through a special relationship between the EU/NATO and Russia and Ukraine. To some extent, this process of engagement has already made headway with the EU-Russian and EU-Ukraine partnership, NATO's Partnership for Peace, the Founding Act between NATO and Russia, and the admittedly slow transformation of the CSCE to the OSCE.

Conclusion

Enlargement is both a cause and an effect of EU foreign policy activity. The more the EU grows in membership, the more it must deal with the problems of a wider world and the more it develops reactive foreign policy positions. For example, as the EU has grown, it has redefined and upgraded its bilateral relationships with the United States, Canada, and Japan; it has taken a more active role in multilateral negotiations at the OSCE and the WTO; and it has extended its preferential trading ties with the members' former colonies in Africa, the Caribbean, and the Pacific. Enlargement itself is an EU foreign policy action that in turn triggers a flurry of other actions as the EU deals with the outside world. The latter is either adversely affected by enlargement and seeks accommodation and/or views the EU as a more unified international political actor than it really is and thus places demands on the EU, which in turn triggers common responses. The EU has extended preferential trading terms and political dialogues with the non-member Mediterranean states following the first enlargement and with the

CEECs following the third and fourth enlargements. The EU has taken political positions on international issues (for example, imposing sanctions on regimes that violate basic human rights, such as Nigeria) at international organizations where it is a member or observer or is represented by the EU Council presidency (such as the UN General Assembly); the EU has also designed and pursued peace plans intended to end various international conflicts (for example, the Soviet occupation of Afghanistan, the Arab-Israeli dispute, and the war in the former Yugoslavia). In short, enlargement brings the EU closer to new international issues and regions.

Enlargement, in the end, has contradictory effects on the EU. On the one hand, enlargement increases the EU's regional and global political clout, extends the EU's reach into other countries, regions, and issues, and catalyzes internal decisionmaking reforms. On the other hand, enlargement increases the diversity of opinion and national interests within the EU, complicating—or even setting back—foreign policy consensus. Overall, though, the benefits have outweighed the costs in terms of the overall growth and development of the EU's foreign relations and policies. However, if the EU fails to deepen before it widens in the next round of enlargement, the CFSP, ESDI, and objectives of a political union will sustain a severe, if not fatal, blow.

Notes

1. In Schmitter, P., "Three Neofunctional Hypotheses About International Integration," *International Organization* 23, no. 1 (winter 1979), pp. 161–166. The author makes progress in theorizing about the impact of enlargement on external relations, which he calls "externalization." In Ginsberg, R. H., *Foreign Policy Actions of the European Community: The Politics of Scale* (Boulder: Lynne Rienner, 1989), I tested Schmitter's externalization hypothesis and found that it explained a large number of EC foreign policy activities.

2. Ginsberg, *Foreign Policy Actions Of The European Community.*

3. Featherstone, K., and Ginsberg, R. H., *The United States and the European Union in the 1990s: Partners in Transition* (London: Macmillan, 1996).

4. According to Miles, Nordic accession will directly affect the international focus of the EU: "Arising partly from the external perspective of the Nordic model . . . [it] will probably bring with it a more formal link between the EU and the Nordic Council. Importantly, Finnish accession will also include new EU borders with Russia and a substantial interest in ensuring friendly EU relations with the Baltic states." Miles further states that Nordic enlargement will help "redress the Mediterranean bias evident in the EU since the 1986 enlargement" and that EU environmental policy "will be strengthened by the inclusion of Sweden and Finland." See Miles, L., "The European Union and the Nordic Countries: Impacts on the Integration Process," in Rhodes, C., and Mazey, S., eds., *The State of the European Union: Building a European Polity?* (Boulder: Lynne Rienner, 1996), pp. 317–337.

5. For additional analysis of the impact of the fourth enlargement on the EU, see Redmond, J., "The Wider Western Europe: Extending the Membership of the EC," in Cafruny, A., and Rosenthal, G. G., eds., *The State of the European Community: The Maastricht Debates and Beyond* (Boulder: Lynne Rienner, 1993), pp. 207–227.

6. Ginsberg, R. H., "Germany in the Stream of Democracy," in Fischer, M. E., ed., *Establishing Democracies* (Boulder: Westview, 1996).

7. Laurent, P.-H., "Widening Europe: The Dilemmas of Community Success," *Annals* (American Academy of Political and Social Sciences) 531 (January 1994), p. 128.

11

Enlargement: Implicit Debates

John Redmond & Glenda G. Rosenthal

The forthcoming process of expansion of the European Union will be the most challenging the Union has ever undertaken. At the same time, it is important not to overlook the continuity of the enlargement process. The EU has been expanding since its inception, and one of the intentions of this book has been to set the future challenge of absorbing the Central and Eastern European Countries (CEECs) within the broader historical framework of the ongoing growth of the Union. As the EU moves from "classical" to "adaptive" enlargement, it will face many critical issues; but most of them are not new. For example, the CEECs' enlargement may act as a catalyst for reform of the Common Agricultural Policy (CAP), but this was already on the agenda—not least because of the impact of previous enlargements.

Nevertheless, while the principal parameters of the debate are clear, there is still a diversity of views on the precise impact of enlargement; indeed, this is reflected to a significant extent in the essays in this book, which do not present a unified view (and indeed it would be surprising if they did). There are a number of "implicit debates" going on, reflecting the differences of opinion among contributors. This is actually instructive because it illustrates very clearly the dilemmas politicians and policymakers in the European Union face today.

Perhaps the most important of these implicit debates concerns the question of the timing of the accessions of the CEECs and the linked issues of changes to the EU budget and structural funds and the reform of CAP. At one end of the spectrum is Inotai (Chapter 8), who argues very forcefully for early admittance of the CEECs; he asserts that the alleged costs of such an enlargement have been overstated and that it could ultimately cost the EU even more (to maintain the stability of these countries) if they are kept waiting at the door of the EU for too long.

More pessimistic views are put forward by other contributors. Josling

(Chapter 5) does not present a "view" in the same way as Inotai does, preferring to work through a series of potential scenarios. But he examines the possibility that the EU will continue to be reactive and not slim down the CAP in the face of budgetary pressures; in this case, enlargement to the east would clearly be difficult. Grabbe and Hughes (Chapter 7) raise similar concerns about the demands the CEECs would place on unreformed structural funds. Specifically they feel that the associated pressures on the EU budget would lead to "a deliberate slowing of the enlargement process and to unnecessary transitional conditions." However, and perhaps surprisingly, Grabbe and Hughes are relatively sanguine about the impact on the "sensitive sectors" in the EU of unbridled competition from the CEECs, and it is Inotai who is concerned that the threat to EU producers and employment (or even the mere notion of it) could have negative effects.

Another area where there is some divergence of opinion is the relationship between enlargement and the EU's efforts to develop a Common Foreign and Security Policy (CFSP), which is a central concern of two authors. Allen (Chapter 6) takes the view that there has been very little linkage between the enlargements of the EU and the development of EPC/CFSP in the Union. Moreover, he is somewhat pessimistic about what the impact of new members will be if the CFSP is a full-fledged policy; indeed, a main element of his argument is that the interaction between enlargement and the CFSP (which he implies would be conflictual) has not materialized so far because the CFSP amounts to so little. On the other hand, Ginsberg (Chapter 10) is much more positive and argues that the development of the EU's foreign and defense policy has been pushed forward by enlargement, and he is much more optimistic about the future contribution of the European Free Trade Association (EFTA) neutrals that joined the EU in 1995 and any of the CEECs that become EU members in future accessions.

A number of the contributors consider the relationship between widening and deepening. This potential dilemma has been a cause for concern since the very first enlargement in 1973. A historical overview of the debate is provided by Edwards (Chapter 3). Allen (Chapter 6) makes two key points. First, he summarizes the positions of three key EU member states. Britain and France, he contends, perceive a conflict between widening and deepening but react in diametrically opposed ways: the British favor widening because it will lead to a "looser" (and less integrated) EU, while the French oppose it for precisely the same reason. The Germans, on the other hand, see no conflict between widening and deepening but regard them as mutually reinforcing processes and support them both. Allen's second point is that, while in the specific context of foreign and security policy it may seem that enlargement has been linked with positive developments, these have involved intergovernmental cooperation and not supranational integration. However, Inotai (Chapter 8) sees the dilemma as short-term and argues that failure to admit the CEECs would cause disruption within the EU—particularly German discontent—that would threaten deepening anyway; his implicit argument is that widening and deepening must proceed simultaneously.

A final issue concerns the possibility of "variable geometry." It is worth being precise about this. Variable geometry may, broadly speaking, take three forms: a multispeed EU in which all members have signed up to all policies but are pursuing them at different speeds; an EU composed of concentric circles in which members signed up to all policies form a hard core and are surrounded by several groups ("tiers") of members signed up to progressively fewer policies;[1] and an à la carte EU in which all members would probably participate in core policies (although in principle this need not be the case, since all policies could be "optional"), but then individual or groups of members would choose from a range of "optional" policies. This is not merely a matter of semantics; different kinds of variable geometry can have quite different implications for the EU's policies and institutions.

However, despite these important distinctions, in the face of some of the seemingly intransigent problems raised by any accession of the CEECs, it frequently seems that variable geometry provides the only means of squaring the circle. Indeed, this is the line taken by Grabbe and Hughes (Chapter 7) in their analysis of how the EU might cope with the budgetary implications of extending the structural funds to the CEECs. The idea is clearly not a new one. As Edwards (Chapter 3) points out, such ideas were very widely discussed even in the 1970s. Moreover, it is a historical fact that the EU has facilitated past enlargements by adopting a kind of multispeed framework (in the shape of extended transition periods for various EU policies for new members). However, these derogations have been temporary, and variable geometry of a permanent nature is much more problematical. These problems take their most acute form in the European Parliament and are described by Neunreither (Chapter 4). Any consideration of the likely institutional impact of variable geometry reveals problems that may well be as great as those such a development is intended to avoid in the EU's budgetary, agricultural, and other policies.

The past history of enlargement provides a rich source of experience from which lessons can be drawn for the future expansion of the European Union. Inevitably the future will be different, because the EU is, by common consent, reaching the limits of its "stretchability" in its present form. Nevertheless, a detailed examination of past enlargements, together with a critical assessment of the impact of likely future accessions on the EU's institutions and major policy areas, can do much to inform the debate that is likely to dominate the European Union in the coming years.

Note

1. Multispeed and multitier Europes are not mutually exclusive. It would be possible to have a multitier, multispeed EU or a multitier, single-speed (within each tier) EU—or a single-tier, multispeed EU, which is arguably what the EU is today (although it also has à la carte elements in the shape of the British and Danish opt-outs).

Acronyms & Abbreviations

AA	association agreement
ACP	African, Caribbean, and Pacific
ASEAN	Association of Southeast Asian Nations
CAP	Common Agricultural Policy
CEECs	Central and Eastern European Countries
CEPS	Centre for European Policy Studies
CET	Common External Tariff
CFSP	Common Foreign and Security Policy
CIS	Commonwealth of Independent States
CMEA	Council for Mutual Economic Assistance
COREPER	Committee of Permanent Representatives
CSCE	Conference on Security and Cooperation in Europe (now OSCE)
CU	customs union
EAEC	(see EURATOM)
EAGGF	European Agricultural Guidance and Guarantee Fund
EBRD	European Bank for Reconstruction and Development
EC	European Commission
ECJ	European Court of Justice
ECSC	European Coal and Steel Community
ECU	European currency unit
EEA	European Economic Area
EEC	European Economic Community
EFTA	European Free Trade Association
EMS	European Monetary System
EMU	Economic and Monetary Union
EP	European Parliament
EPC	European Political Cooperation
ERDF	European Regional Development Fund

ESDI	European Security and Defense Identity
ESF	European Social Fund
EU	European Union
EURATOM	European Atomic Energy Community
FDI	foreign direct investment
FEOGA	Fonds Européen d'Orientation et Garantie Agricoles
FYROM	former Yugoslav Republic of Macedonia
GATT	General Agreement on Tariffs and Trade
GMP	Global Mediterranean Policy
GSP	Generalized System of Preferences
IGC	Intergovernmental Conference
IMP	Integrated Mediterranean Programs
JHA	Justice and Home Affairs
MEP	member of the European Parliament
NATO	North Atlantic Treaty Organization
NMBC	nonmember Mediterranean Basin countries
OECD	Organization for Economic Cooperation and Development
OEEC	Organization for European Economic Cooperation
OOP	Office of Official Publications (of Commission)
OSCE	Organization for Security and Cooperation in Europe
PKK	Kurdish Workers Party
QMV	qualified majority voting
SCA	Special Committee for Agriculture
SEA	Single European Act
SME	small- and medium-sized enterprises
STABEX	Stabilisation of Export Earnings Scheme
TEU	Treaty on European Union
TRNC	Turkish Republic of Northern Cyprus
UNPROFOR	UN Protective Force (in former Yugoslavia)
VAT	value-added tax
WEU	Western European Union
WTO	World Trade Organization

The Contributors

David Allen is senior lecturer in politics and head of the Politics Section of the Department of European Studies at Loughborough University, UK.

Desmond Dinan is director of the Center for European Integration Studies at George Mason University, Arlington, Virginia.

Geoffrey Edwards is Jean Monnet Director of European Studies at the Centre of International Studies and Pembroke College fellow at Cambridge University, UK.

Roy H. Ginsberg is director of the International Affairs Program at Skidmore College, New York.

Heather Grabbe is a research fellow in the European Programme at the Royal Institute of International Affairs, London, UK.

Kirsty Hughes is head of the European Programme at the Royal Institute of International Affairs, London, UK.

András Inotai is director of the Institute for World Economics, Budapest, Hungary.

Tim Josling is professor at the Food Research Institute and director of the Center for European Studies at Stanford University.

Karlheinz Neunreither is professor at the University of Heidelberg, Germany, and former director-general of the European Parliament.

John Redmond is professor of European Studies and Jean Monnet Chair in the Political Economy of European Integration at the University of Birmingham, UK.

Glenda G. Rosenthal is director of the Institute on Western Europe of the

School of International and Public Affairs at Columbia University, New York City.

Birol A. Yesilada is associate professor and chairman of the Department of Political Science at the University of Missouri–Columbia.

Index

About the Book

The Expanding European Union examines the effects of successive increases in EU membership, drawing comparisons among the 1973, 1981, 1986, and 1995 enlargements, during which the Union grew from six to fifteen members. The authors also look ahead to the likelihood of a twenty- or even a twenty-four-member entity by the year 2000.

The main sections of the book deal with the impact of enlargement on institutions and selected policy areas (agriculture, external relations and security, trade and industry) and address issues related to the future inclusion of the Central and Eastern European and the Mediterranean countries. A concluding chapter discusses the role of an expanding European Union in world politics.

John Redmond is professor of European studies and Jean Monnet Chair in the Political Economy of European Integration at the University of Birmingham (England). His numerous publications include *The Next Mediterranean Enlargement of the European Community: Turkey, Cyprus and Malta?* and (with J. D. Armstrong and L. Lloyd) *From Versailles to Maastricht: International Organisation in the Twentieth Century.* **Glenda G. Rosenthal** is director of the Institute on Western Europe at Columbia University's School of International and Public Affairs. She most recently edited (with Alan Cafruny) *The State of the European Community: The Maastricht Debates and Beyond.*